WARE AT WAR
1939-1945

Also by Derek Armes

Our Boys : Ware Men in the First World War
(Rockingham Press, 1998)

Derek Armes

Ware at War
1939-1945

To Joy
with kindest regards
Derek Armes

The Rockingham Press

First published 2002
by The Rockingham Press
11 Musley Lane,
Ware, Herts SG12 7EN

**A catalogue record of this book is available
from the British Library**

ISBN 1 873468 873

Printed in Great Britain by
Biddles Limited
Guildford & King's Lynn

CONTENTS

ACKNOWLEDGMENTS

I would like to give my grateful acknowledgements for all the help they have given to the Hertfordshire Archives and Local Studies and their friendly staff; Ware Town Council; Ware Museum; Hertford Museum; The Imperial War Museum at Duxford; Helenswood School Hastings; City of Liverpool Library; National Museums & Galleries of Liverpool;The National Maritime Museum at Greenwich; Public Records Office; The Commonwealth War Graves Commission; The Royal Navy Museum and GlaxoSmithKline at Ware. Also to the townspeople of Ware for their encouragement, suggestions, photographs and mementoes with special thanks to:

Alan & Nona Wallis
Arthur North
Audrey Campkin
Beryl Tyder
Chris Nicholls
Doris Gilbey
Win Stalley
Jean Mowett
Jim Myers
Kath Bardwell
Maisie Webb
Ron Wall
Tony Fleetwood (ATC)
Wally Ling

Derek Young
Des Furze
Frank Prior
Fred & Mary Munt
Ian Chivers
John & Pat Carter
Fred & Barbara Morris
Geoff Chandler
George Webster
Jack Bowman
John & Ann Bridges
Richard Prior
Pat Kemp
Stewart Lawrence

Charlotte Chamberlain
Doreen Chapman
Dorothy & Jack Gilbert
Fred Church
Henry & Nell Page
Hilda Long
Michael Jennings
Michael Ottley
Monica Hale
Pat Greenhill
Reg Rand
John & Charlie Stockwell
Ted Whybrew

To my son Christopher for his help on the internet and finally to my wife Veronica for her patience and forbearance during my endless hours of research.

Ware, February 2002   Derek Armes

Opposite: The certificate sent by King George VI to every school child in the country on VJ Day, 8 June 1946, when the war in Europe and against Japan was finally over. On the reverse (page 8) was a list of important dates during World War II.

8th June, 1946

To-day, as we celebrate victory, I send this personal message to you and all other boys and girls at school. For you have shared in the hardships and dangers of a total war and you have shared no less in the triumph of the Allied Nations.

I know you will always feel proud to belong to a country which was capable of such supreme effort; proud, too, of parents and elder brothers and sisters who by their courage, endurance and enterprise brought victory. May these qualities be yours as you grow up and join in the common effort to establish among the nations of the world unity and peace.

George R.I.

IMPORTANT WAR DATES

1939

SEP   1. Germany invaded Poland
SEP   3. Great Britain and France declared war on Germany; the B.E.F. began to leave for France
DEC 13. Battle of the River Plate

1940

APR   9. Germany invaded Denmark and Norway
MAY 10. Germany invaded the Low Countries
JUNE 3. Evacuation from Dunkirk completed
JUNE 8. British troops evacuated from Norway
JUNE 11. Italy declared war on Great Britain
JUNE 22. France capitulated
JUNE 29. Germans occupied the Channel Isles
AUG   8–OCT 31. German air offensive against Great Britain (Battle of Britain)
OCT 28. Italy invaded Greece
NOV 11–12. Successful attack on the Italian Fleet in Taranto Harbour.
DEC   9–11. Italian invasion of Egypt defeated at the battle of Sidi Barrani

1941

MAR 11. Lease-Lend Bill passed in U.S.A.
MAR 28. Battle of Cape Matapan
APR   6. Germany invaded Greece
APR 12–DEC 9. The Siege of Tobruk
MAY 20. Formal surrender of remnants of Italian Army in Abyssinia
MAY 20–31. Battle of Crete
MAY 27. German battleship *Bismarck* sunk
JUNE 22. Germany invaded Russia
AUG 12. Terms of the Atlantic Charter agreed
NOV 18. British offensive launched in the Western Desert
DEC   7. Japanese attacked Pearl Harbour
DEC   8. Great Britain and United States of America declared war on Japan

1942

FEB 15. Fall of Singapore
APR 16. George Cross awarded to Malta
OCT 23–NOV 4. German-Italian army defeated at El Alamein
NOV   8. British and American forces landed in North Africa

1943

JAN 31. The remnants of the 6th German Army surrendered at Stalingrad
MAY   Final victory over the U-Boats in the Atlantic
MAY 13. Axis forces in Tunisia surrendered
JULY 10. Allies invaded Sicily
SEP   3. Allies invaded Italy
SEP   8. Italy capitulated
DEC 26. *Scharnhorst* sunk off North Cape

1944

JAN 22. Allied troops landed at Anzio
JUNE 4. Rome captured
JUNE 6. Allies landed in Normandy
JUNE 13. Flying-bomb (V.1) attack on Britain started
JUNE   Defeat of Japanese invasion of India
AUG 25. Paris liberated
SEP   3. Brussels liberated
SEP   8. The first rocket-bomb (V.2) fell on England.
SEP 17–26. The Battle of Arnhem
OCT 20. The Americans re-landed in the Philippines

1945

JAN 17. Warsaw liberated
MAR 20. British recaptured Mandalay
MAR 23. British crossed the Rhine
APR 25. Opening of Conference of United Nations at San Francisco
MAY   2. German forces in Italy surrendered
MAY   3. Rangoon recaptured
MAY   5. All the German forces in Holland, N.W. Germany and Denmark surrendered unconditionally
MAY   9. Unconditional surrender of Germany to the Allies ratified in Berlin
JUNE 10. Australian troops landed in Borneo
AUG   6. First atomic bomb dropped on Hiroshima
AUG   8. Russia declared war on Japan
AUG   9. Second atomic bomb dropped on Nagasaki
AUG 14. The Emperor of Japan broadcast the unconditional surrender of his country
SEP   5. British forces re-entered Singapore

MY FAMILY'S WAR RECORD

Chapter 1
PREPARATIONS FOR WAR 1935 – 1939

The Great War of 1914-1918 was acknowledged as the "War to end wars" and these feelings were reflected in the setting up of the League of Nations in 1920 following the ratification of the Versailles Peace Treaty. However the League's authority was soon flouted when Greece attacked Turkey in 1922. From 1920 Britain's defences were rapidly run down although it was appreciated that the nation was vulnerable to an attack by air as had been demonstrated by the Zeppelin and Gotha bomber raids on the Home Counties and the East Coast towns in 1916. To counteract this danger the Government set up a secret subcommittee of the Imperial Defence Committee in 1924 to plan air raid precautions and create the Observer Corps under the guise of special constables to track enemy bomber movements.

The acts of aggression continued, Japan occupied Manchuria in 1932, Italy invaded Abyssinia in 1935 despite League of Nations sanctions, Germany reoccupied the Saar and had started to rearm. Against this darkening background Britain reluctantly began to prepare its defences. On 6th July 1935 the Home Office wrote to every Local Authority enclosing Air Raid Precautions (ARP) Memorandum No.1 which detailed the responsibilities of Central and Local Governments should the country be subjected to air attacks by a foreign power. The former would be responsible for general co-ordination, provision of equipment and training instructors while the later would be responsible for the preparation of schemes to deal with casualties, recruitment and training. Emphasis was placed on gas attacks. At the same time the Home Office asked the Order of St. John (St. John Ambulance Brigade) and the Red Cross Organisations "that their organisations will as far as practical be placed at the disposal of both Central and Local Governments to supplement official resources". Both organisations readily agreed and the Ware branch of the Brigade immediately started training in gas warfare. The seeds of Ware's preparations for war had been sown.

When Germany remilitarised the Rhineland in 1936 contrary to the Versailles Treaty and used the Spanish civil war as a training ground for its newly formed airforce the British Government, while still pursing a policy of appeasement, accepted that war was inevitable and the time for disarmament was over. Memorandum No.1 was updated based on the new type of aerial warfare in Spain and reissued to all Local Authorities. Its purpose was to outline the type of organisation envisaged for the recovery and treatment of civilian casualties caused through aerial high explosive, incendiary and gas bomb attacks. The organisation was set up at County Council level. Hertfordshire was divided into areas and sub-areas, Hertford, Ware and Hoddesdon together with their Rural Districts formed sub-area No.2 of Area A. The onus for setting up the ARP in Ware rested with Town Council working to general directives issued from Central Government via the County headquarters. The first stage required was to draw up a general plan for the town including the personnel required, preparing lists and schedules of buildings needed including details of any necessary changes and modifications. Once the plan had been prepared further action fell under two headings, (a) recruitment and training personnel and (b) the assessment of additional equipment required. Ware elected its Air Raid Precautions Committee on 19th May 1936. Its members were Councillors Tom Burgess, J G Wright and Dr Walter Stewart, Superintendent Charles Forbes of the St. John Ambulance Brigade, Harold Sharp from the British Legion, Miss Garforth the Commandant of the Hertfordshire 14th Detachment of the British Red Cross Society (the Voluntary Aid Detachment nurses or VAD), Leslie Southall the Town Clerk and Robert Grantham the town's Engineer and Surveyor.

At their first meeting the ARP Committee proposed that a Gas Decontamination Centre should be built in the old malting behind 87 High Street (the Library) and to use Western House laundry to clean gas contaminated clothing together with its "casuals ward" for air raid casualties. During the next six months Wright and Grantham prepared an overall defence plan for Ware based on a national formula using figures taken from the 1931 census returns. Further air raid precautions were introduced in 1937 under the Air Raid Precautions Act, these included the formation of the Auxiliary Fire Service (the AFS) and the Wardens Service. Wright, who was appointed Chief Warden with Harold Sharp as his deputy, revised his lists which were presented to the Council before submission to the County Authorities on 10th June. New training courses were organised for the few recruits who came forward.

In the meantime Leslie Southall was dealing with a multitude of directives and information pamphlets arriving from the Home Office. Based on Home Office guidelines Robert Grantham was busy surveying business premises to see if they were suitable for air raid shelters, assessing how many gas masks the town required and arranging for their storage space in the harness room at the Priory Street Council Depot as well as a myriad of other tasks. July 1938 saw the resignation of Mr Wright as the Chief Warden and Robert Harradence took over the role. He immediately pressed for a Council building for the sole use of his wardens and wanted Priory Lodge (Ware Museum) as his headquarters. More will be heard of this a little later.

September 1938 – The Munich Crisis

Hitler annexed Austria early in 1938 and soon had his eyes on his next acquisition, Czechoslovakia, which led to the Munich Crisis in the September and the immediate threat of war. This created a flurry of activity within the ARP Service, gas masks were issued, trench shelters were set out at the Buryfield recreational ground and at the town's schools although the excavation work was not started. Local businesses were asked to make their own arrangements to protect their employees and most were able to do so. Records of the precautions taken at Western House show that a trench shelter was actually dug there in the nurse's garden and remained in use during the war. Tension eased with the signing of the infamous "Peace in our Times" agreement under which the Czech Sudetenland, the German speaking border land, was ceded to Hitler. However it was an uneasy peace and focused the country's need to protect its inhabitants. At last the authorities sensed that the main danger would come from high explosive and incendiary bombs rather than gas and there was now much more

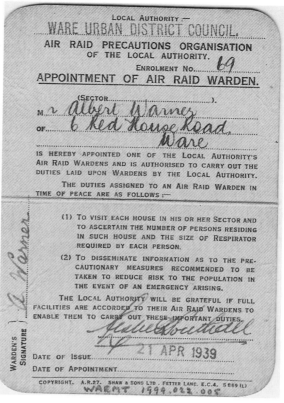

A warden's card issued in April 1939 and signed by Leslie Southall

urgency into the forward planning for the forthcoming conflict. A definite line of command was put into place around this time, the country was divided into thirty-two regions and Hertfordshire came under area No.12 – the Cambridgeshire area with a regional headquarters at Cambridge. The regional headquarters eventually co-ordinated evacuees and the fire services. Equally important money was made available from central funds on "an equitable apportionment of the cost between national and local funds" which in reality meant that Ware received a 65% refund of its expenditure on air raid precautions. Soon after the Munich Agreement, Leslie Southall was appointed as the ARP Officer to coordinate the activities of all the ARP services.

With some two hundred of the town's citizens now trained or undergoing training for ARP work a large scale exercise designed to test all sections of the service together with the Fire Service was held in the town on the night of the 5/6th November 1938 under "black out" conditions. It was assumed that gas bombs had fallen outside the Drill Hall in Amwell End, incendiary bombs on the Old Town Hall and high explosive bombs in Tower Road. The exercise was considered to be an all-round success.

A gas training exercise at Western House on 18th July 1939.

1939 saw an ever increasing volume of paper work flowing from the Home Office via the County headquarters to the Priory to accelerate the civil defence preparations so it was agreed that two female typists should be recruited whose salaries would be recovered from Central Government. One would be employed in the Clerk's department and the second with the Surveyor, the positions were advertised and Miss Joan Pamphilion together with Miss Hollands were appointed at a weekly salary of thirty shillings (£1.50). They were supplied with new typewriters, chairs and filing cabinets costing £80. The Town Clerk's work load was further increased further when Ware was declared a safe area to receive evacuees and he was appointed as the town's Chief Evacuation Officer.

February 1938 saw one major change to Ware's ARP Service. The Ambulance and First Aid Post Services now became the responsibility of the Ministry of Health and administered by the County Council, in broad terms the County bore the cost of the service while our town provided the personnel and facilities etc. required. The town's hopes of using Western House as a local air raid casualty hospital were dashed when the Ministry of Health declared that it was not classified as a reception and treatment area for casualties but would receive up to 200 chronically sick cases from other hospitals. With the loss of Western House fears were raised in the town that if Ware bridge and the railway viaduct were bombed it would be difficult to transfer casualties to Hertford so a sensible compromise was reached if this eventuality occurred then Western House could be used. The County also recognised that more ambulances were required and contingency plans were made to commandeer suitable vehicles within Ware for that purpose. The Council's financial accounts for the year ending 31st March 1939 show that £607 had been spent on general air-raid precautions with a further £200 on fire precautions.

In the spring the Home Office booklet "The Protection of your Home against Air Raids" was sent out to every householder. The booklet described how a householder could select and prepare a refuge room and how to make it gas proof, how to blackout their house and basic First Aid. Another official publication encouraged people to stockpile canned food and gave advice as to the contents of these emergency rations.

Although the calls for volunteers to serve with the ARP services had been encouraging there was an imbalance of numbers between the various branches, the town's First Aid sections were well over establishment and those for the wardens and AFS below strength. This was noted at County level and Ware was told to stop recruiting First Aiders, however the Committee felt that it was wise not to turn volunteers away and ignored the instruction. Several of the town's local businesses such as Thurgoods and the Tottenham & District Gas Board trained their own wardens and fifteen of the mistresses at the Girls Grammar School became day-time wardens.

Guidance was received from County level as to the numbers of whole time ARP staff who could be employed whose salaries would be grant aided. Unlike many towns Ware did not take full advantage of this

3

(4) LIGHTING RESTRICTIONS.

All windows, skylights, glazed doors or other openings which would show a light at night must be screened with dark blinds, curtains, or with brown paper fixed on to the glass so that no light is visible from outside. All lighted signs and advertisement lights and other outside lights must be turned out.

All street lighting will be stopped till further notice.

(5) FIRE PRECAUTIONS AND METHOD OF DEALING WITH INCENDIARY BOMBS.

Clear the top floor of all inflammable materials, lumber, etc. See that you can get easily to any attic or roof spaces.

Water is the best means of putting out a fire started by an incendiary bomb. See that water is available about the house. Have some ready in buckets, but do not draw off water if you can help it during an air raid. Be careful not to throw a bucket of water directly over a burning incendiary bomb. The bomb would explode and throw burning fragments in all directions.

You may be able to smother a small bomb with sand or dry earth.

(6) CLOSING OF CINEMAS, THEATRES AND PLACES OF ENTERTAINMENT.

All cinemas, theatres, dance halls and places of public entertainment will be closed until further notice. When it is seen how the air attacks develop it may be possible to allow the re-opening of such places in some areas. They are being closed because if they were hit by a bomb, large numbers would be killed or injured. Football matches and outdoor meetings of all kinds which bring large numbers together are prohibited until further notice. Never crowd together unnecessarily.

A page from the Home Office booklet "The Protection of your Home against Air Raids"

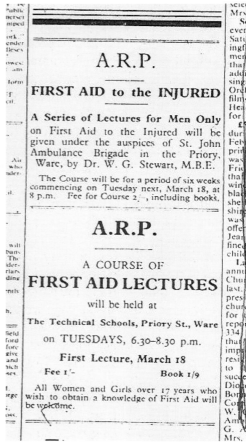

Dr. Walter Stewart, who was appointed ARP Controller in April 1939 and held the position throughout the war. Right: advertisement in the Mercury for First Aid training – the top one was segregated for "Men Only"!

regulation, a full-time Chief ARP Officer or at least a deputy could have been appointed at little cost to the ratepayer and relieved an overworked Town Clerk of some of his tasks. One can only assume that the traditional inbuilt frugality of our town councillors prevailed – a decision that effected the efficiency of the town's civil defence service until William Reed was appointed Southall's deputy in January 1942. Instead they passed a resolution in April 1939 that the Chairman of the ARP Committee would automatically become the ARP Controller with overall responsibility for Ware's air-raid precautions with the exception of the fire services. Dr Walter Stewart held this position throughout the war with Tom Burgess as his deputy. Ware owes much to Walter Stewart: in World War I he ran the VAD hospital in The Priory, he was associated with the St. John Ambulance Brigade for many year, and he served as a Town Councillor, chairing the Emergency Committee which was to run the town in the event of an invasion. Many of his spare evenings were devoted to teaching First Aid to the wardens and the fire service. Dr. Stewart, together with Leslie Southall and Robert Grantham, were the driving forces behind the town's civil defence. The names of Southall and Grantham are commemorated in roads named after them – it seems a pity that Walter Stewart was not honoured in the same way.

May 1939 saw a flurry of activity. Robert Grantham submitted detailed plans to the full council of the air raid precautions proposed for the town, these included: a Report and Control Centre adjoining Priory Lodge, wardens posts and air raid shelters including an interesting proposal to construct a public convenience at Parrott's site in the High Street which could be rapidly adapted as an air raid shelter sufficient for sixty people. (Parrott's was a butcher's shop at 100 High Street and had been burnt down, the site is between The Wine Lodge and Harold Freeman's chiropody shop.)

Grantham's proposals were accepted and he was instructed commence work on the Report and Control Centre immediately and to open negotiations with landowners so that construction work could be put in hand on the other facilities without delay should war breakout, this proved to be a wise decision since the acquisition of a couple of the proposed sites were problematic. Other items Grantham had to consider were buildings for First Aid posts, gas decontamination and cleansing posts as well as facilities for the fire fighting services. 45,000 sand bags and a sand bag filling machine were ordered in May to build blast walls at key installations such as the Musley pumping stations, the police station in Watton Road, the First Aid post at the swimming pool and the sewage works at Stanstead Abbotts.

At the request of the County Medical Officer a register of trained nurses, assistant nurses and nursing auxiliaries was prepared. The Civil Defence Act received the Royal Assent on 13th July 1939 enabling The Home Office to instruct Local Authorities to call up a percentage of their ARP volunteers on a full-time basis. The last Council meeting held prior to the outbreak of war normal business was suspended and the entire meeting was devoted to civil defence matters. For once there was little or no dissension among the Councillors, it was agreed that the telephones at The Priory, Allen & Hanburys together with the top waterworks would be manned twenty-four hours a day. The Council's workmen were to start building the wardens posts while orders were placed with Crook Brothers and F Hitch & Company to build the public air raid shelters. Instructions were given that all street and public lighting were to be put out, notices were served on vehicle owners requisitioning their cars and vans for ambulances and offices made available within the Priory for the Food and Fuel Control Authorities. Nineteen trained ARP personnel were appointed on a full-time basis with a weekly salary of £3.00, many a rumour spread through the

The plate fixed to James Ling's house at South Lodge at Presdales who was a warden at the Scotts Road ARP post—photograph by Michael Ottley.

town when this was announced with many volunteers thinking it applied anyone connected with civil defence. And so by the outbreak of war the town's ARP services were in place albeit understaffed in some sections and with some facilities substandard. A considerable sum of money had been spent by the Council on the town's defences which can only have come from the reserve funds since Ware, unlike Hertford and Hoddesdon, did not raise the general rates in October 1939. As the war progressed the service and facilities were gradually improved, fire watching introduced and the whole organisation rationalised on 2nd September 1941 when the service changed its name to Civil Defence – a much more appropriate one.

On Friday, the 1st September, Germany invaded Poland in spite of the guarantee made by England and France in May 1939 that should this happen then the Anglo-French Alliance would come to Poland's aid. An ultimatum

WAR EMERGENCY

INFORMATION AND INSTRUCTIONS

Read this leaflet carefully and make sure that you and all other responsible persons in your house understand its contents.

——————

Pay no attention to rumours. Official news will be given in the papers and over the wireless.

Listen carefully to all broadcast instructions and be ready to note them down!

One of the leaflets issued by the government with information about the wartime emergency.

was given to Germany that if they failed to give an undertaking to cease their warlike actions by 11.00 am on 3rd September then the Allies would declare war. Ware was a hive of activity that day, the Territorials had been mobilised, the first of 441 evacuees arrived in the town, air raid shelters were being dug and blackout screens were frantically being made. The Prime Minister, Mr Neville Chamberlain, broadcast to the nation on Sunday the 3rd soon after the ultimatum had expired. Few who heard the broadcast will forget the fateful words delivered in a voice of a man wearied by his efforts to avert war and in falling health when he said "I regret to tell you that no such undertaking has been received and we are therefore at war with Germany". King George VI broadcast to the nation at 6.00 pm in the evening.

Blackout restrictions were immediately imposed, the air raid siren sounded for the first time on the 6th September, the schools were closed until work had started on their air raid shelters, petrol rationing was soon to start, food became short at the grocers and was soon to be rationed too. Service reservists were recalled to the colours and Ware knew it was at war.

Chapter 2
WARE'S WARTIME GUESTS – EVACUEES

Towards the end of 1938 Ware was considered to be a safe area and designated to receive evacuees from London, these would be school children, children under school age accompanied by mothers, expectant mothers, the handicapped and registered blind persons. In January 1939 the Ministry of Health instructed Local Authorities to compile a "Government Evacuation Scheme Register of Accommodation" designed to show the accommodation available for evacuees throughout the country. In Ware this task fell on the shoulders of Leslie Southall who had been appointed the town's Chief Evacuation Officer. Fortunately for Southall the newly formed Women's Voluntary Service offered to undertake this task which he willingly accepted since little or no cost would be incurred by his council.

The WVS ladies visited practically every house in the town to record the name of the householder, the number of inhabitable rooms, the number of people normally resident in the house and if additional bedding would be required should an evacuee be billeted there. Their findings were entered in a specially printed ledger which established that there were 9062 inhabitable rooms within the town and that a maximum of 2329 additional people could be accommodated in Ware should mass evacuation prove necessary. Taking an example at random from the survey No.16 Park Road, then occupied by the Rooke family, had four inhabitable rooms normally occupied by three people and it was assessed that one unaccompanied child could be accommodated but the householder would require another single mattress and three single blankets. The register also records that in the event of war several householders would be making their own arrangements to receive relatives as evacuees and their numbers were recorded as well.

Southall attended a series of meetings at the Ministry of Health's regional office at Cambridge with the Regional Evacuation Officer Reginald Bouttell, whose home, by a strange coincidence, was at 29 Musley Lane in Ware. It was considered that Ware could accommodate up to 1,200 evacuees. Detailed planning was left to the local area centred at Hertford, here the number was reduced and arrangements were made for Ware to accept some 800 children, their teachers and helpers. The local plan was that the evacuees would arrive at Hertford North station where they would be met by railhead representatives who, in the case of Ware, would be Charles Lucas, the Sanitary Inspector. Transport to their dispersal points at Musley Hill Infants and the St Mary's schools would be by London Transport buses. Before being taken to their new billets each child would be issued with a carrier bag of rations for their hosts consisting of one can of meat, two cans of milk (one sweetened and one unsweetened), two packets or 1lb of biscuits, 1/4lb of chocolate or two chocolate crisps all packed in a carrier bag. Adults would receive the same with one extra can of meat.

Now that the anticipated numbers were known the accommodation register was updated in May 1939 with many houses having the number of inhabitable rooms reassessed and reduced by one. Robert Grantham was given the task of organising the suitable "blanket and rations dump" which, with the co-operation of Hubert Martin, he established at Western House. Two of the WVS ladies who took part in the survey, Miss K Cavell of Walton Road and Miss R Gibbs of Hunsdon Hill were appointed as the towns unpaid billeting officers. From time to time Southall was advised that he should allocate accommodation for 50 blind people, 80 nurses who might be sent to Western House and possibly "civilian billets" for soldiers. As far as it is known no blind people were evacuated to the town although some did arrive in nearby Nazeing and private properties such as Alpha Cottage in Princess Street were requisitioned by the military. Evacuees from the Wellhouse Infirmary at Barnet and the St Mary's Hospital Paddington were received at Western House in 1939 and 1941 respectively. Wellhouse Infirmary had been earmarked as a military hospital and it was for this reason that its elderly patients were evacuated to Ware, the majority of its 202 patients were housed in the men's annexe built in 1934 on the opposite side of Collett Road from the main complex. The infirmary wards normally held eighteen patients, to accommodate those from Barnet the beds were doubled up and Kath Cannon (now Bardwell) recalls that the wards were overcrowded and incredibly warm. Those from Paddington were unmarried pregnant women who were kept at Western House for about two months, the laying-in ward was below the Octagon. The babies were either adopted at the end of the two month period or taken away from their mother and sent to Great Cozens near Fanhams Hall to join other young evacuee children from the St Mary Abbotts Hospital of Chelsea. The County Council also used Great Cozens as an Emergency Maternity Home.

With a plan in place, extra bedding and rations in store, it was time for a dress rehearsal so in July it was arranged that this would take place on Monday 11th September when 45 children and 5 teachers were to be taken to Bayford by bus, entrained and met at Hertford North station where the railhead evacuation procedure would be carried out. As events turned out Reginald Bouttell who was on holiday with his young family was recalled to his Cambridge Office on the 27th August and the full evacuation plan, operation "Pied Piper," swung into action on Friday and Saturday, the 1st and 2nd of September. Emergency instructions issued to the evacuees parents stated that *"Each child should have a handbag or case containing the child's gas mask, a change of underclothing, night clothes, house shoes or plimsolls, spare stockings or socks, a toothbrush, a comb, towel, soap and face cloth, handkerchiefs; and, if possible a warm coat or mackintosh. Each child should have a packet of food for the day."* They all had a stamped addressed post card so that they could inform their parents of their new home. One of the author's poignant memories of the war was the arrival of a group of children of his own age from Bermondsey and their reaction at seeing rural Sussex for the first time, the scenario was almost identical to the following taken from the *Mercury* dated the 9th September describing the arrival of evacuees at Hertford North Station:-

The first train load of evacuees arrived at Hertford North Station at 9.33 am on Friday and within a few minutes the children had descended onto the platform and had been transported into an orderly array. Each school was separated, each teacher bore his or her name on a coloured ticket and to each child was attached a luggage label bearing its name and school number, while each contingent was headed by a banner bourne by two boys or girls.

Many of the children had come well prepared, with their skeleton kit in haversack or bag, but others presented a pitiable spectacle. Clutching their few clothes in paper bags or other containers in a greater or less degree of completeness, some of them obviously wore the coat or mackintosh shared by the youngest members of the family and had ragged plimsolls on their feet.

The state of mind shown by the youngsters varied to an amazing extent. One school went down the station steps singing cheerily 'We'll have a barrel of fun.' While others looked sad and forlorn. Others again, and these were mainly the older children, talked of their 'holiday in the country'. A teacher told the Hertfordshire Mercury reporter 'They are all right now but it will be tonight when they have not got their mothers to tuck them up in bed the trouble will come'. They were shepherded down steps by the evacuation officers and special constables across the road to the waiting buses.

And so 485 evacuees from Holloway consisting of 441 unaccompanied children and 44 others from three catholic schools arrived at Musley Hill where they were met by staff from Allen & Hanburys, Wickhams and A B Swain together with local school teachers who had been placed at the disposal of the billeting officers. Soon small groups of children set out carrying their hand luggage, name labels round their necks and their bag of rations. There were a few unhappy doorstep scenes where either the hostess did not like the look of the child offered or where the child realised that the new home was not all he or she imagined it would be. However it was recorded that apart from a few minor problems everything went well. A panel was formed which acted as a tribunal in the event of a dispute or problems, a few children were subsequently rehoused when their billets proved unsuitable or overcrowded. The evacuees hostesses were paid 10s-6d (£0.52) per week per child, there were a few isolated cases of fraudulent payment claims which were quickly dealt with by the billeting officers. Some of the children rejected being evacuated and showed this by bed wetting and claims for damage were dealt with sympathetically. The children must have been happy in Ware since very few returned to London in the early days of

Left: Valerie Clarke (now Mrs Baldwin) who was billetted with the Perry family in Watton Road. Right: another Hastings girl, Heather Johnson, photographed in 1943 with Beryl Bouttell on the right. Beryl's parents at 29 Musley Lane were hosts to four evacuees: Olive Bater, a teacher with the Shelburne School who returned to London at Christmas 1939; Mrs Teague, a teacher from the Sion Convent School; Heather Johnson and finally Mrs Marjorie Bradshaw, a nurse at the children's nursery in Bowling Road.

the war. As the winter nights set in St. Mary's Schools launched an appeal for books to set up "an evacuees library". Ware showed its true hospitality to their guests over the Christmas holiday period; entertainment, cinema shows, rural walks and numerous parties were arranged for the evacuees and the children they were billeted with.

Soon after the arrival of the evacuees there were cases of diphtheria at St. Mary's School, none had been immunised against the disease and even if this was done immediately it would be three months before the vaccine was fully effective. A call by Dr Alan Whitelaw, the town's Medical Officer for Health, to immunise all children in Ware against the disease was rejected by the Councillors on the grounds that it would cost 6s-0d (£0.30) per head and considered that the London County Council should bear all the costs since it was the London children who brought disease to Ware; it comes as no surprise that the LCC 'passed the buck' to Islington Borough Council. Some sort of compromise was reached since a clinic staffed by a nurse was set up for the evacuees coinciding with three further cases of diphtheria among the Londoners attending Musley Infants School, the clinic may well have been at Balls Park, Hertford. This gave Dr Whitelaw the opportunity to asked the Council to reverse their previous decision not to immunise the Ware school children. A motion to do so proposed and seconded by Councillors Tom Burgess and Arthur Swain was carried but not unanimously. As a result of their tardiness in acting quickly the Council had put the town's children at risk and now faced a claim for loss of earnings from one man when the evacuee billeted with his family caught the disease.

And so things remained static, the Town Council announced in March 1940 that no more evacuees were anticipated but things were soon to change in the summer months with the Battle of Britain and the bombing of London. On Sunday the 21st of July 1940 Ware station buzzed with the voices of 188 girls Hastings High School girls who had been evacuated to the town. This was a complete reversal of the policy adopted in September 1939 when thousands of south London children had been sent to the towns along the south coast and Hastings High School had been the hosts to St. Ursula's High School from Greenwich. During the summer of 1940 Hastings and St. Leonards had been hit by "tip and run" bombing, shot up by aerial machine gun attacks as part of the "softening up" process before the launch of Hitler's proposed invasion of our country, operation "Sealion" (the beaches between Hastings and Eastbourne had been correctly identified by the British Army as one of the proposed landing areas). The Hastings girls were taken to Ware Grammar and Central Schools before proceeding to their billets which had been arranged the previous week. Miss F M Cummin, the headmistress, and her girls shared the Grammar School for the remainder of the war. Every summer some twenty to thirty East Sussex County Council scholarship winners from the junior schools in and around Hastings came to Ware to continue their education.

Writing in the school magazine after the war Miss Cummin recalls the school's stay in Ware, *"Lining up in our schools in the car park, and parents watching as we climbed into buses which took us in the rain to the station; and so our train, one of many, carried us off to Hertfordshire, and Hastings was left, like Hamelin of old, without its children. We reached Ware in the afternoon, and soon found we had indeed left the sea, and all the attractions of a sea-side resort behind us. We did learn the joy of a beautiful school garden. This garden became our chief standby and refuge throughout our years in Ware. At first, in holiday time, we were able to make expeditions, and nearly every one went to Whipsnade, St. Albans, Windsor and Cambridge; but as petrol became more difficult to acquire, and we were more hemmed into Ware, the school garden played a greater part in our free time.*

"The school buildings we used in the afternoons; only VI. and V. were able to work there in the mornings, the rest of the school being scattered in a Church and Church halls. We were within earshot of the bombing of London, and during the Blitz spent much time in shelters, or even rolling under the pews of the Church. Life fairly

soon fell into a regular routine: lessons, Guides, medical inspection, nurses inspection, visits to the dentist; and for me, almost daily visits to the billeting officer. Even the noise of the gunfire and the wail of the siren seemed part of everyday life".

Miss Cummin went on to say that as the years passed the urge for the School to return to Hastings grew, the school did in fact reopen in Hastings to give tuition classes late in 1943 but with the onset of the "Doodlebugs" in August 1944 eighty-two girls returned to Ware.

Valerie Clarke (now Baldwin) came back to Ware on a nostalgic visit sixty years after she was evacuated from Hastings. Following her visit she wrote to the Curator of Ware Museum telling him of some of her experiences as an evacuee in Ware:

In July 1940 I remember gathering with a large crowd of children and teachers on the platform of Hastings railway station together with a lot of worried parents. The children were wearing labels (I think they were luggage labels tied on to the buttonholes) and carrying gas masks in cardboard boxes. We also had suitcases and food to eat on the journey. The steam train seemed to take forever to reach our destination. Did it go through London I wonder? Did the boys stop at another town? My own brother was nearly 18 and about to join the army.

On arrival at Ware we were formed into crocodiles and walked round the town dropping off children at the various houses where kind people of Ware had agreed to look after the evacuees. Elsie (Myles) and I were the last, or almost last, in our group. We were surprised to be taken into this large house, Cambridge Villa, 4 Watton Road, but were told that it was a temporary arrangement until Mrs Perry next door at No.6 could have us. We were given postcards to write to our parents giving our addresses and told that we were in Ware which caused a lot of confusion with us asking where? and being told Ware and thinking that they were repeating the question. Both the Gilberts and the Perrys were very kind to us.

I remember that we shared Ware Grammar School on a half day basis but I have no idea how we spent the rest of the day. My parents came to see me on a few occasions. My father was in a reserved occupation as a manager of three ice and cold storage factories. When the convoys got through with meat etc. he had to have storage ready at any time. So he had an extra petrol ration which he must have misused in coming to see me. My mother was evacuated to Devizes for some time. Some time at the beginning of 1941 we were moved from Watton Road to Star Street. This was a house where you walked off the street into the front room. It was not a nice billet with the sheets rarely changed and an occasional bath in a 'tin' bath in the kitchen with everyone using the same water. I was very unhappy and one day my father appeared at the school and Miss Cummin agreed to let me go home to St. Leonards.

Two evacuees who arrived from Holloway on 1st September were brother and sister Joe and Hilda Varley who attended the Pakeman Street School returned to Ware recently. Before they left north London the school's headmistress had told the mothers that they could accompany their offspring to Ware, when they arrived at the station the mothers found this was not so – hardly the best way of parting and many and extra tear was shed. Joe and Hilda were billeted with the Horsnell family at 8 Amwell Terrace. At first Mrs Horsnell was only willing to take Hilda as a companion for her daughter Janet but relented and took in seven year old Joe as well. Joe relished the freedom of the open countryside by the river Lee. With the lack of aerial activity in either Ware or Holloway the two youngsters returned home in the summer of 1940 before the Battle of Britain and remained there for the rest of the war.

Several small north London companies relocated their factories and employees in Ware during the Battle of Britain and others came during the "Blitz", more details can be found in chapter 12. The relentless bombing of London officially started on 7th September 1940 and continued for fifty-seven consecutive days. This saw an influx of bombed out and homeless people who had made their way down the Lea valley to the relative safety of Ware, the problems the town faced were summed up in an article which appeared in the *Mercury* dated the 13th September which read:-

HOMELESS LONDONERS IN WARE

Many homeless families from London have found their way to Ware. The first problem raised by this exodus is that of accommodation, the second is clothes. In their flight from the bombing they have been able to bring but a few personnel possessions and many were without winter clothing. The Women's Voluntary Services organisation in the district have taken the situation in hand, and from their general organiser, Mrs May, comes an appeal this week to all householders in the district to turn out their wardrobes for all the children's, men's and women's clothing they can spare for the evacuees. These should be sent to Mrs May, 87 High Street, Ware. The clothing will go to those evacuees billeted in the villages around Ware as well as those in the town itself. Miss Cavell, the WVS billeting officer, is arranging for accommodation. Some families have been temporarily taken care of by Captain Carter, of the Salvation Army, in the Army Hall.

Others made their way to the villages surrounding villages. Eileen Lynch, then living at the Windmill pub at Thundridge, worked in the RDC food office at 30 Baldock Street (now demolished) and recalls that it was often full with bedraggled, dirty and tired Londoners wanting to register their ration books with retailers in the town. The plight of these people was raised and discussed at the next full Council meeting where it was accepted that homeless families were sleeping rough in the town's shelters at night including young children. Although it transpired that many had not approached the Ware billeting officers the Council agreed a resolution by the chairman of the housing committee "that the Emergency Committee should be given power to put into a reasonable condition for occupation in an emergency certain homes which were subject to demolition orders. Such action would not be taken until the authority were satisfied that additional housing accommodation had to be made available immediately and when all billeting accommodation had been fully utilised."

Ware was now bursting at the seams, towards the end of October 1940 the Food Control Officer estimated the town's population had increased by some 2,000 – 2500 as a result of official evacuation schemes and the influx of others seeking respite from the London Blitz. To put it another way the town's population had grown by 25% in a matter of months and it is hardly surprising that the billeting officers were now finding it difficult to obtain voluntary billets for evacuees although they could still resort to the compulsory powers invested in them. Their problems were not helped by the news, which would travel quickly in a small town such as ours, that in several cases the evacuees had caused damage to their billets. One such example happened to Mr Fordham of 84a High Street who was eventually paid £5-5s-0d (£5.25) compensation by the Council for damage to his household effects.

With accommodation within the town at a premium it was inevitable that some people took advantage of the Londoner's plight and charged exorbitant rents. This was brought to Councillor Walter Thurgood's attention, he was told that some council house tenants were charging evacuees ten shillings a week for a single room in which families cooked, ate and slept. To give but one example a tenant in Fanhams Road let his three bedrooms to evacuees while the occupier, his wife and three children slept and lived in one room, he was served a notice by the Council requiring him to abate the overcrowding. Another family were luckier, the occupier of 56 King George Road relinquished the tenancy and the evacuee family living with him were entitled by law to become the new tenants. Pressure on the town's accommodation was increased in October 1941 when it was announced that war workers (factory workers) were to be billeted in the town, possibly these were people drafted in to repair army tanks at Wickham's. This proved to be the last straw for the two voluntary billeting officers, Miss Cavell and Miss Gibbs, who resigned and were replaced by Mrs D M Bennett on a full-time basis at a salary of £2.00 per week which was increased to £3.25 some five months later.

Forty-two Barnado boys from Bayfordbury House, Hertford, came to the Central School in September 1942 – it appears that they were evacuees from Lewisham since a Council minute reads: "School at Lewisham bombed on 20th January 1943, a number of children killed. This School had been evacuated to Ware". For a while in 1942 Fanhams Hall was used as a temporary home for Cheyne Hospital for children with heart problems (*see the photograph on the next page*). During 1943 Widbury House was used as a nursery by London County Council.

With the end of the war in Europe in May 1945, evacuees returned to London and

Children from the Cheyne Hospital in London in the garden of Fanhams Hall in 1942 and (left) playing with toys in the Library. The little boy in the centre with the bricks was Jim Myers, now 65 and living in Sawbridgeworth. He wrote to the Hertfordshire Mercury *in 2001 about his memories of Fanhams Hall during the war.*

Hastings at the end of the summer term. Many lasting friendships continued well into peacetime. For example, when Margaret Morris married, Mrs M Huggins with whom she had been billeted in London Road provided the reception at her home. It was not until 1952 that the town's people who had taken in evacuee children received official thanks for their kindness when they were presented with a certificate from Queen Elizabeth. One who received the certificate (*see below*) was Mrs A H Wall of 100 Canons Road – she was hostess to a lad from Holloway and, when he returned home, she then took in two girls from Hastings High School.

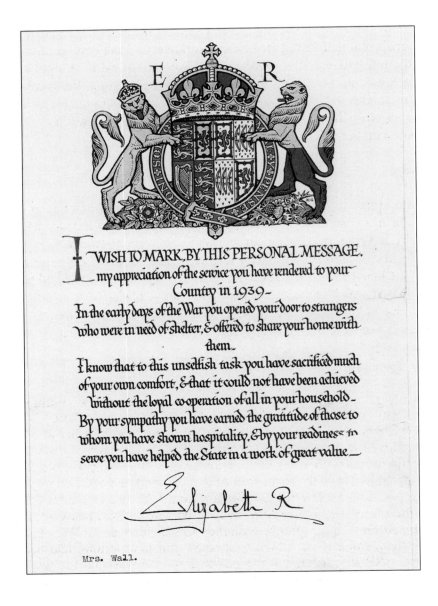

I WISH TO MARK, BY THIS PERSONAL MESSAGE, my appreciation of the service you have rendered to your Country in 1939.

In the early days of the War you opened your door to strangers who were in need of shelter, & offered to share your home with them.

I know that to this unselfish task you have sacrificed much of your own comfort, & that it could not have been achieved without the loyal co-operation of all in your household. By your sympathy you have earned the gratitude of those to whom you have shown hospitality, & by your readiness to serve you have helped the State in a work of great value.

Elizabeth R

Mrs. Wall.

Chapter 3
THE BLACKOUT AND AIR RAID SIRENS

The blackout was the first wartime irritation Ware's townsfolk had to accept. Under the Lighting Restriction Order of 1939 any form of street lighting was prohibited, all domestic and business premises had to screen windows to prevent lights being seen by enemy aircraft. Motor vehicles and cyclists were subjected to restrictions too, life for pedestrians wasn't easy either since torches had to be shielded. Bonfires were prohibited during the hours of darkness and as a cowman from Standon was to find out the regulations covered the movement of cattle at night as well. At first the blackout was treated as a bit of a joke but not for long, the number of road accidents rose and more casualties were caused by the blackout than from any form of German activity. The general public finally got the message when the authorities clamped down on the offenders.

Street lights

Ware's street lighting was entrusted to the North Metropolitan Power Company who had sensibly ensured that most lights were supplied by independent lighting cables controlled by a master switch, it was therefore a simple task to switch the lights off for the duration of the war. Full scale blackout trials were undertaken on 8th and 11th August 1939 and proved successful. To help motorists and pedestrians alike in the blackout white lines were painted on the roads in the town centre as were alternate kerbs on key roads, the Engineer and Surveyor reported that these were in place as hostilities were declared. Later road studs were added at road junctions.

"Put that light out!"

Under the Lighting Restriction Order it was an offence to allow a glimmer of light to be seen from any domestic or industrial building during the hours of darkness regardless whether an air raid was in progress or not. Within the home this was normally achieved with heavy lined curtains, black roller shutter blinds or wooden shutters while in many factories the windows were often simply covered in black paper or painted black. In the early days of the war the Ware Police apparently took little action against breaches of the regulations until the German air raids started in earnest in the summer of 1940. From then on breaches of the blackout regulations were strictly enforced by the Police with the cases being heard at Ware Police Court in Watton Road. Initially the offenders pointed out that nothing had been said to them by the ARP authorities but the police response was that the wardens only patrolled the streets once the siren had sounded and were therefore in no position to comment whereas they, the police, patrolled the streets regardless whether a raid was taking place or not. The first prosecutions were reported in the *Mercury* dated the 28th June 1940:

> *Two Ware residents were each fined 10s-0d each at Ware Police Court on Tuesday for failing to screen indoor lights. They were Frederick P Ward, aged 42, a foreman of 14 Cross Street and Frank Watson, aged 40, a coach driver of 26 Fanshawe Crescent.*
>
> *Giving evidence in the case of Ward, Special Constable Hammond said that on 7th June he was on duty at Clements Street when he saw an unscreened light at the back of a warehouse owned by Messrs Albany & Son Ltd. He was unable to gain admittance so he broke a window and smashed the bulb. Ware Reserve Constable Corne gave evidence of interviewing Ward on 9th June when he made a statement in which he said he was a foreman at Albany & Son Ltd and that on 7th June he was doing his books and had a light on, when he left the building he forgot to switch the light off.*
>
> *PC Pearman giving evidence in the case of Watson said he pointed out an unscreened light to Watson, he said my wife must have forgotten to pull the blackout. The light was showing from an inner room and reflected through frosted glass windows.*

Father Francis Macirone of the Presbytery in King Edward's Road came before the Bench on 9th July for showing a light at 11.00 pm The good Father was fined £1, he was a persistent offender being fined £4 for his second offence and when caught for the third time on 5th November the fine was increased to £10 with the threat of imprisonment if he offended again. With so many blackout infringements in Hertfordshire, the Chief Constable flew over the county with the Royal Air Force and singled out Bishops Stortford as "appalling". Ware was not put on the black list but the offences continued. When Harry Jackson of 27 Croft Road was cautioned by a warden he replied "what's wrong there isn't a raid on" – the magistrates reply was "fifteen shillings to pay!". When Arthur Spencer of 4 New Road received his summons he wrote to the court saying " a stray cat must have got in and switched the electric light on". Cat or no cat he still had to pay a fine of ten shillings! However early in the New Year of 1941 an alleged interview with a captured German pilot was printed in the *Mercury,* who is reported as saying *"we always drop bombs where we see a light".* After this piece of propaganda fines became less frequent and more severe.

Motorists and cyclists

All motor vehicles had to screen their lights. The bulbs of side lights were restricted to seven watts and the glass was to be obscured with two layers of tissue paper or replaced with ground glass; rear lights were masked so that light was emitted through

Head lamps had to be fitted with narrow apertures (as here) or hoods which directed the light down on to a narrow stretch of the road.

a single aperture of not more than one inch (25mm) diameter.

Other war time regulations stated that cars had to be immobilised when left unattended for any length of time; if parked in the road at night they to face in the direction of the traffic flow and show a light front and rear, all sensible requirements in unlit streets. The regulations were strictly enforced as local residents were to find to their cost. Geoffrey Parker of Westmill Road was fined 15s-0d (£0.75) when he left his car without lights in Ware Road on the 26th July 1940. In comparison Ernest Rednall of Hampden Hill got off relatively lightly when he failed to immobilise his car and parked on the wrong side of the road during the hours of darkness, his fine was 5s-0d (£0.25).

Cyclists had to have shielded front lamps, rear lights and red reflectors on the rear mudguards, another sensible precaution since shielded car head lamps were about as effective as a glow worm in an unlit street. The town's police enforced the regulation and many a Ware cyclist found himself before the local Magistrate. The reason for some many offences possibly stems from the fact that few people owned a car in 1939 and therefore didn't realise that the mere presence of a windscreen filtered out the little light the drivers had. The first recorded offence by a Ware cyclist was by Arthur Brown of 42 Star Street who was caught riding a cycle without lights in Ware Road on 1st November, he was fined 2s-6d (£0.12). He was quickly followed by Harold Clue of 31 Baldock Street, James Ward of 20 High Street and Alfred Bradshaw of 59 Fanshawe Crescent all whom appeared at the Magistrate's Court in Watton Road. Many other cases followed, various excuses for not complying with the regulations were given such as the cyclist from Ware Park who said he had difficulty in getting batteries – it still cost him a 5s-0d fine! With an increase in the number of military vehicles on the local roads an ever increasing number of accidents involving cyclists it was not long before common sense prevailed, lights were used and the number of court appearances dropped dramatically.

With unlit streets and vehicles fitted with shielded headlights it was not long before accidents happened, the first blackout victims in Ware were two dogs run over and killed in mid September, this prompted an article in the *Mercury* urging dog owners not to let their pets out at night. Probably the first accident involving pedestrians happened on 29th October, a moonlit night albeit cloudy, when H Stanion of 12 Church Street knocked down four soldiers in Ware High Street, fortunately there were no serious casualties. Stanion was fined ten shillings for careless driving. Young Joseph Clibbon was not so lucky. Clibbon, a seventeen year old lad, was knocked down and killed by an army lorry in Amwell End after leaving a dance at the Drill Hall on a dark and very foggy night. His mother and step-father, Mr and Mrs P W Rolfe, lived at 17 Clement Street. Joseph, who was in the ATC, was employed by H Page & Company. Maurice Brett of 160 Musley Hill who was with Joseph at the time was injured and taken to Hertford hospital. Pedestrians struggling in the darkened streets fell foul of the authorities, Reginald Walters of 39 Croft Road was caught flashing an undimmed torch towards a building in Maidenhead Street, Hertford on 10th December 1939 and fined 2s-6d (£0.12) for the offence. On Monday, the 8th January 1940, two trains collided in the dark to the west of the level crossing at Amwell End. Fortunately there were no serious casualties but the rescue operations were severely hampered by the blackout regulations. Air Raid Warden F G Stockwell of Bowling Road fell over during an air raid alert on 7th June 1940. Stockwell injured his leg, broke his glasses and tore his clothing, the Council reimbursed him £3-10s-6d (£3.53) for replacements.

The most bizarre blackout infringement court case was heard in Ware on the 2nd January 1940, the caption in the *Mercury* read:-

COWS MUST BE LIT UP
Standon man pleads ignorance of the Law at Ware
Lamps for and aft!

Pleading ignorance of the law a Standon cowman, Cecil Hitchens of Eleanor Cottage, Stortford Road, Standon was summoned at Ware Police Court on Tuesday for failing to cause lamps to be carried while driving ten cows in the hours of darkness at Standon on the 20th November last. The prosecution was brought under the Lighting Restriction Order of 1939. Unfortunately the report does not give the outcome of the case.

"Wailing Winnies" – Air raid Sirens

As enemy aircraft crossed our coastline their movements were tracked by the Observer Corps operating from posts placed in strategic positions throughout the country. They estimated the aircraft type and numbers, their height and direction of flight passing the information to their Control Centre who in turn transmitted the reports to Fighter Command at Stanmore. The nearest observer post to Ware was in Hertford which came under the control of No. 17 Group based at Watford. The post at Hertford, code number B3, was originally located in Brazier's pit on the Ware to Hertford Road. However it proved to be unsuitable since it had a poor view of enemy aircraft approaching from the south, furthermore it was considered too close to the road and noisy and so it was relocated to a site near Titmus's farm on the Hertford to Welwyn Road. Fighter Command correlated the information supplied by the Observer Corps and assessed the likely targets the bombers were making for and, in the case of Hertfordshire, relayed warnings to the County ARP Office at Hertford. Should Ware be affected then Hertford would telephone a warning message to the Report and Control Centre of an impending raid on the town. The messages were colour coded, yellow for information raid expected, purple for raiders expected to pass overhead, red meant attack imminent and white for raiders passed.

At the outbreak of war the works siren at Allen & Hanburys was used to warn the town of an impending enemy air attack. At first it was manned by company employees during work hours and by paid civil defence members at other times. After a few weeks it was linked by land line to the Report and Control Centre adjacent to Priory Lodge and operated from there. The siren was tested on the first Sunday of month at lunch time between 1.00 and 1.10 pm

The Allen & Hanburys siren proved to be inadequate from the outset of war and Robert Grantham considered using a second factory siren, however two new sirens were installed in 1940. It was proposed that the first one should be at Western House Public Assistance Institution but the Council were concerned that the noise would disturb the residents many of whom were elderly and frail so enquiries were directed to the "Master", Hubert Martin. His response was that many of the elderly did not mind at all since it would save them straining their ears and it would cause them no stress at all! After much debate the second was eventually placed on the roof of 87 High Street, the present day Library. Both were operated from the Control Centre. There were two other sirens in the town although there is no reference to these in either the Council's minutes or ARP documents. Both were located on poles at the Musley Lane Waterworks and adjacent to the railway line near Wickhams. Most of the sirens were still operational long after the war ended as a flood warning system, each siren was fitted with an electricity meter which was read annually as late as 1963.

"There's one coming over John"

With so much production time lost at Allen & Hanburys while the workforce sheltered beneath L and R blocks during an air raid alert Ken Samways decided to adopt the roof spotting scheme operated by Wichams, so every time the siren sounded about six men were despatched to the roof as aircraft spotters. However, as we shall see, there was a flaw in the scheme. Samways had instructed the Air Training Corps cadets in aircraft recognition and he knew that their "star spotter" was a young John Carter who just so happened to work at the factory. John was summoned to see Samways and was told that it would be his job to identify any aircraft in the area during a raid and should they be German ring the alarm bell so that the workforce could take cover. During one raid a dog fight was spotted some way off and John decided that the Priory Street factory was no in danger, however some five or six aircraft broke away and flew very low towards A & H. In fact they were so low that they were below roof level. Now all the wartime aircraft spotting charts gave side and head views together with a plan view as seen from the underside of the plane, faced with an unfamiliar view John decided that they were German Messerschmitts and sounded the alarm bell. With the workers safely ensconced in the shelters it was realised that the planes were in fact British Hurricanes and that no system was in place for the spotters to advise those sheltering that it was safe to return to work so John and his colleagues let them stay there! For a long time after John was greeted with the words "there's one coming over John!"

The air raid sirens were "stood down" on the 2nd May 1945, the one at Allen & Hanburys was returned for their own use, however this was to cause problems since the pitch wasn't altered initially and complaints were made that it frightened young children into thinking that a raid was to take place. The County Council's ARP records show that Ware's sirens sounded in anger for the last time on the 29th March 1945. They also show that the number of warning messages received in Ware for the whole of the war were:

Yellow messages (information only)	348
Purple (raiders expected to pass overhead)	185
Red (attack imminent)	1073 *
White (raiders passed)	1143

*   *The number of times the siren sounded, the figure is confirmed from other sources.*

Like the rest of the country, Ware did not have to sound the different type of alert for a gas attack – wardens would then have toured the town frantically waving wooden gas rattles and, when the danger of gas was past, ringing handbells. The rattles were put to good use after the war by the town's football fans.

Chapter 4
AIR RAID PRECATIONS AND CIVIL DEFENCE

Before looking at the roles the townsfolk played as full-time staff and volunteers within the various Civil Defence sections, it is worth looking at how the overall plan would be operated and on factors common to all branches of the service. In the event of an air attack the town's civil defences were co-ordinated and directed from a Report and Control Centre which was manned day and night throughout the war.

If bombs fell during a raid it was one of the air raid warden's duties to report the damage and assistance required at the scene to the Centre. Where there were casualties members of the mobile First Aid parties (ambulances and their attendants) would go to the scene of the incident, render First Aid and help to remove the badly injured casualties to the First Aid post established at the Priory Street swimming pool or to the County Hospital at Hertford for further treatment. Sitting wounded were to be conveyed to the First Aid Post by "sitting casualty" cars. Where casualties were within a building the First Aid teams were only allowed to enter and treat casualties after it had been secured by the rescue parties. Road clearance crews would be summoned if necessary and in the event of a gas attack nobody would be allowed near the scene until declared safe by the gas clearance squad.

To have an effective Civil Defence organisation a nucleus of full-time members was essential to man key points during daylight hours when many of the volunteers were working out of town. This had been recognised by Ware Town Council who proposed that in the event of war forty-eight people should be directed to full-time civil defence appointments. However, at the outbreak of war the number of trained volunteers willing to exchange their employment to take up civil defence work fell far short of the town's requirements and it was mooted that townsfolk should be called up to fill the vacancies. Nevertheless after much debate in the Priory council

chamber the proposed number of full-time Civil Defence members was reduced slightly, Tom Burgess agreed to a reduction in the First Aid Parties to five, Robert Harradence cut his wardens from sixteen to seven while the other sections remained unchanged. Even so it proved impossible to recruit full-time members to meet these lower targets so in October 1940 three of the

Council's employees were seconded to full-time civil defence work, Alf Trundle and B Smith went to the First Aid section while lorry driver E. Devonshire, a retained fireman with the Town Brigade since 1921, became a full-time fireman.

Training exercises were held regularly through 1940 into 1941, gradually the town's Civil Defence units became much more efficient although an exercise held on the 29th July 1941 turned into a "fiasco" when tear gas was used to simulate a gas attack revealed that there were serious deficiencies within the Rescue and Gas Decontamination Services. After one scheme in Ware the umpire, Dr W G (Bill) May, recorded *"In future exercises I would suggest that more volunteers are required to act as casualties, this would give the First Aid Post more work to do in dealing with large numbers of cases at the same time; if there are not enough Scouts, perhaps those Wardens not on duty could act as casualties"*. Dr May was also surprised to see that the Wardens on patrol were not wearing steel helmets. Major exercises involved the military and the other Civil Defence units in Essex and Hertfordshire: one took place in the first weekend of November 1942 when the general public were asked to co-operate by keeping off the streets. The scheme envisaged that Hertford and Ware were being invaded, that a heavy air attack had neutralised the telephone system and that Ware was surrounded by a pincer movement. The Scouts and Guides acted as casualties while the ACF and the ATC were messengers. ATC sergeant Eric Smith became a real casualty when he was involved in an accident with a motor cycle driven by a member of Ware's First Aid team! The Home Guard enjoyed themselves too letting off "thunder flashes".

From October 1942 people could be directed into Civil Defence work but this did not happen in Ware. In recognition of the part the Civil Defence played in the defeat of the German air attacks in 1940/41 Sunday the 15th November 1942 was declared "Civil Defence Day" – a National Day of Remembrance and Thanksgiving Day in honour of all members of the Civil Defence services. With little enemy activity in the summer of 1943 the full-time members helped out at Western House to relieve the boredom and to gain some practical experience at the same time.

As the risk of aerial attack decreased during after the D-Day landings cuts were made to the town's Civil Defence establishment, wardens posts were only manned when the siren sounded and finally the whole service was "stood down" on the 2nd May 1945 and disbanded on 30th June. Ware's ARP Committee held its last meeting on 7th June having been in existence since the 19th May 1936. The last of the full-time staff, Mr Reed the Deputy ARP Office, Kath Cannon at the First Aid Post, Fred Woodhouse in the Rescue Service and Alf Norman the Senior Warden were given notice that their employment would be terminate at the end of the month. Ambulance drivers Lawrence and Trundle obtained posts with the County Ambulance Service. The equipment was packed up and arrangements made for the Civil Defence vehicles to be put up for sale – an exercise which two years to complete. All civil defence members were entitled to apply for and receive the Defence Medal.

Chapter 5
THE REPORT AND CONTROL CENTRE,
THE WARDENS AND AIR RAID SHELTERS

The original thoughts were that the Report and Control Centre would be located in a first floor room at the Priory. In April 1939 County ARP Officer correctly stated that this arrangement was totally unsuitable since it offered little or no protection against bombs and suggested that a purpose built structure be erected at the rear of the Priory Lodge. Within a month Robert Grantham, with advice from the County Technical Advisor, had designed a reinforced concrete surface structure and commenced building works using the Council's direct labour force. The Centre was fully equipped and operational a few days after hostilities commenced. The money expended on its construction and fittings came to £406-18s-0d (£406.90).

The telephone switchboard at the Centre had two direct lines to the town's telephone exchange as well as direct links to the Fire Station, the Police Station, the Priory and other civil defence posts. It was from here that the air raid sirens were operated and calls for mutual assistance from Great and Little Munden, Thundridge, Standon and Wareside were received. The bunker was fitted out with sleeping accommodation, maps showing the location of the wardens posts etc. Other facilities such as toilets were available within Priory Lodge to which it was linked with a covered way.

The concrete bunker which formed Ware's Report & Control Centre – now incorporated in Ware Museum to show how the town managed enemy air raids.

At the outbreak of war the Council decided to man the Centre by day and night with four full-time Wardens but until they were recruited it was manned by Council staff. Labour shortages meant that only three wardens were recruited two of whom manned the post at night together with the Controller or his Deputy or the ARP Officer, the town's Engineer and Surveyor or his Deputy, a member from the Fire Brigade and the Police. The team was completed by lady volunteers who assisted in the evenings as telephone operators and secretaries. One of the ladies, Monica Skipp (now Mrs G Hale), recalls that a lot of the time was spent reading books etc. and that it was the telephonists job to hit the siren button as soon as the "red alert" was received from the ARP Centre at Hertford. In the event of a breakdown in the telephone system messenger boys based in the Priory Lodge were to convey orders and instructions to the outlying posts by bicycle. Arthur North relates that he and his pal Norman Murphy shared on duties sleeping there every other night on camp beds. Most nights were extremely boring broken by reports of drifting barrage balloons and other similar incidents. The messengers used their own bikes and one lad had his stolen from the Lodge in 1941, it took the Council six months to agree that he had not been negligent and reluctantly agreed to buy him another – second hand of course!

The third paid warden was allocated to the Centre during the day with back up staff being drawn from the Council Offices at the Priory whenever there was an air raid. Approval was given in April 1942 to employ one additional person in Centre, the post was offered to both Charles Spencer of 106 Watton Road and Mr B Wade of 8 Park Road but both declined. A back up Report and Control Centre was established at the Christ Church Mission Hall in Amwell End and remained functional until the end of 1944 when the Hall was closed for civil defence activities.

With hostilities in Europe rapidly drawing to a close the County ARP Officer wrote to Leslie Southall in February 1945 saying that the full-time wardens must be reduced by one and that other cost cutting savings should be effected. Warden Cecil Hartmann was given notice (and thanks). The Rescue Centre closed down on 10th March and its full-time members transferred to the Priory Lodge where they trained to assist in the Control Centre, the services of the lady volunteers operating the telephones were terminated as well. The full-time members were put on a twenty-four hour shift basis until the Civil Defence organisation was stood down on the 2nd May. The Centre still stands today and is in a remarkable state of preservation, following refurbishment it now forms part of Ware museum.

The Wardens and their posts

Although a considerable number of volunteers came forward and trained as wardens after the Munich crisis in 1938 they did not have a room or building to use as a headquarters. This obviously caused resentment since their colleagues in the First Aid and Ambulance Parties had use of a room within the Priory. In October 1938

The wardens from the Scott's Road post in 1945. Some of the wardens have been identified by Michael Jennings as follows: Back row (standing behind the ladies)—Albert Warner Snr of Red House Road, Hubert Reynolds and Stan Hall, both of Chadwell, Esme Styring of Chadwell Lodge, Reg Jennings of Myddleton Road, unidentified and unidentified. Front row—unidentified, Robert Ackford of North Lodge, Hoe Lane, Senior Warden Henry Storey (with the board), Frank Burgess of Amwell End, John Ling of South Lodge, Hoe Lane, and unidentified. If you can identify other wardens, please leave a note at Ware Museum – thanks.

Councillors Gardner and Harradence proposed that the Priory Lodge was taken over and used as the ARP headquarters, the suggestion was deferred by the remainder of the Councillors who wanted a month to think things over. The result was that Gardner and Harradence resigned from the ARP Committee although the later continued as chief warden. Three months passed and still no decision had been reached so on 1st February 1939 Robert Harradence issued an ultimatum to the Council to the effect that if you don't let us have Priory Lodge as an HQ then we, the wardens, will consider resigning "en bloc". While one can understand the frustration felt by the wardens the Councillors had a duty to their tenant living there.

Reports of the Town Council meetings were published almost ad verbatim in the *Mercury* pre-war so whether the ARP Committee liked it or not news of Harradence's threat would have reached the County ARP Officer in a matter of days. It is clear that within a month he had reviewed Ware's defences since he condemned the proposed Control Centre in the Priory, suggested its new location behind the Priory Lodge which he recommended should be used as the wardens' headquarters. The Council now agreed to this and placed their tenant, Fred Woodcock, on the priority list for a council bungalow. Early in May Robert Grantham suggested that as a temporary measure the wardens' headquarters should be in a wooden building in Church Street which had previously been used by the Fire Brigade to store their escape ladder. He also proposed to link the Report and Control Centre to the Lodge which would become the wardens' headquarters in the event of hostilities and that and three combined warden/First Aid outposts should be built. At long last there was a sense of urgency to get things done prevailed. The wardens posts were subsequently increased to four and were finally located at:

(a) The Council's Waterworks at the corner of Trinity Road and Musley Lane.
(b) In Watton Road by the entrance to the Buryfield recreation ground.
(c) On Sid Hornsby's land at the junction of Star Street and Clements Road (Star Street Garage).
(d) On County Council land at the lower end of Scotts Road where it was dug into the bank roughly at the entrance to Hertford Regional College.

The four Wardens Posts were Nissen type shelters large enough to accommodate twelve people but the proposal to locate a First Aid Posts within them did not materialise. Constructed by the Council's work force and linked to the Report and Control Centre by telephone they were operational as war was declared. The capital expenditure for these works including the modifications to Priory Lodge which was handed over as the wardens' headquarters at the start of hostilities is recorded as £272-5s-6d. (£272.28) in Council's financial accounts for May 1940. The posts were fitted with iron beds and blankets, First Aid kits, log books, gas protection clothing, service type respirators, gas rattles and hand bells but were primitive and devoid of electricity, heating and creature comforts. The winter of 1939/1940 was the coldest for forty-five years and a night in a Nissen hut without heating would have been grim.

The wardens had statutory and reporting functions. Along with the Police they enforced the blackout regulations, "Dads Army" was not all fiction since there were several Mr Hodges in Ware known for shouting "put that light out". Their main role however was to observe and report to the Control Centre where bombs fell so that help could be sent, assist people to the air raid shelters and later when the shelters were kept locked following vandalism it was the wardens who opened them when the siren sounded. Since the wardens generally worked in their home area they were invaluable in providing the rescue and First Aid parties with information as who was likely to be in a damaged building. Another of their functions was to check on the condition of the townspeople's gas masks. For most of the war in Ware it was a matter of standing to when the siren sounded, training and practices broke the discomfort and boredom of long night watches.

The Council provided the senior wardens in each section with rations to make hot drinks such as tea, coffee, cocoa, Oxo and Bovril when on duty but in March 1941 a voucher system was introduced. Each voucher was worth 4d (about 2p) which had to be spent within seven days at one of the named tradesmen within the town after it had been signed by a section head. This system caused a great deal of unrest since the full-time members were receiving a nightly subsistence allowance of 3s-0d (15p) and it was not long before every member of the Civil Defence, AFS and Home Guard were placed on an equal footing and were in receipt of standardised nightly subsistence rates set by the Ministry of Home Security.

Things did not run smoothly within the wardens' hierarchy since in April 1940 the senior wardens passed a vote of no confidence in Robert Harradence, the chief air raid warden, who was asked to resign and his services were terminated on the 27th

---

WARDEN'S REPORT FORM.

A.R.P./M.1.

Form of Report to Report Centres.

AIR RAID DAMAGE (Commence report with these words)

Designation of Reporting Agent
(e.g., Warden's Post No.   )

Position of occurrence

Type of bombs : —HE/Incendiary/Poison Gas

Approx. No. of Casualties : —
(If any trapped under wreckage, say so)

If fire, say so : —

Damage to mains : —Water/Coal Gas/Overhead electric cables/Sewers

Names of Roads blocked

Position of any unexploded bombs

Time of occurrence (approx.)

Services already on the spot or coming : —

Remarks : —

ORIGINAL ⎰ These words are for use with a report sent by messenger.
DUPLICATE ⎱   Delete whichever does not apply.

A Warden's Report Form

April. He was replaced by William Ward of Warner Road, Harold Sharp continued as Ward's deputy. The wardens' first real test came on 18th September 1940 when a bomb fell in New Road, Charles Grover was on duty in the immediate vicinity and was seriously injured by the blast. His colleagues aided by the rescue squad toiled in the fallen debris to release people trapped in the two houses severely damaged by the bomb.

After the bomb fell in New Road, it was revealed that the Musley Hill wardens were holding a meeting in a pub since their post was unlit – this resulted in both electric lighting and heating being installed in the posts by the end of the month and well before the onset of another extremely cold winter. The lighting to both the wardens posts, public and school air raid shelters was a 12 volt battery system, Arthur North who worked on their installation recalls that the work was carried out by candle light. Water supplies were installed in July 1941 and the added luxury of conveniences in January 1942 all of which cost nearly £100. Little appears to have been altered at the Priory Lodge which had a dual role as the wardens' headquarters and wardens post for the High Street area until a Morrison table shelter was added in 1942. The wardens' hierarchy in 1942 was:

Chief Air Raid Warden: William Ward, Deputy: Harold Sharp.
Full-time Wardens: Alf Norman (Senior Warden), Cecil Hartmann and one other.
Senior Wardens at posts:

High Street:	Senior Warden Mr RT Trundle, Deputy Warden Mr JE Brierlsey
Trinity Road:	Senior Warden Mr FC Chapman, Deputy Warden Mr FJ Weatherly
Park Road:	Senior Warden Mr JH Slater, Deputy Warden Mr Vaughan
Star Street:	Senior Warden Mr AH Hall, Deputy Warden Mr FP Ward
Scotts Road:	Senior Warden Mr HJ Storey, Deputy Warden Mr S Hale.

On 12th January 1943 Trinity Road and the High Street wardens posts were discontinued at night with the men agreeing to turn out when the siren sounded, the bedding from these posts was withdrawn, cleaned and put into store. The Star Street post continued to operate but the men didn't draw their nightly subsistence allowance. The others remained open but were closed a couple of months later in March. With an increasing shortage of labour coupled with experiences painfully gained in bombing raids it made sense that the wardens took part in rescue operations and training in the elementary principles of rescue work started in February 1944. As we have already seen the whole of the town's Civil Defence arrangements were gradually scaled down as the Allied Forces gained ground in Europe, the last full-time warden ceased to be employed on 16th June 1945.

Some eighty wardens attended their last meeting at the Priory on Thursday the 18th June – a "Wardens' Victory Party". Among the many toasts proposed by the chief warden, William Ward, was one to the wives of all the Civil Defence personnel who were often left alone at home with their young families, a nice gesture on his part. It was a lively evening with entertainment concluding with community singing. Soon after the end of the war the Priory Lodge was refurbished and let to Mr Butler, a local postman on condition that his wife acted as the cleaner at the Priory which she agreed to. The other four posts were demolished.

Air Raid Shelters

It was the Council's duty to provide shelters for ten per cent of its population, that being the number the Home Office thought might be caught in the street during an air raid. Robert Grantham prepared plans in association with the County Air Raids Precautions Technical Advisor for public shelters located at the following locations:
— The present car park at Kibes Lane adjacent to the "Warehouse" for 375 people.
— At 100 High Street for 130 people, mention has already been made of this site but work on the proposed underground toilets had not been started.

— The basement under 87 High Street was to be strengthened with heavy timber supports and had a covered entrance from the High Street on the left hand side of the building. This shelter was capable of accommodating a further 135 people.

— A trench type shelter at Chapel Yard Amwell End for 100 people.

These provided shelter for 740 people, approximately ten per cent of the town's population so the Council had met their obligations under the regulations.

It was late in August 1939 when the go-ahead was given to construct the public shelters and by now the whole of the Council's workforce were fully engaged on the construction of the control centre, the wardens posts, the conversion of the town's swimming pool to a First Aid post and sandbag protection walls at vital installations such as the water works so it was decided to call in outside help from the town's main builders. Crook Brothers were given the task of constructing the trench style shelters while F. Hitch & Co. were entrusted to build the others. Both companies were paid on a cost plus 10% basis and worked round the clock to complete the works in a short a time as possible. Gas curtains were to be hung in all public shelters but proved impractical and so the idea was dropped. The shelters cost £1,884 to build.

So far public shelters had been built only in or near the town centre and concern was expressed that the outskirts of the town were without protection. Councillor Relton raised the resident's anxiety at the height of the Battle of Britain, at the end of August 1940 when he enquired if a public shelter could be provided for residents in the Musley Hill area. He was told that the Council had no powers to construct shelters for the general public apart from those people caught in the street during a raid. However things were to change quickly when the Germans changed their tactics and switched from day to night attacks on London and other major cities and Londoners were arriving in Ware to spend the night in Ware's shelters. The Engineer and Surveyor, now Frank Cornhill, prepared plans for adapting the town's public shelters for use at night which were quickly approved by the ARP's Regional Technical Advisor. Another public surface shelter was built at Walter Clark's slaughter house in Amwell End (to the east of David Morris's car sales area). Work started on the dormitory shelters in December 1940: bunk beds were installed, the trench shelters were made damp proof since they leaked like sieves due to the speed of their construction, sanitary accommodation was added or improved and lighting installed. It was not long before a problem not uncommon in the town today was encountered – vandalism – it was considered that the High Street shelters should be kept open from dawn to dusk and locked at night providing suitable arrangements could be made to open them when the "alert" sounded.

It was suggested that the school's shelters (see chapter 15) be converted to dormitory shelters by installing hammocks – initially the idea was rejected by the County Council's Education Department but in January 1941 the County had a change of heart and agreed that they could be used on the condition that they were left clean and tidy by 8.30am. The County Authorities were probably unaware that the Musley Hill School shelter was being used by the public in October 1940. The Ware Magistrates Court recorded that a well-known town drunk entered this particular shelter on the 24th October and terrified the women and children sheltering there. He was fined £5. The Surveyor arranged for electric lighting and heating provided by small coal stoves to be installed in all the town's school shelters. An indication of how cold the school trench shelters were in February 1941 is given by Miss Metcalf, the headmistress of St. Mary's school, writing in the school log book: "In trenches from 10.25 to 11.30 am – children sent straight home as they were so cold". In March 1941 the Ministry of Health authorised the Town Council to raise a loan of £950 for "the provision of trenches and shelters for air raid precautions". That brought to some £2,612 the money spent on public shelters in the early war years.

Individual householders had to provided their own shelters so in 1938 the Home Office prepared a pamphlet which contained plans and specifications and enabled householders to build, or have built, their own surface shelters in their back gardens to a relatively high standard. The design gave protection against blast and splinters from a 500lb high explosive bomb detonating not nearer than 50 feet. Several were built in the "middle class" areas of the town, one family in King Edward's Road used theirs every night of the war regardless as to whether the siren had sounded or not. Several households shared shelters, for example Walter (Wally) Crook built one in his back garden which was used by his relatives and neighbours. However the cost of materials for the Home Office shelter was beyond the pocket of the average working man in the town who, if he wanted to protect his family, had to use whatever materials he could lay his hands on – from the descriptions of some of these given to the author it is just as well that so few bombs fell on Ware. Soon after the onset of war local companies such as Concrete Utilities in Lower Road, Great Amwell designed and produced a precast concrete shelter which they advertised for sale to the general public for £7-10s-0d.

The most famous of all the war time shelters was the curved corrugated steel Anderson garden shelter was partly set below ground level and usually entered by three brick steps. These shelters, designed by David A Anderson, were acceptably safe and could withstand considerable damage except for a direct hit. One historian wrote, 'to be inside an Anderson shelter felt rather like being entombed in a small, dark bicycle shed, smelling of earth and damp'. Anderson shelters were not made available in Ware free of charge to householders earning less than £350 per annum until June 1944. Just over one hundred were issued in the town. A testimony to the Anderson's robust construction is that one still exists in Mrs Parker's back garden in Myddleton Road where it is disguised as a rockery complete with a waterfall built by her late husband Ralph (Ted). Where an Anderson was not practical the Morrison steel table was issued, this was made with steel angle iron legs with a thick steel top

Have you a Safe Shelter for your Family?

ASK YOUR BUILDER TO GET IN TOUCH WITH US
Our Reinforced Concrete Shelter is a permanent
useful addition to your garden.

CONCRETE UTILITIES, Ltd.,
Great Amwell, Ware (Phone 84)

and steel mesh sides and as its name suggests was intended to fit under a kitchen or dining room table. Some twenty-five were issued and the local Boy Scouts volunteered to put these up for elderly householders.

Letters were sent to some 700 householders enquiring if they wished to take advantage of the offer to be provided with "refuge room". In essence a "refuge room" was a ground floor room protected by baffle or blast walls built externally in front of doors and windows, they were not very popular since they made the rooms very dark. Crook Brothers and F Hitch & Company started work on "refuge rooms" in the Watton Road area in February 1941 as soon as men and materials became available. 128 homes in this area were protected over a twelve month period at an average cost of £15 per house. Similar works followed to homes near the factories at Crane Mead.

Ware was fortunate in that many of its older buildings had dry cellars and basements – the Council pursued a policy of strutting these with heavy timbers on the condition that the householders allowed them to be used by the public at large during raids. The remains of one such basement shelter constructed at Brook House in London Road can still be seen, access was via a flight of covered steps from the footpath. Michael Ottley remembers using it on his way home from school. Such shelters were denoted a black plate with the letter "S" painted in white on an adjoining wall.

We have already seen that the major employers in the town were expected to make their own preparations to protect their employees which the larger employers did voluntarily. In January 1941 Ware UDC came under the Ministry of Home Security's Civil Defence (Specific Areas) Order 1940 which made it compulsory to provide shelters in factories, premises and public buildings which meant that it was now obligatory for companies such as Allen & Hanburys, Wickhams, Thurgoods etc. to review their air raid precautions. The order meant that many of the town's maltings had to provide shelters for the first time and are described by some of the surviving maltmakers as being primitive sand bag blast walls built below the barley storage areas.

Arrangements were made soon after the war to dismantle and demolish the town's public air raid shelters, it was suggested that some of the 800 German Prisoners of War from the camp established at Much Hadham were employed on the work but eventually the demolition was undertaken by local contractors. The remains of the one at "Parrott's" (the shop that used to be in the gap next to the Wine Lodge) was uncovered a two or three years ago when the High Street was repaved.

Dr. Bill May with the staff of Western House – to the right of the doctor Nellie Rutter and Arthur Brazier Jnr; to the left Mrs Myrtle Martin, the Matron (in dark dress), behind her Emily Munt, Sister Maunders, Joan Morris (née Keane) with the Master, Hubert Martin behind her and on the extreme left Bridget Snee.

Air Raid Precautions – Western House

Plans for protecting public buildings were made and a dusty file in the Hertfordshire County Council's archives tells the story of the air raid precautions taken at Western House. The file starts in September 1938 at the height of the Munich crisis with a letter from the Clerk of the County Council to Hubert Martin, the Master of Ware Union at Western House, stating "In the event of an emergency Institutions under the control of the Ministry of Health will become emergency hospitals". Enclosed with the letter was an extremely detailed list of air raid precautions which were to be put in place even listing specific tasks to be undertaken by named members of the staff.

An intensive staff training programme was introduced. On Tuesday 18th July the first of three demonstrations and exercises in air raid precautions was carried out. The first was a rehearsal of the evacuation of the patients to the shelters, the second assumed that an incendiary bomb had fallen on the laundry building roof to demonstrate the use of the stirrup pump and finally a rescue exercise was carried out in the infirmary yard. Dr G W (Bill) May, an Ophthalmic Surgeon and Practitioner of New Road, was appointed as the Medical Officer in charge of the Area First Aid Post at Hertford Hospital where two wards were reserved for use in a major emergency – his wife Phylis was a nursing sister there.

Chapter 6
FIRST AID AND RESCUE SERVICES

It has already been noted that in 1935 the Order of Saint John and the British Red Cross Society were asked by the Home Office to participate with air raid precautions. Ware's St. John Ambulance Brigade (the Ware Division was founded in 1902) was commanded by Superintendent Tom Forbes and together with the Voluntary Aid Detachment (VAD) under Miss Garforth it was to form the nucleus of the town's wartime ambulance and First Aid services. Indeed it can be said that during the war their members virtually ran the town's Civil Defence organisation.

One facet they were not trained to deal with was gas warfare, so training courses were quickly organised and run from a room set aside for Brigade's use at the Priory. On 17th March 1936 ten of their members passed an examination in First Aid for Chemical Warfare. The successful candidates were: Superintendent T C Forbes and Messrs F Beazley, A Blake, T H Burgess, E Dyer, P Lawrence, G Smith, R W Jackson, H J Storey and J W Trundle.

In the years leading up to the outbreak of war more men and women were trained and those who qualified were able to join the Air Raid Precautions Auxiliary Reserve of the St. John Ambulance Brigade. From February 1939 the First Aid services became the responsibility of the Ministry of Health and were administered by the County Ambulance Service with Ware providing the necessary facilities.

Mobile First Aid Service – the Ambulances

In March 1939 the County Ambulance Authority asked Ware to earmark suitable vehicles which could be requisitioned and converted into ambulances should war be declared. The vehicles were to be driven by volunteers, aged between 30 and 50 years old, and tested by Messrs J Street of Hertford for their suitability as ambulance drivers. Private cars were also to be earmarked as "ambulances" to carry sitting casualties to the First Aid Post. The task of organising the vehicles fell on the shoulders of Robert Grantham who had to check with the Royal Army Service Corps that the vehicles he selected were not required for military purposes. On 3rd August 1939, the Brigade's ambulance, together with a Morris van from Crooks Stores and three vans belonging to Robert Kay's Snowdrop Laundry, were requisitioned. The commercial vehicles were modified to take four stretchers.

With two Ministries now involved with air raid precautions there appears to have been a breakdown in communications at County level. When Robert Grantham presented proposals for his combined wardens/First Aid posts in May 1939 he was under the impression that all ambulances were to be based at the Priory and was unaware of an early guideline issued by the Ministry of Health stating that ambulances should not be concentrated in one area which made them vulnerable to aerial attack. This error was not recognised until August when vehicles were requisitioned as ambulances. Clearly the wardens' post were simply not big enough to accommodate the wardens, ambulance drivers and their attendants, the car drivers and First Aid teams. The outcome was that the headquarters and main ambulance station remained at the Priory where the crews occupied a large room on the ground floor together with a smaller room behind the present Town Council reception area as an office. Matching satellite stations were established at Musley Pumping Station and within the domestic science block at Ware Grammar School for Girls (Amwell House).

The Outbreak of War

The day after war was declared the Brigade called volunteers to serve on a full-time basis. H Lund, A Flood, Fred Woodhouse and Bob Jackson stepped forward and served with the Civil Defence throughout the war years. By 9th September 1939 the ambulance station at The Priory together with its satellites had been set up. Resources such as steel helmets, gas protective clothing and service-type gas masks issued from Council's Priory Street depot, were kept at the various posts and not issued to individuals. The ambulances at the Priory were kept in the Priory's timber laundry building – the remains of which still stand today behind the East Herts and Citizens Advice Bureau offices. More equipment arrived in a piecemeal fashion over the ensuing months. The members of the St. John Ambulance Brigade could either wear their own uniforms or, if they preferred, the standard issue overall type "bluette" uniform with the St. John badge on the right breast pocket.

The accommodation at the outposts were as bleak if not bleaker as those endured by the wardens. The one at the Girl's Grammar School was moved from the domestic science room to a shed within the school grounds where the ambulance crews must have suffered real hardship in the harsh winter of 1939/1940. The following October the post was transferred to the Christ Church Mission Hall in Amwell End which the Council rented for £20 per annum. The Mission Hall (on the west side of Amwell End roughly where Ocean Fish Bar now stands) was lit by gas until February 1941 when electricity was installed. It was shared with St. John's Cadets, the 3rd Ware Scouts and the AFS who had established an "action station" there. Mr Kay's converted van was attached to this post and garaged in a shed rented at five shillings (25p) a month from French's Flour Mill until both garage and ambulance were destroyed by fire on 25th November 1941.

The posts were manned at night and at least one person had to remain awake to answer the phone. Their shifts were long – an undated roster for car drivers at the top waterworks First Aid Post shows that one of the three drivers, Ernest Crook, Tom

A car converted into a war time ambulance. It is probably the car purchased from Mr Skipp in 1940 and converted by Walter Thurgood at his Park Road Works. At the wheel is Alf Trundle, who worked for the Town Council, joined the Brigade in the 1930s. After the war he became a member of the County Ambulance Service.

Crook and Charles Ward, was on duty every night with a shift lasting from 9 pm to 9 am – this after a day's work and the prospect of going to work again at the end of the shift.

A directive was issued in August 1940 stating that the "sitting casualty" cars should carry stretchers so they were fitted with roof racks. The cost allowed for this was twenty five shillings (£1.25) and in some cases entailed drilling through the roof of the car – a guaranteed certainty for corrosion with a pre-war car. Four steel stretchers and eight blankets were issued to each vehicle, the object was not to stack the patients on the roof rack but to make them nice and comfortable for transfer to an ambulance when it arrived!

In October Robert Kay received the good news that only one of his vehicles was required on a full-time basis and that the other two would only be required in an emergency. Bad news was to follow, within a month he heard that his retained van had been destroyed in a fire at French's Mill. The replacement ambulance was a converted Morris 21HP car purchased from Horace Skipp of Ware Garage for £30, converted by Walter Thurgood at his Park Road works for £27 and ready for use as an ambulance early in December.

In November 1941 the post at the Musley waterworks was closed and its resources transferred to the Priory. The post at the Mission Hall remained operational with its ambulance stationed in a garage in Chapel Yard until the general stand-down on 5th May 1945. Training continued, in March 1942, when Fred Woodhouse and Alf Trundle

First Aid Party Leaders Course No 12 held at Southend in March 1942. Second from the left in the third row is Fred Woodhouse of Myddleton Road who joined the St. John Ambulance Brigade in 1929 and became a full-time member of the ARP First Aid Party the day after war was declared. After the War he became the Superintendent of the Ware Division of the St. John Ambulance Brigade. When he retired on 13 May 1964 after 35 years the Brigade recognised his devotion to public duty by making him a Serving Brother of the Most Venerable order of St. John of Jerusalem, The St. John Ambulance Brigade.

attended a week long First Aid Party Leaders Course run by the Eastern Regional Training School at Southend. May 1942 saw the purchase of a 1938 25HP Vauxhall car for the First Aid Section from Mr Abbiss's Garage at Hertford for £100; Charlie Adams was put in charge of maintaining all the section's vehicles which were now being inspected on a regular basis by the ARP Eastern Regional Transport Officer. The Mobile First Aid Section ceased to exist in December 1942, when it amalgamated with the Rescue Squad to form the Civil Defence Rescue Service.

Rescue and Demolition Squad

The brief of the Rescue Service was to secure bomb damaged buildings before the First Aid teams were allowed to enter in safety and recover casualties and bodies. Ware's Rescue Squad consisted of seven men based at the Council's Priory Street Depot, they were all volunteers and it would appear that they were without a trained squad leader, without transport and had very little equipment. In spite of this they attended the town's one major bombing incident on 18th September 1940. A training exercise held on 5th August 1941 highlighted the deficiencies within the squad who were the last to arrive on the scene, hardly surprising since they were still without transport. As a solution to the transport problem the Council suggested that their

1932 Morris Commercial lorry could be modified to suit the Rescue Service's requirements; the offer was accepted and Walter Thurgood carried out the conversion works for £45. The Regional ARP Authority authorised the purchase of floodlights together with additional rescue equipment and the appointment of seven men employed on a full-time paid basis to form the nucleus of the squad.

Eric Cullin, recently appointed as the town's Engineer and Surveyor, took on the role of Rescue and Demolition Officer assisted by his deputy William Lewis. Cullin came to Ware from Broadstairs and had experience from "tip and run" raids which were all too common on our coastal towns. By March 1942 he had recruited five men including Mr W H Killon, a Londoner who was then living in Ware. Killon had experienced rescue work during the London Blitz. In an effort to improve moral and relieve the boredom of inactivity Lewis organised a social club for the Rescue and Decontamination squads. Darts matches were played against the Home Guard and whist drives held at the Priory with Killon as the M.C.

In December 1942 the Ministry of Home Security reorganised the teams and the Rescue Squad and Mobile First Aid Service were amalgamated to form the Civil Defence Rescue Service. This was a logical move based on experiences gained in the Blitz on London and other major cities where the two services had learned each other's skills. The new section was run by the Chief Officer of the Mobile First Aid Service, Tom Burgess.

Civil Defence Rescue Service

Tom Burgess and his ambulance men with their St. John Ambulance background were far more professional in their outlook but lacked training and experience in rescue works. To overcome this deficiency a series of lectures and demonstrations were organised and given by Eric Cullin, similarly the rescue team were instructed in First Aid. New quarters for the former full-time rescue members were made available in the Council's Town Depot while the ambulance crews remained at the Priory. However the reorganisation did not immediately solve the ever present problem of manpower and transport. Tom Burgess went to Regional Training School at Southend to learn more on the general organisation required for his new section in May 1943 and on his return he applied to the Labour Exchange for men suitable for rescue work but no suitable applicants came forward. It was not until November 1943 that the manpower problem was solved, with the risk of invasion past members of the Home Guard were made available to make up the numbers of volunteer members.

The transport problems were finally overcome when three ex-W.D. Fordson 30cwt vehicles together with a Commer lorry arrived in 1943. These were housed in a new timber garage built for the sum of £229 by Crook Brothers behind the Report and Control Bunker. Percy Lawrence was put in charge of the maintenance of these vehicles. It was the Council's policy that the Civil Defence vehicles should be garaged, since pre-war vehicles left out in the open were notoriously difficult to start in a cold and damp night even with the aid of a starting handle.

In common with the other civil defence units November 1943 saw the full-time members of the Civil Defence Rescue Section commencing 24 hour shift work apart from Charlie Adams who worked six twelve hour day shifts a week. Not unreasonably the men hoped that other more suitable quarters would be made available for their use. They were soon moved to new quarters in the Council's Town Depot and at long last the former rescue men, ambulance drivers and First Aid attendants finally formed an integrated unit. Here they remained until the 10th March 1945 when the centre was closed down and the full-time staff transferred to the wardens headquarters at Priory Lodge. Ambulance drivers Percy Lawrence and Charlie Adams remained responsible for greasing and generally maintaining the ambulances, First Aid car and rescue vehicles.

With so little German air activity in 1944 (there was virtually none in Ware apart from the "doodlebug" which fell the September) the full-time members qualified in First Aid helped out at Western House. The Civil Defence Rescue Services were stood down in conjunction with the rest of the Civil Defence organisation on 2nd May 1945 and disbanded on 30th June. Ware had hoped to retain a full-time ambulance station in the town after the war when the County Council Ambulance Service was formed, this was not to be although two of its war time ambulance drivers, Lawrence and Trundle were employed by the new authority.

VAD and First Aid Post at the pool

It was probably in February 1939 that the Ministry of Heath and Ware Town Council agreed that in the event of war the main First Aid post combined with a gas cleansing centre would be located at the Priory Street swimming pool. The readiness of our Councillors to co-operate was possibly tempered by the £75 annual rent they would receive from the Ministry! The post was staffed by Red Cross and St. John Ambulance ladies and came under the supervision of the Commandant of the Herts 14 Detachment British Red Cross Society, first Miss Garforth of Widbury Hill and later in 1943 by her successor Miss Gwen Dixon. They also ran the adjacent gas cleansing station. Miss Garforth wasted no time in kitting her ladies out with uniforms, in March 1939 she requested and was duly supplied with eight indoor uniforms, thirty-six overalls and caps which cost £33. It would seem that the Ministry of Health were far freer with their money than the Home Office.

The works required to convert the Priory swimming pool into a First Aid Post were completed a couple of days after war broke out and soon operated day and night for the duration of the war in the Europe. Kath Cannon (now Mrs Bardwell) recalls that working at night did have its compensations since Mrs Lempriere allowed

Right: Kath Cannon (now Mrs Bardwell) of Garland Road who served with the British Red Cross at the Priory Street First Aid Post throughout the war, first as a volunteer then in 1940 full-time. She and colleagues helped with the blood donor scheme and carried out numerous ambulance duties, including taking expectant mothers to Haymeads Hospital at Stortford which was used as the area maternity hospital when the wards at Hertford were set aside for air raid casualties. When diphtheria broke out among the evacuee children from Islington, Kath remembers going to visit them at a hospital at Balls Park, Hertford with Gwen Dixon of Myddleton Road (Gwen was to become the Commandant of the Ware Red Cross Detachment). At other times they helped out at Western House and at Gallows Hill. During a 'flu epidemic in the early spring of 1943 she spent six weeks at Haileybury College Infirmary – when it was time for her to leave she was

presented with a large bunch of daffodils which she soon discovered "the little devils had pinched them from the college grounds." Her saddest memories relate to the a spell she and Gwen Dixon spent at Tring Hospital tending repatriated prisoners of war, many in a terrible state. After the civil defence services were disbanded Kath continued with a nursing career at Western House.

her girls to have free use the pool at the end of the shift, no doubt this would have been frowned on if certain Councillors had known. As the war progressed, four salaried First Aiders were added to their ranks: Kath Cannon, Kath Brazier, Mrs Blake and Mrs Lond. The staff dealt with all the minor air raid casualties as well as some 408 minor casualties not due to the war. Their Commandant, Gwen Dixon, was responsible for the First Aid Post at Thundridge manned by members from the village. Gwen Dixon was a dedicated and well respected Commandant who took a keen interest in her staff, putting their welfare to the forefront especially when away on an ambulance at night. The post closed soon after VE Day and on 1st July 1945 all the members who had served there, including Miss Garforth, were entertained at an informal farewell gathering at Miss Dixon's home in Myddleton Road.

COUNTY OF HERTFORD

LIEUTENANCY OFFICE,

HERTFORD.

Date 12th October, 1945.

DEAR Mr. Ling,

It is a great privilege to me now that the Civil Defence Organization has been disbanded to convey to you this expression of appreciation for the service you have so ably rendered towards the general defence of this Country.

It must be a satisfaction to you and a legitimate cause for pride to know that the local authority and the general public will long remember with gratitude the unfailing trust and confidence they vested in you during the long period of the war.

His Majesty's Lieutenant
of the County of Hertford.

The letter of thanks which James Ling and other members of the Civil Defence services received when the services were disbanded in 1945.

Chapter 7
THE FEAR OF GAS ATTACK

The Council's Surveyor, Robert Grantham, attended a course at the Government's anti-gas school as early as January 1937 so that he could prepare schemes to protect the townsfolk should the need arise. The air raid wardens undertook a survey to establish how many gas masks would be required in the town and publications on "How to make your home gas tight" were made available at the Priory. As time passed, it was gradually realised that the main threat would come from high explosive bombs rather than gas and the priorities changed.

Gas Masks

The survey undertaken by the ARP wardens in the summer of 1938 showed that the town would need 7800 gas masks made up of 2700 large, 2900 medium and 2200 small sizes excluding the special ones for youngsters and babies. These were duly delivered by the Home Office (via the County Council) minus their carrying boxes as the Munich crisis peaked in September 1938 and assembled by Miss Garforth and her team of VAD ladies. Distribution to the townspeople was undertaken by the wardens working from schools throughout the town on Tuesday the 27th September and the following day at the Priory Street swimming pool – a considerable feat by the team of volunteers. Some 7358 lightly waxed carrying boxes, less their carrying strings, arrived in November and were stored in the old stable block in the Council's Priory Yard Depot since it was decided not to issue them until after Christmas. The supply and distribution of the special masks needed to protect the very young was left until war was a certainty. 180 red white and blue "Mickey Mouse" respirators for small children together with 180 helmet type ones for children under the age of two arrived in Ware in July 1939. Another 197 helmet type arrived in December followed by more "Mickey Mouse" ones in the New Year.

As soon as war broke out, everyone had to carry their masks with them whereever they went. The cardboard cases being flimsy soon started to fall apart, the Metal Box Company produced a range of metal containers which were far more robust and practical. They had other uses too. The author's was a cylindrical one which was treated as a rugby ball, we practised our ball handling skills with it on the way to school and by the end of the war it was so battered that I doubt if the mask would have come out of its case in an emergency! Many of the rectangular metal ones ended up as lunch boxes after the war.

Soon after war was declared there was a serious discussion in the Council Chamber relating to small children and their gas masks, a question was asked on what precautions should be taken against children being terrorised during a gas attack. Walter Thurgood, always an inventive man and perhaps with a glint in his eye, suggested that a device could be formed by which a child's arms be could comfortably fixed behind its back to avoid the child panicking and tearing off its gas mask! Councillor Miss Abbot was not amused. Schools in particular had gas and gas mask drills. The full-time wardens toured the town and visited schools to check, repair respirators and fit additional filters. Dorothy Gilbert tells of one gas drill staged at

Iris Whybrew and Margaret Bouttell wearing their gas masks in the summer of 1942.

the Grammar School "we had to hurry through a gas filled tent without our gas masks so that we would recognise a gas attack, needless to say we would all have been Olympic Champions the speed we reached!" (the gas would have been tear gas commonly used in Ware's ARP exercises). The Council minutes show that free gas mask repairs were still being carried out in 1944 when an entry records "Wardens to assist in inspection at St Mary's and Musley Hill Schools. Hastings High School and LCC Schools already done".

The Gas Decontamination Squad

It was anticipated that 50 kilogram bombs containing skin blistering agents such as mustard gas would be used by the Germans, and that a heavily "splashed" area would give off vapour and remain dangerous for at least a day until the droplets had settled. The recognised plan of action was that decontamination squads would be the first to arrive on the scene wearing protective clothing and respirators, cordon off the affected area, remove any casualties to a cleansing centre for treatment and finally decontaminate the area by hosing down with water or treating the surfaces with a bleach material before other services were allowed to enter the area. This plan would work provided the Germans were considerate enough not to drop a mixed cluster of high explosive and gas bombs, none of the guide lines issued covered this possibility!

CONFIDENTIAL

TO BE USED IN CIVIL DEFENCE
INSTRUCTION AND TRAINING

AN ASSESSMENT OF A GAS ATTACK

Introduction

Though much information is available on the subject of war gases, their effects, and the counter measures required to combat them, it is difficult for anyone without access to the data compiled from secret official sources to visualize the probable sequence of events or to assess the magnitude of the effects which might result from a heavy gas attack on a city from the air. There may be a tendency to exaggerate certain potential dangers or to minimize others according to the viewpoint of the individual.

It has accordingly been felt that it would be of value to present a properly balanced assessment of this form of attack, and this memorandum, based on the most accurate and reliable information available, endeavours to outline a general picture of such an event in its proper perspective.

General discussion

Either non-persistent or persistent gases may be discharged from aircraft. Both can be released in the form of bombs, while the latter can also be discharged in the form of liquid spray from the air. Air spray is, however, essentially a weapon for use against persons in the open and likely to be less effective against cities than a heavy attack with gas bombs, to which attention will be confined in this assessment. Other forms of attack may be devised by the enemy but the problem is essentially one of a gas cloud being generated at a point from which it spreads before the wind.

For convenience, phosgene will be taken as typical of non-persistent gases, since it is not only a very likely war gas but is also one of the most deadly. Similarly, in discussing persistent gases, mustard gas will be taken as the prototype as it is one of the most potent blister gases and also gives rise to the most difficult problems associated with defensive measures.

To be completely effective a gas attack must have an element of surprise and it may be expected that if the enemy decides to use gas, the first attack will be a heavy one. In the light of experience of air raids in general, a night attack is more likely, but an attempt to use gas during the day, at the time when most people are in the streets, cannot be ruled out. At night, gas could be more effectively used in conjunction with incendiary and H.E. bombs. The former would bring fire-fighters out of doors, while the latter, by breaking windows, would facilitate the entry of gas into houses where the bulk of the population would be at night.

Though the effectiveness of a gas is influenced by the weather conditions prevailing at the time of the attack, mustard gas can be used in almost any weather. Phosgene is most dangerous in still air conditions and least so in high winds, but if a bomb drops in a town it will create a small area of extreme danger whatever the meteorological conditions may be.

Methods of attack

A phosgene bomb forms a cloud of relatively brief persistence (except in an enclosed area), which drifts along a street before the wind. This cloud is capable of causing numerous casualties, with many fatalities, amongst people who are unprotected at the time of the passage of the cloud, unless they know how to put on their respirators properly and immediately. Phosgene, to be most effective, might be used in large bombs—say 250 kilos or more.

A mustard gas bomb heavily contaminates the immediate area with liquid. In addition, people within 100 yards of the point of burst are exposed to a most dangerous cloud of droplets and vapour which travels down wind. The area round the bomb remains dangerous until it has been decontaminated. Mustard gas, except when used against special targets, would, in general, be more effective and contaminate a larger total area if 50-kilo bombs were used in preference to larger ones.

Precautions to be taken in the event of a gas attack – a leaflet which belonged to Councillor Tom Burgess, Chief Ambulance Officer and Deputy ARP Controller.

The seven man volunteer Gas Decontamination Squad, their vehicle and equipment were based in an old building located in the Council's Town Depot in August 1939, showers had been added so that the men could wash after an incident but other facilities were lacking. When the centre was inspected by the Regional Office of the Ministry of Health in August 1941 it was declared to be unsatisfactory mainly because it was located in an old and inappropriate building. The centre was rebuilt by Norris and Sons of Hertford to meet the Ministry's requirements for the treatment of gas casualties and also scabies. Later in the war it was realised that food stocks could become contaminated with gas so a small treatment centre was built within the Council's yard at the Priory Street where Charles Lucas, the Sanitary Inspector, and his staff would be able to test suspect food. In the late summer of 1943 the ARP Committee decided that a gas attack would most likely take place in daylight hours it would be far better if Council workmen were trained to undertake this task rather than rely on volunteers who, if the truth was known, were thin on the ground.

Gas cleansing centres

Two Gas Cleansing Centres were also set up, the first was adjacent to the First Aid Post at the swimming pool in Priory Street. Two empty cottages in Amwell End were requisitioned for the second where showers and gas geysers were installed. These were numbers 6 and 14 on the west side of the road where the row of shops built in the 1960s now stand, the former was for men and the latter for ladies. The centre at Amwell End with an establishment of four men and four women was never manned during the war, maybe the intention was to rely on people from the nearby Mission Hall ambulance post to treat casualties. The cost of building works to deal with the effects of gas attacks came to £631-12s-7d (£631.63) and was paid for by the County Council.

Apart from the treatment of eyes and skin blisters the other function of the centres was to allow casualties to shower with plenty of soap and warm water and to have a complete change of clothing stored there. Arrangements were made with the Snowdrop Laundry in Baldock Street to decontaminate the clothing at 6d per dry pound with the Council contributing £15 towards the cost of the addition equipment required. Hertford enquired if they could make use of the same special facilities which was readily agreed to. Later facilities were established adjacent to the Wonder Laundry in Hertford which was to treat all clothing from not only Hertford but Hatfield, Ware, Braughing, Bishops Stortford and Sawbridgeworth as well. In the spring of 1942 the storeman who had been in charge of the spare clothing store left the Council's employ, following a stock audit it was found that certain items of clothing were missing including nineteen pairs of men's socks and thirty-two pairs of ladies silk knickers. Was the storeman a transvestite or a black marketer? Police proceedings followed.

Chapter 8
BOMBS ON WARE

A lmost all the bomb damage and casualties the town suffered during the war took place in September and October 1940. The first and worst incident occurred at 9.15 pm on 18th September 1940, a clear and moonlit evening, when a high explosive bomb from a lone raider caught in the beam of a searchlight fell in Vicarage Paddock in New Road. The front page of *The Hertfordshire Mercury* for Friday 20th September 1940 (reproduced on the next page) began its report as follows:

Enemy Bombs Fall on Hertfordshire Town
6 KILLED AND 2 INJURED IN WEDNESDAY NIGHT S RAID
Churches and House Property Damaged

Two houses in a Hertfordshire town were demolished by a high explosive bomb on Wednesday night, resulting in 6 persons being killed in one of the houses.

A Hertfordshire Mercury reporter visited the scene early yesterday (Thursday) *morning and found demolition squads busy at work clearing up the debris. Two houses were completely destroyed, and the roadway was a mass of bricks and broken glass. A Vicarage opposite the two houses also caught the full force of the blast, and doors and windows were torn off, and the roof was pitted with holes.*

CHURCH DAMAGED

The roof of a church was also damaged and a Methodist Church also suffered considerable damage: some distance away the stained glass window of a Congregational Church was practically blown out.

Plate glass windows in the shopping district of the town suffered, and the whole of the row of houses in the street where the two houses were demolished were badly damaged.

The bombing occurred at about 9.15 pm, and many people were having their supper, when suddenly there was a terrific explosion and people scurried to shelter in all directions.

The occupant of a nearby house told a Hertfordshire Mercury reporter that they were reading when they were suddenly thrown out of their chairs by the force of the explosion.

RAIDER CAUGHT BY SEARCHLIGHT

Another eye-witness declared that the raider was caught by a searchlight some distance from the town, and within a few seconds afterwards the explosion followed. A man who was on the scene within a few seconds of the explosion said that the ARP workers responded to the call with great promptness, and in spite the handicap of falling debris, did what they could to release the trapped occupants of the houses. "Their work was magnificent" he said.

A number of soldiers were in the vicinity and they too worked "like Trojans" said an eye witness (they would have been the troops billeted in the Parish Hall of the Roman Catholic Church). *Fortunately the bombing did not cause any fire, although the fire brigade was in attendance.*

KILLED AND INJURED

The six dead persons are:-

Mr Webster, Mrs Webster, Edna Richland aged about 18, Arthur Seaman, R H Harris and Miss Brooks.

Another occupant of the demolished house, Doris Webster, was taken to hospital with severe injuries (she lost a leg)*, and an air raid warden, Charles Grover, was also taken to hospital with serious injuries, having been injured whilst on duty in the vicinity of the house.*

People whose houses were affected were given temporary accommodation in an air raid shelter, and were provided with food and refreshment.

War time reporting restrictions prevented the *Mercury* from stating where the bomb fell but the demolished house was No.63 New Road, now the entrance to Tesco's car park. The house was rented by Stadium for their employees when they moved their premises to Ware from London to escape the bombing. Normally some ten people were in the house but that evening four had gone to the cinema. However there were two visitors there when the bomb struck. One was George and Annie Webster's seventeen year old son George Junior, the second was their son-in-law Arthur Seaman married to their daughter Annie. Arthur's wife together with their three young children had been evacuated to Berkhamstead while Arthur, a journeyman butcher with the London Meat Company, remained in London. George and Arthur used to visited their relatives in Ware a couple of evenings a week. On the fateful evening the four men in the house were playing cards in the front parlour when the bomb fell, three were killed immediately by falling debris but young George, who was sitting with his back to the window, was blown into New Road where he found himself trapped under a timber beam and debris. Through the dust he could see a shaft of moonlight, he wriggled himself free and found himself alone in the street. Contrary to the report in the *Mercury* George says it was some time before the ARP services appeared on the scene with the first arrival being Mr Bishop in his car who wanted to take him to

The entrance to Tesco's car park is where Nos. 61 & 63 stood, No.65, originally a two storey house, was partially rebuilt as bungalow and it is probable that the asbestos roof to its rear extension and workshop are part of the bomb damage repairs.

hospital. This would have been Mr G Bishop of Musley Lane attached to First Aid Post at the swimming pool with his car used as an ambulance for "sitting casualties".

Other people's recollections related to the author confirm George's memories of the delay he experienced. When the bomb dropped some people ran to Mr Bishop's house and others to that of the section air raid warden only to be told that they, the wardens, were in the pub for an "official wardens meeting". The obvious question is why were the wardens at the pub and not at their post? The answer is simple, electric lighting had not been installed at their posts and therefore the pub was a much more convivial place for a meeting and so it is not surprising to learn that electricity was provided to all the ARP posts immediately after this incident.

Why was there a delay? Arthur North who, as a sixteen year old, was on duty as a messenger with the wardens at the Report and Control Centre behind the Priory Lodge when the bomb fell (the messengers were based in Priory Lodge used as the wardens High Street post) provides the answer. He has vivid memories of the incident and he says: "It was ironic that of the few bombs that fell on Ware one could have killed me, just before the bomb fell I was on my way to the head warden's home (Arthur Dickenson) at 65 New Road to collect the tea rations etc., a regular chore, and stopped to talk to a warden outside the Priory gates and spoke to him for about ten minutes which was the time of my journey to New Road. A searchlight at Colliers End picked up a German bomber just over Ware in its beam and it dived to let his remaining bombs go. The house next to the chief warden was demolished. The head warden who worked in London was late home that night due air raids over the capital and was going down his cellar stairs to greet his family a few seconds before the bomb hit the house next door and escaped injury as the top of his house disappeared above him. Two old wardens were walking opposite the houses when one received a shrapnel wound below the heart but walked back to the Control Room to report the incident." The "two old wardens" were Charles and Frederick Grover who ran a ladies and gents outfitters shop at 28 High Street (next to the Bell Inn). They acted strictly in accordance with procedure and reported the incident to the Control Centre who alerted the rescue services

All the unfortunate victims of the New Road bombing were taken to the unconsecrated Chapel within the grounds of the Old Cemetery in Watton Road. Deaths through enemy action were recorded in a Government issued book called the Local Authority's Record of Civilian Death Due To War Operations for Ware Urban District Council. The cause of death entered for the New Road victims given as "due to bomb explosion and falling debris".

The following day reports circulated throughout the town that more than one bomb was dropped on Ware the previous night and these stories still persist today. However the official ARP records show that only one bomb fell in New Road and there were no others in the town that night although there was considerable enemy activity in the area – three bombs fell at Horn's Mill in Hertford with a further four at Tonwell, none of which caused any casualties or damage. The Head of Ware Central School, Albert Evans, was even more specific in his school log where he wrote *"H E bomb in Vicarage Paddock* (now Hanbury Close) *about 25yds from rooms 5 & 6 and 30yds from the Memorial Hall, severe damage to the school with broken windows and collapsed ceilings."* The school remained closed while Crook Brothers effected repairs. The Council minutes show that the demolition of No. 63 New Road together with the adjoining No. 61 which was beyond repair was completed within a week by local builders F Hitch & Co. and Crook Brothers. The remainder of the house repairs were completed by mid February. At Christ Church the windows in the north aisle were replaced with plain glass in May 1942 while the remainder were not fully repaired and restored until 1948, the new east window together with those in the south aisle were unveiled at a service of rededication held on 18th April 1948.

Bombs fell in Great Amwell the following night causing damage to the rail track between Ware and St. Margarets near Concrete Utilities Works. Ware's Fire Brigade attended a fire caused by an oil bomb in Great Amwell that night. Several parachute mines fell in the vicinity of Ware in the next few days including one in Tamworth Road, Hertford which caused considerable damage and killed four people. Among these was twenty-two year old Elsie Wright who worked in the Co-op Stores in Star Street, Ware. Mrs Elizabeth Chivers of 7 Vicarage Road in her weekly letter to her daughter Ethel Brazier, then living at Milton Keynes, described how their next door neighbour, Harry Munt, saw this mine floating down and thinking it was a German parachutist started to run towards it – until he realised "it" didn't have legs! Unfortunately Mrs Chivers doesn't describe what happened next! Raids were a nightly occurrence starting round about nine o'clock with lots of gunfire: Ted Titmarsh had told her that if he wasn't issued with a tin helmet he would have to give up courting since shrapnel from the guns made it too dangerous to be outside – he didn't appear to be too concerned about his young lady!

An amazing sequence of events happened when a parachute mine fell 115 yards (106 metres) from Ware Park Sanatorium on 24th September 1940. The parachute became entangled in a tree and failed to explode. The Sanatorium was evacuated while the mine was made safe by the Royal Navy. An unknown patriotic person suggested that if the mine was displayed in the Priory grounds it could be used as a show piece to raise money for the "Ware Boys at the Front Fund" (*see chapter 19*) and was taken there by Council workmen. It remained for several days before a serviceman walking by with his young son pronounced that the mine had not been fully defused. This caused much panic and an Army bomb disposal team was immediately called in and removed it to Brazier's gravel pit in Watton Road. Despite protests by both the Surveyor, Frank Cornhill, and the Chairman of the Council, Dr Walter Stewart, that it was in close proximity to houses the military decided that this was the place to blow it up. The County Council records note that the blast effect from this sort of mine was considerable, covering a radius of some 500 yards so why did the army detonate the mine there? People over a wide area including Cromwell Road in Hertford were advised by the air raid wardens to leave their doors and windows open to avoid blast damage. The mine was exploded during the evening of Friday 30th September. A large crowd assembled at Widbury Hill to watch the explosion which one person likened to "the rising of the sun."

The explosion caused considerable damage over a wide area, one house was totally destroyed and three more had to be demolished. The Cemetery Lodge together with several houses in Watton Road lost their roofs and another 300 or so (including ten in the Ware RDC section of Westmill Road) suffered various degrees of damage. It seems incredible that no casualties were recorded. Strong words were voiced in the Council Chamber with the members insisting that the town should not foot the bill for the damage repairs which was not in effect caused directly by enemy action. The Council won the day since the Ministry of Health sanctioned the cost of the damage at the end of January 1941. One member of the Council staff working at the Priory at the time felt that this was a vote of "no confidence" in Frank Cornhill and it was he who "took the can" for the fiasco which was neither recorded in the ARP records nor reported in the local paper.

On 9th October twenty-three bombs fell in the Stanstead Abbots area two of which caused damage to Ware's sewage works at Rye Meads, although the buildings and pipework were badly damaged with lesser damage to two of the tanks the plant remained functional. The cost of repairs came to £1704. The same night a goods train was bombed and damaged between St Margarets and Rye House with a result that the line was put out of action for the best part of a day. Railway lines were particularly vulnerable due to glow from the steam engines and more so in the case of passenger trains when the carriage windows "pull down" blackout blinds were not securely fixed.

On 16th October a high explosive bomb hit Walter Thurgood's Coachworks in Park Road at 7.15 pm causing a small fire and heavy damage to a couple of factory buildings. Fortunately the works were closed for the night and the fire watchers had yet to report for duty so there were no casualties to Thurgood's workforce although two men at the adjoining Warerite factory were slightly injured. Upon seeing the damage Mr Thurgood's reaction was typical, "lets clear up and start rebuilding." After the raid a rumour spread through the town that this was a precision bombing attack intended for the Warerite factory. The basis of this story was that two young Germans had worked there before the war and that it was they who had given the factory location to the Luftwaffe. Bearing in mind that this was a night raid by a plane with basic navigation aids and with no other bombs falling in the area that night it can only have been another rogue bomb from a plane fleeing a formation which had been broken up and had lightened its weight for the flight home.

Fred Morris possibly provides the answer to how the "precision bombing" myth started. When the bomb fell Fred, then eighteen, was one of some fifteen or twenty men working under charge hand Con Saunders on the 2.00pm to 10.00pm shift at Warerite whose policy was to carry on working during an air raid alert. However to give their workforce some protection whenever there was a raid a plane spotter was posted outside to watch out or listen for enemy aircraft and warn the workers when to take shelter. On 16th October an elderly firewatcher was performing this duty, he spotted a plane and shouted out "its diving on us". Fred, more out of curiosity that concern for his safety, went outside and realised that there was indeed an aircraft virtually overhead and started to dash for the shelter which was fifty yards away. At the same time he heard a noise in his words "sounded like an express train" and dived for cover. As the bomb exploded he saw the asbestos roof of the Warerite factory cave in and the widows of Skinner's butcher's shop and Smith's grocery in Watton Road shatter. Two of the workers were slightly injured by falling debris which was scattered over a wide area. By the time the story had been repeated a dozen times it is easy to understand how Warerite's works had been damaged in "a precision dive bombing attack." Crook Brothers, assisted by the factory workforce, started the repair works the next morning and three weeks later full production had been resumed.

Although other bombs fell in the town during the war no serious damage was caused nor were casualties sustained until a VI Flying Bomb or "doodle-bug" fell in a gravel pit 100 yards to the south-west of the new Cemetery in Watton Road on 5th September 1944. The blast caused considerable damage to roofs, windows and ceilings over a half mile radius and injured one small child. A considerable number of chickens kept by Allen & Hanburys nearby were also killed. The following report appeared in the *Mercury* on 8th September:

Flying Bomb in Gravel Pit

Residents in a country town in Southern England on Tuesday morning heard the intermittent throbbing of a flying bomb. Many people watched it limp across the sky towards them. It was low, exceptionally low, and after it had barely cleared a row of houses it suddenly dived.

Fortunately the "doodle-bug" picked a gravel pit for its last resting place and the only casualties were a few chickens. Houses had their windows and doors blown in and roofs were damaged. One woman, who watched the bomb approach, was blown down a passage but was unhurt.

Some of the houses damaged were knocked about earlier in the war by a mine. The main grouse that morning was that doors were damaged and could not be shut, and housewives were not inclined to leave their homes to go shopping.

The variation in the roof tiles to some houses in Fanshawe Crescent shows where the damage caused by the "doodle-bug" was repaired. A few weeks after this incident reporting restrictions were lifted and the *Mercury* and the locations where bombs fell could be published. Fortunately the town was not hit by the most feared weapon Hitler used against the civilian population – the V2 rocket, the nearest one to our town landed in a field on the SW corner of the Amwell roundabout. The total cost of repairing bomb damage within the town's boundaries came to £6400 with most of the repairs being undertaken by F Hitch & Company assisted by Crook Brothers.

A number of bombs fell in the surrounding districts. In Ware RDC which was served by Ware's civil defence services, 418 high explosive bombs fell together with some 900 incendiary bombs, 7 land mine and 5 flying bombs. There were two fatalies.

Mortuaries

The chapel in the old cemetery was used throughout the war as a mortuary. It was upgraded in 1941 by Hitch & Co at a cost of £115 to accommodate 18 bodies. Specially printed identity labels were issued by the Home Office and arrangements for photographic identification by the relatives. A temporary mortuary was set up in the Council's Town Depot behind 87 High Street for another two bodies and in the event of a major disaster occurring it was proposed to utilise the Council's garage as well. The chapel was cleared of its war-time fittings and handed back to the Burial Joint Committee in June 1945.

Chapter 9
THE FIRE SERVICES

Ware always had a well trained and efficient Fire Brigade run by the Town Council to protect the many maltings and timber framed buildings in the town. The Brigade was manned by men on a "retained and on call basis" based at the Old Fire Station in what is now the library car park – in the event of a fire members were summoned to the fire station through a series of alarm bells activated from the police station and linked to their homes or place of work. The Ware Brigade also provided cover for Ware Rural District Council. In 1937 the Brigade consisted of a foreman, four motor men, a turncock who knew the location of all the fire hydrants and valves, eight firemen, two reserve firemen and two messengers. There was a wealth of experience within the Brigade – the "old hands" together with the dates they became firemen are shown below:

Fire Captain A Brazier, October 1905   Lieut. W Sheppeard, April 1900
Motorman WC Hart December 1907   Foreman W Hammond Dec. 1914
Fireman F Devonshire February 1916   Fireman B Lambert July 1919
Fireman E Devonshire May 1924 (Messenger in 1920)
Fireman F Davey August 1924   Fireman J Newton 1925

Their equipment consisted of a relatively new Merryweather "Hatfield" Fire Engine complete with an escape ladder purchased in the early 1930s, backed up by a 1912 Strand Mason BV Type 350 gallon Steam Fire Engine drawn by a pair of the Council's horses which were still on the payroll in 1939. One wonders how long the Strand Mason pump took to raise a head of steam!

Auxiliary Fire Service (AFS)

The Home Office recognised that in the event of war the risk of fire through bombing would require increased fire protection. The Air Raids Precaution Act of 1937 enabled the Government to raise, train and equip a body of volunteers or auxiliaries to assist the regular brigades. Fire Captain Brazier and his crew played a vital role in formulating Ware's fire fighting defences against the anticipated fire bomb attack. Not only did the Brigade actively encourage recruits to join the newly formed Auxiliary Fire Service (AFS) by giving fire fighting demonstrations, they prepared lists of extra equipment required and in conjunction with Robert Grantham rectified some of the deficiencies and shortcomings in the town's water supplies. Above all else

Ware's Merryweather "Hatfield" Fire Engine outside the Priory in the 1930s.

they trained and imparted their knowledge to the auxiliaries.

Early Home Office guide lines stated that "fire posts" (where pumps etc. were based) should be about 500 yards apart but the "goal posts" were changed before Ware's plans had been finalised, the new requirements were that the town should be covered by a series "fire beats" from "action stations" based no more than ten minutes travelling time between each. Under the revised plan equipment was ordered for three "action stations" which would be and were subsequently established at the Upper Waterworks, the Girls Grammar School and Park Road.

Arthur Brazier ensured that his volunteers were properly kitted out with uniforms and received recognition for all the training they undertook in their spare hours. His tactics to secure the uniforms were novel to say the least since in July 1938 he told the Council that his first batch of recruits could not complete their wet drills until they had proper uniforms! This worked although it was a further four months before fifteen uniforms were purchased from Hobson & Son of Tooley Street in London. Although Brazier proved to be unpopular with several of the Councillors he clearly showed that he had a flair for man management and realised that it was imperative that the auxiliaries required experienced men to lead them. In November 1938 he suggested that motorman W C Hart be promoted as a Lieutenant with the AFS together with firemen B Camp and John Page Senior as foreman and instructor respectively. Bill Hart, a World War I veteran, had fireman's blood in his veins since his father Joseph had been the town's Fire Captain for many years, John Page had been the Fire Chief in the 1920s and Camp had served in the Brigade for some twenty years. The Council coughed and spluttered when Brazier suggested that Hart's retainer was increased by £3 a year but as usual he got his way! November saw the arrival of the first piece of major equipment to be supplied by the Home Office when the Brigade took delivery of a Coventry Climax trailer pump quickly followed by a second. These pumps, each with a capacity of 120/150 gpm (gallons per minute) and capable of throwing a twin jet of water 150 feet, could be towed by a medium sized car or lorry. By the outbreak of war a third had been delivered as well as a larger Apex heavy trailer pump with a capacity of 350/500 gpm together with an unknown number of canvas dams (reservoirs). With more pumps and hoses Brazier asked for and got a hose winder and brushes which cost £17-15s-0d (£17.75).

The AFS now had pumps but no towing vehicles, it was left to Robert Grantham to select suitable vehicles which could be requisitioned in the event of war – a repeat of the exercise he had carried out for ambulances. Having completed this task Grantham then turned his thoughts to emergency water supplies. He interconnected the rising mains from the town's two pumping stations to the water tower and reservoir so that supplies could be maintained should one of the main pumps be put out of action, new style fire hydrants were ordered and all the valves on the older water mains were replaced to ensure easy operation. This cost £650 most of which was recoverable through government grants. Another precaution was to order diesel generators as standbys at the pumping stations in case the electricity supply failed during an air raid, these together with the new fire hydrants were delivered and installed in December 1939.

Another proposal made to the Home Office was that a fire float should be made available on the basis that much of Ware's industry was adjacent to the river, however this suggestion was turned down. This may be the reason why Robert Grantham came up with a novel idea of storing emergency water supplies for fire fighting purposes, he reasoned that he could dam the town's surface water drains by building in penstock valves at key points and four such valves were ordered at an estimated cost of £50. The idea would have certainly have worked in the low lying areas such as the High Street, Amwell End, Star Street and the culverted part of the Bourne under Baldock Street, unfortunately the records where the penstocks were installed have not survived the passage of time.

The larger companies within the town formed their own factory brigades or held appliances. Allen & Hanburys formed a fire fighting crew under Fire Brigade Captain J Smart and purchased their own trailer pump in July 1939 which could be towed by a company car. Wickhams, with ample experience in manufacturing their well known diaphragm pumps for the civil engineering industry, made their own fire fighting pump manned by members of their workforce who had joined the AFS. Warerite Ltd. of Watton Road, The Ministry of Works at Crane Mead and flour millers French & Co. of Viaduct Road also had fire pumps.

At the end of August 1939 the AFS equipment was removed from its storage place with the pumps first being checked by Wickhams to ensure that they operated at peak efficiency before being distributed to the "action stations", towing vehicles were requisitioned, tow bars were fitted and insurance cover arranged by the Council. Forty-eight efficiently trained volunteers were ready to go into action alongside the Town Brigade, Ware's fire services were prepared for war although events proved that they lacked transport.

Town Brigade and AFS at war

During the early days of the war the station log book records that their call outs were restricted to dealing with breaches of the blackout regulations such as domestic and chimney fires and had assisted at a major fire at Botsford & Wright's premises in Hertford in February 1940. Nearer home they fought a major incident on Tuesday, the 28th May, when the Ware Joinery Works in Star Street were completely destroyed. In the early months of 1940 the Brigade made arrangements with the military to protect their installations, these included the army camp at Colliers End. Correspondence stamped "Secret" shows that the Commanding Officer of a Reserve Supply Depot run by the Royal Army Service Corps at Fanhams Hall was most anxious to be assured that the Town's Fire Fighting Services would be able to provide adequate cover in the event of a fire. The Brigade's first call out as a result of enemy activity occurred during the evening of the 18th September when the bomb fell in New Road killing six people, fortunately there wasn't a fire and the Brigade attended on a "standby basis". They were called out just before midnight the following night when an incendiary oil bomb set fire to a bungalow called "Four Trees" in Great Amwell. However when they arrived at the scene they found that the Hoddesdon Brigade had the situation well under control and that their services were not required.

Ware's fire crew were in action again on the 27th September to deal with a wheat or straw stack at Rowney Priory Estate (Sacombe Green) which had been set alight as the result of an air raid. This incident showed that the Brigade needed a fire tender to back up the Merryweather when tackling a blaze in an outlying area. As a result, a Ford V8 car was purchased for £35 and converted to a tender for a further £37-9s-0d (£35.45). This vehicle was also used to tow the large trailer pump.

Arthur Brazier always looked after the welfare of his men and with the onset of winter he requested that the AFS be issued with waterproofs and recommended that the same type as used by the regular brigade be purchased which they duly were in January 1940. The out stations housing the fire appliances were inspected in November to ensure they offered full protection to the vehicles and pumps, and where necessary improvements were effected.

The AFS training programme continued and by May 1940 at least 59 of its members had passed the prescribed efficiency test on the auxiliary equipment, ladder drills and stirrup pump drill. For their efforts each man was given a £1 bonus. Those known to have passed their efficiency test by the end of May 1940 are given in Appendix

No.8. German air activity increased following the retreat from Dunkirk in June 1940 and the risk of fire through incendiary bombs increased. So in July the Clearance of Lofts Order was enacted, and Ware and Hertford placed a combined public notice in the *Mercury* dated 2nd August 1940 to explain its implications to their townspeople. Following its publication, concern was voiced in the town whether adequate supplies of water would be available in the event of a major fire. A temporary solution came to Robert Grantham when he realised that the maltings did not work in the summer and that their steeping tanks could be used as auxiliary water storage tanks for fire fighting purposes. The Ware maltsters readily agreed to co-operate and store as much water as possible out of the malt making season. These arrangements remained in place until 1942 when three 5000 gallon Emergency Water Supply (EWS) steel static tanks were built in the town, one at the Canons Hotel with the second at the Western Maltings in Collett Road. A third was constructed in King George's Road. Residents on the south side of the town expressed a view that the water pressure in the mains south of the New River was too low to be effective in the event of a major incident. It was soon proved that the poor water supply to Warner and Myddleton Roads did not comply with the requirements of the 1938 Fire Brigade Act – rather odd since the mains and roads were laid in 1939. An exercise by the brigade showed that a Coventry Climax could pump water from the New River to Warner Road, however the Metropolitan Water Board (MWB) were adamant that this would not be allowed until a formal agreement had been drawn up and signed. Under its terms the M.W.B required an annual fee of £2.00, payable in advance of course, and in return they would allow the town to draw water from four access points along the Hertford/London Roads. Three of the points were via existing gates and the M.W.B constructed a fourth, a single leaf gate between the Broadmeads pumping station and Myddleton Road.

Numerous requests were made to and refused by the Home Office for an additional fire tender to convey water and their canvas dams to the scene of a fire. However one incident was to change the Home Office's attitude. In December 1940 a detachment of Ware's full-time and AFS spent 48 hours in London fighting fires at the height of the Blitz, they had left Ware with their only fire tender capable of towing their large pump and upon arrival in London were criticised for not having brought their dams with them! Within a space of a month the Council received Home Office approval to purchase a suitable truck to carry the dams provided the cost did not exceed £150, a Guy lorry was soon to be added to the fleet of fire fighting vehicles.

During an air raid in the early evening of 19th of October 1940 a lone high explosive bomb hit Thurgood's coach works in Park Road damaging and setting fire to the main building in Park Road. The AFS under Lt. Hart were the first on the scene and tackled the blaze.

At the end of October the town had six AFS members employed on a full-time basis, however with frequent calls to fight fires in London they were fully stretched so authority was given to engage another eight AFS men or retained firemen on a full-time basis bringing the total to fourteen, enough to form two twelve hour watches. Conditions at the old Fire Station were primitive and it wasn't long before the full-time crew were asking if the premises could be extended to allow proper sleeping quarters and showers which were agreed to. Eric Cornhill called for tenders to build new accommodation above the recreation room at the rear of the fire station. Crook Brothers submitted a successful bid of £115, bunk beds and twenty blankets (later increased to forty) were provided along with cooking facilities. The "action station" at the Girl's Grammar School was

WARE FIRE BRIGADE.

WARE URBAN DISTRICT COUNCIL.

Report of Fire.

122

Fire at *Thurgoods Works Park Rd* on *Wednesday 16th October 1940*

Called by *A.R.P. Warden* Time *7.15 pm*

Cause of Fire *Enemy activity*

Owner of Property *W.L. Thurgood* Tenant

Estimated Loss { Property, £ _____ Contents, £ _____ } Total _____

Building Insured with _____ Agent _____

Contents Insured with _____ Agent _____

Firemen present :—

Captain *1*

Lieut. *2*   Foreman *1*

A.F.S. *14*

Motor engineers *2*   Firemen *10*   Messengers *2*

Remarks *I was informed that the Brigades services were required at Thurgoods Works Park Rd entrance. On arrival found that an H.E. Bomb had struck the main building, wrecking it & causing fire, the A.F.S. with Lieut Hart were quickly on the scene and attacked the fire from hydrant, I also despatched the main pump, and reserve pump from Fire Station & got to work from second hydrant, fire was quickly subdued and all men were back at their stations by 8.30 pm. Owing to the promptitude of the A.F.S. in getting the fire under control, no pumps were brought into action.* Signed :—

A. Brazier

Chief Officer, W.F.B.

The report of the raid which destroyed the Thurgood's works in Park Road in October 1940.

deemed unsuitable for winter use so the AFS moved to and shared accommodation with the ambulance crew at the Mission Hall in Amwell End. The fire tender and pump were kept in the adjoining Chapel Yard. In March 1941 Arthur Brazier expressed his concern that using part-time cars for towing the auxiliary Coventry Climax pumps was not a satisfactory arrangement and requested the Council to purchase three cars for the purpose. As usual he got his way.

The spring of 1941 saw a flourish of activity by the Ware fire-fighters, besides dealing with local fires at Hardmead, Walnut Tree House at Widford, Mardocks at Wareside, Concrete Utilities at Amwell, pumping out bomb craters at Plashes Farm for the military and a cottage fire at Standon. Calls were made on the Brigade for assistance outside of their normal "patch" and saw them in action at Barking, Enfield, Hendon and as far afield as Swindon on the 24th April. During May they travelled to Trent Bridge (Nottinghamshire) on 9th and two days later they were fighting fires in Enfield. The strain was now beginning to tell on the Fire Captain Brazier, in May he fell out with Councillor Arthur Swain because the Fire Brigade Committee always over ran its allotted time and delayed Swain's Health, Housing and Public Works Committee meeting which followed. It is obvious that there were words between the two since Swain complained to the full Council that Brazier had "a truculent attitude" and poor old Brazier was reprimanded. Whoever was in the wrong it soured the relationships between the Fire Brigade and the Town Council and the "bickering" continued throughout the war with both parties finding fault with each other.

The Councillor's annual Fire Brigade inspection took place on 10th June 1941, the regular firemen and forty-six AFS took part in the march past together with the Merryweather fire engine, four light pumps (including Allen and Hanburys pump) towed by cars and the heavy duty pump by the V8 fire tender. Various displays were drills were carried out by the light pump crews, the fire engine crew and the heavy pump team.

The demise of Ware Fire Brigade came on 1st August 1941 when all the country's fire brigades together with all their auxiliary units became a nation wide organisation and renamed the National Fire Service (NFS). As a grand finale the AFS demonstrated their efficiency and skills by using their pumps and portable dams in relays to pump water from the river in Star Street to King George Road where they played two 150ft high jets of water before the Town Councillors.

The last meeting of the Town Council's Fire Brigade committee was held on the 24th September when they recorded that "the fire service has now been transferred to the Government". However the bitterness between the Council and their ex-Fire Captain continued, at a subsequent meeting it was suggested that Mr Brazier was given an ex gratia payment for the services he had rendered to the town. It was recorded that he had been paid £30 in January 1940 in respect of training AFS members, he received £15 per annum retaining fee and eight guineas per annum for fire practices, it was resolved that "no further payments be made". The saga does not end here either, the Brigade were called to a fire at French's flour mill on the 25th November 1941 when the Merryweather fire engine became bogged down in the mud, to make matters worse one of the trailer pumps would not start. In spite having relinquished all control over the Brigade the councillors still demanded an explanation from Brazier as to how their beloved Merryweather suffered the indignity of being stuck in the mud, this time he was backed by his superiors in the NFS and it was resolved "that no further action be taken." The hatchet was buried at long last.

The National Fire Service (NFS)

The Fire Services (Emergency Provisions) Act of 1941 provided for the unification of the 1600 or so full or part-time Municipal Fire Brigades and their Auxiliaries into the National Fire Service (NFS) for the duration of the war. The Act standardised the nation's fire fighting services so that mutual assistance was possible throughout the country. Until its formation fire hydrants and hose couplings varied from area to area, the designation of staff and ranks varied throughout the country as did rates of pay. From now on the fire brigades were organised on military lines and all equipment could be manufactured and used far more effectively. Like their colleagues in the civil defence Ware NFS came under regional area no.12, sub area four with a station number 12B/2X. The Home Secretary publicly stated that the brigades would be returned to "local control" at the end of the war. Arthur Brazier remained in charge of the NFS in Ware as Section Leader and was now a full-time fireman receiving a weekly wage of £5-15s-0d (£5.75). Bill Sheppeard, his deputy, remained in the town as the Liaison Officer between the Fire Station and the Civil Defence Report and Control Centre. Mr J Riddle was appointed as leading fireman receiving £4 per week.

The provisions of Fire Services Act meant that AFS volunteers could be called up as whole-time firemen and posted anywhere within their region. This happened to three Ware men, R H (Bob) Cruse, C E Gould and J W Wicks who were called up for service with the Cambridge and Wisbech Fire Brigades. Leslie Southall managed to get Cruse's papers deferred "on account of the importance of his occupation being one of the town's bakers". The new NFS continued with routine domestic fires including a major one at Allen and Hanburys on 16th September, here the fire broke out at 10 pm and was confined to four nissen huts built in 1940 which were gutted. Assistance was provided by the Hertford Brigade since it was feared that the fire would spread, many employees return to the site and they together with the Home Guard and Police cleared the contents from the threatened buildings. More fires in hollow trees were dealt with which were probably caused by the local boys having a crafty smoke of a Wills Woodbine or Players Weight which could be purchased in packets of five for about 2p if my memory is correct! The following month NFS officials inspected Ware's fire station, a few minor modifications were required to the sleeping quarters and maps were required to indicate where the static water supplies were – local knowledge was no longer good enough. Another potentially dangerous fire broke out at 11.15 pm on the 25th November at French's Mill where two timber storage sheds were destroyed including a lorry and a Civil Defence ambulance garaged there.

By April 1942 a Dennis 350/500gpm fire tender was received and stationed at Amwell End replacing the converted Ford V8 car and all the water mains had been fitted with standard fire hydrants. The number of NFS fire-fighters had increased to

15 whole-time men and 2 whole-time women backed up by 71 part-time men and 4 part-time women. The NFS attended numerous call outs during 1942, these ranged from putting out bonfires on the town's allotments after dark, two stack fires at Easneye and various domestic fires in Ware and Stanstead Abbotts. On the 6th May the Ware NFS were called to Norwich to help with the fire fighting in the City. When the fire crews returned it was reported that the Ware men were lined up for inspection before being allowed to go into action and fight the fires which raised a few eyebrows in the Council Chamber. In January 1943 the NFS vacated their action stations at the Mission Hall and at Musley Hill Water Works, in both cases the reason given by the Divisional Fire Officer was that "the accommodation was very indifferent".

The Town Council's long association with the fire brigade lingered on, it was an established custom for the Councillors to watch an annual fire drill demonstration and 1943 proved no exception when the NFS duly obliged. Throughout 1943 the NFS were kept busy with dealing with domestic incidents, fires in old trees, bales of straw etc. in and around the district. On 3rd of December they attended a crashed aircraft in which four members of the crew were killed and another two seriously injured. January 1944 saw a major fire in the town when Henry Page's malting in Star Street caught fire, the NFS column based in Hertford were called in to assist Arthur Brazier and five pumps relayed water from the river to fight the fire. Another major fire broke out at Crane Mead Mills owned by F Dixon and Son on 8th June, twelve pumps from Ware and Hertford tackled the blaze with river water. In another incident they went to the aid of a military glider bound for Arnhem which became detached from its mother plane and landed safely in St Margarets Road.

At the end of the war Ware, in common with many other local authorities, fully expected to run their own brigade again bearing in mind the promise made in 1941. However this was not to be, Central Government decreed that Hertfordshire County Council would be responsible for providing and running the fire service in future and argued that they had not gone back on their word since the County Council was local – politicians haven't changed over the years!

Fire Watching and the Fire Guard Service

As a direct result of the 1940 Blitz on London and other cities the Ministry of Home Security were given more powers under the Defence Regulations to combat incendiary bomb attacks. These were announced by the Minister of Home Security, The Rt. Hon. Herbert Morrison, in a broadcast to the nation on New Year's Eve. His appeal was reproduced in a pamphlet delivered to every householder by the WVS and introduced possibly the most disliked of wartime duties – fire watching. The new regulations were quickly introduced. Ware was declared as a "non compulsory area", in other words it was obliged to prepare a fire plan and call for volunteer fire guards or fire watchers but it was not compulsory for them to sign enrolment forms which left them free to join other organisations such as the Home Guard. The Fire Prevention (Business Premises) Order required all businesses employing over thirty people to set up their own fire watching schemes and to deal with incendiary bombs falling on their premises. Another instruction issued in July 1942 stated that all unoccupied buildings had to keep their upper windows unobscured so that any fire developing could be seen and dealt with.

Leslie Southhall, as ARP Officer, acted quickly. He held an initial meeting with the heads of the various ARP sections on Wednesday, the 8th January 1941, to discuss and act upon the new legislation. Southall drafted a circular outlining the Council's proposals which was printed and circulated to every household in the town.

A card was displayed outside every house where a stirrup pump was kept bearing the wording "Stirrup pump & water", 250 such cards were printed (at a cost of £0.44 each) which gives an idea of the number of houses possessing their own pump. Small sand bins provided by the Council were placed outside front doors, larger ones located at strategic street corners such as the junction of Musley Lane and Trinity Road became a common sight in the town too.

Allen and Hanburys set up sleeping accommodation in the basement of their building fronting Priory Street for their fire watchers who were obliged to put in 48 hours per month normally operated in four shifts on a "two hour on and four hour off" basis. They were entitled to a small subsistence allowance but not to overtime. Walter Thurgood organised fire watchers at his Park Road Works (including Warerite), the factory air raid shelter was fitted out with bunks and the male members of his work force manned the scheme during the week. Nell Swallow (now Mrs Henry Page) recalls that the staff ladies provided cover at the weekends when four were on duty together with the manager, Mr Ledger, and a trimmer by the name of Hayward both of whom slept in the office. The Post Office in the High street organised a rooftop watch as did the Northmet Power Company at Bridgefoot where Arthur North recalls that he was one of eight volunteers to assist the office cleaner/firewatcher every eighth night. Wickhams, The Ministry of Works Depot at Widbury Hill and J W French & Co (Frenlite) were among other firms operating fire watching schemes in the town. J W French installed an automatic fire sprinkler system in their works in March 1944, probably the first company in the town to do so.

Although the larger businesses were organised it is clear from a letter dated 1st September 1941 written by Mr Tom Forbes, proprietor of Charles Forbes Ltd the outfitters at 54 High Street (now Phelps Travel and Change of Address), to the Deputy Controller, Tom Burgess, that the smaller traders were far from happy with the situation. Forbes complained in no uncertain terms that the whole scheme was a farce, no training had been given on how to deal with an incendiary bomb and that there was a complete lack of discipline among the volunteers due to poor leadership. It soon came to light that the main reason the town found itself in this highly unsatisfactory state was that the ARP Controller had failed to act on circular 174/

1941 issued by the Ministry of Home Security which allowed the town to employ a full-time grant earning Fire Guard Officer and an Assistant Officer to organise and train the fire guards. The chief air raid warden, William Ward, confirmed that little or no training had taken place since he told the ARP Committee that "in his opinion a full-time person was required as the three full-time wardens in the town would not be able to organise and train the fire guards".

Forbes's letter and Ward's remarks stirred the Council into advertising for a suitable person to be responsible for training the fire guards and wardens, keeping Civil Defence records and to act as a general "dogsbody" when he had nothing else to do! Candidates were interviewed in November and eventually Mr W J Reid of 46 Trinity Road was appointed as the Deputy ARP Officer on the 2nd January 1942 with a salary of £300 per annum and given an office within the Lord Brough Lodge of the Odd Fellows in the High Street. Reid had served as a volunteer ambulance driver since the early part of the war and was preferred to several other far more experienced candidates from out of town. No attempt was made to recruit an assistant for Reid.

With positive direction the senior wardens resolved to find further volunteers within their own sections so that an acceptable and practical fire guard plan could be formulated. This was completed at the end of June and submitted to and approved by the Regional Commissioner. There were now 643 enrolled volunteers compared with 224 a couple of months previously but more were required so the ARP Officer approached Major Ian Buxton, Ware's Home Guard CO., asking for volunteers from within his organisation.

In February 1944 Ware was declared a "compulsory area" and was required to set up a Fire Guard Sector Organisation under the Fire Guard Order of 1943. Although the town had an approved fire guard plan and had trained sector captains and deputies very little practical training had been given to the rank and file fire guards. Furthermore the fire guards, now numbering 700, would neither volunteer as leaders as street party leaders nor attend training sessions at the Priory. Once again in a belated attempt to regain lost ground the full Council voted to appoint an Assistant Fire Guard Officer in Ware at an annual salary of £275 plus a wartime bonus of £49 – the position was never filled – and to give practical training on "the doorstep". One wonders if the response would have been different had the town been firebombed earlier in the war.

By September 1944 it was decided that the German firebomb threat was over and the fire guard service in the town was stood down on 12th September, the task of reporting fires to the NFS was now a warden's job. In common with the Civil Defence services the fire guards were disbanded on 30th June 1945.

Special constables from Ware who served in 'A' Division of Hertfordshire Constabulary 1939-1945

Chapter 10
LAW AND ORDER

Policing in Ware throughout the war was effected from the Police Station in Watton Road. In 1939 it was manned by Inspector Charles Hollands and Sergeant James Lee backed up by four full-time constables, together with an "old time special" S.C. 772 Hubert Culver of Westmill Road. Hubert had joined the force in 1926 and served in Ware throughout the war years. A police reserve was formed in 1939 staffed mainly by retired officers supplemented by War Reserve Constables, four of the latter were to serve in Ware at various times during the war. More "Specials" were called for at the outbreak of war with John (Jack) Adams and Stan Ball being sworn in within the first couple of weeks serving in their civilian clothes until uniforms became available. The police were issued with service style respirators and steel helmets painted blue and lettered "Police" in white. In 1941 the Women's Auxiliary Police Corps were formed to help with administrative work, Hazel Camm was one of the first to join and she served at Ware until January 1944 when she was sworn in as a full-time member of the Herts Police Force.

The "Specials" main role was to work in conjunction with the Wardens to enforce the blackout or lighting restrictions to both property and vehicles, the offenders being quickly dealt with at the Petty Court Sessions held fortnightly adjacent to the Police Station. The court records show that Ware was a peaceful place and practically crime free as would be expected with police patrolling the streets on a regular basis. The odd poacher appeared before the magistrate, very few cases of petty larceny mainly by soldiers and a couple of people were caught selling clothing coupons. There were virtually no recorded problems with the town's youngsters who, as all of pensionable age know, would have been dealt with on the spot! In two of their annual reports the magistrates recorded no cases of drunkenness and congratulated the town's publicans accordingly although the general shortage of beer in the war years must have helped too!

The only major crime in Ware happened on Tuesday the 30th May 1944 when 14,000 new ration books were stolen from the food office in Star Street in the early hours of the morning. These were destined for the black market and the robbery was considered serious enough for questions to be raised in the House of Commons. The police also had to deal with a spate of traffic accidents the majority of which were caused by military vehicles.

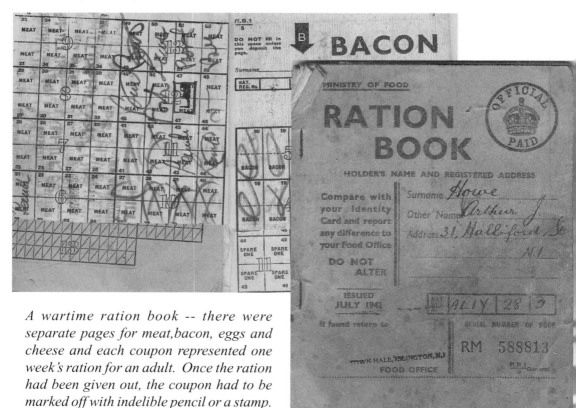

A wartime ration book -- there were separate pages for meat, bacon, eggs and cheese and each coupon represented one week's ration for an adult. Once the ration had been given out, the coupon had to be marked off with indelible pencil or a stamp.

Chapter 11
The Home Front

Although everyone in the town was expecting war few would have anticipated the immediate effects on their daily lives. Apart from the civil defence precautions being put in hand, the influx of evacuees and the blackout regulations, it must have come as a shock to learn that all places of entertainment were to be closed indefinitely. This affected cinemas and football grounds, but fortunately the order was rescinded after two weeks. With the mobilisation of the town's Territorials, Ware Brass lost most of its musicians and Ware Football Club a goodly number of its players so both decided to suspend suspended their activities. Ware Brass resumed in 1942 but the Football Club was closed for the duration of the war although a football league continued to run in the district with teams from the REME, the RA (searchlights), the Army Dental Corps and Allen and Hanburys participating. Identity cards were issued, coal and petrol rationing introduced, food supplies soon became short in the shops. Rationing followed to ensure that everyone received a fair share and stocks were conserved. Days and nights of uncertainty followed with the Battle of Britain and the almost nightly air raids. Clothes rationing was suddenly introduced in 1941 and took everyone by surprise. Gradually the town settled into a war-time routine with the housewife at the forefront struggling to eke out the rations, endless queuing, making-do-and-mend as well as playing a role in charitable organisations.

Identity cards

Friday, the 29th September 1939, was National Registration Day when enumerators visited every household in the country noting the names, date of birth and marital status of people normally resident there. This formed a National Register and every resident was given an individual national registration number entered on a buff coloured Identity Card, which Elsie Woodhouse recorded in her diary were issued in Ware on the 2nd October. It was obligatory to carry the card, usually in a cellophane case, wherever one went. The National Register was also used for the issue of food ration books in 1940 and again when the National Health Service came into being after the war, a person's national registration number appearing on both documents.

Petrol rationing

The first items to be rationed during the war were petrol and coal. The pre-war average monthly mileage of a private car was 600 miles, rationing immediately reduced this to 150 miles at the start of the war, to 125 miles in April 1941, in May 1942 this was reduced to 52 miles and in July of the same year petrol for private motoring was abolished for the duration of the war A supplementary fuel ration was available for those engaged on essential war work but even this was subject to stricter control as the war progressed. In the post-war period petrol restrictions were eased but it was not until 1950 that rationing ceased.

Coal

Coal rationing was introduced under the Fuel and Lighting Order of 1939 enacted on 7th September 1939. Coal merchants were licensed and every householder had to register with their chosen merchant. Rationing started on 1st October which enabled those who could afford it a chance to lay in extra stocks of coal. Local Authorities were required to appoint a Fuel Overseer backed up by a Fuel Advisory Committee. Coal rationing remained in place throughout the war years and further restrictions were placed on the amount which could be stored on the premises.

Charles Lucas, Ware's Sanitary Inspector, was appointed the Fuel Overseer and remained so throughout the war. A room was made available in the Priory as a Fuel Office which the Council received a weekly rental of £1.50 from the Mines Department and to cope with the paperwork Arthur Powell of 25 Baldock Street was engaged as a temporary clerk at a weekly salary of £3.00. Powell was succeeded by Monica Skipp in 1942 and at the end of the war by Charles Spencer.

In the summer of 1940 the Town Council agreed to a request from the Mines Department to store 5000 tons of coal within the town and it was left to the Fuel Overseer and the Surveyor to find suitable storage areas. Transporting the coal from the railway goods sidings to the selected sites at the Old Gas Works, Broadmeads and Caroline Court was undertaken by the town's coal merchants.

Food rationing

Mindful of the food shortages during the First World War, the Government actively encouraged the public to stockpile canned food in 1938, this they achieved through a series of pamphlets and booklets produced by the Canned Food Advisory Bureau. Initially suggestions were made on the sort of items which could be purchased through weekly budget sums, later in the spring of 1939 advice included possible items to provide a weeks food supply together with recipes and storage tips.

In August 1939 all Local Authorities had to appoint a Food Executive Officer and form a Food Control Committee. In Ware Leslie Southall, the Town Clerk, held the position until William Toone of Jefferies Road was engaged as a full-time Food Officer in 1943. The purpose of the Food Committee was to ensure that the regulations were carried out in a practical and efficient manner. The Council provided a large

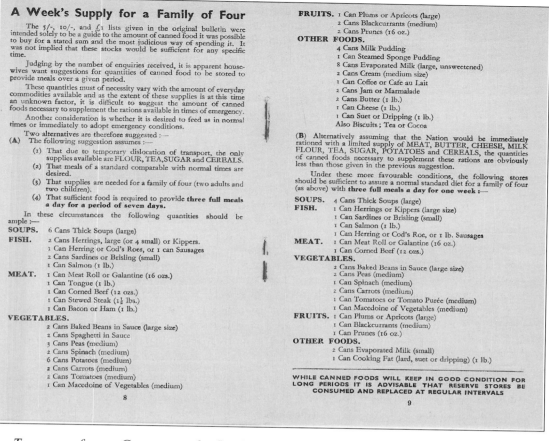

A Week's Supply for a Family of Four

The 5/-, 10/-, and £1 lists given in the original bulletin were intended solely to be a guide to the amount of canned food it was possible to buy for a stated sum and the most judicious way of spending it. It was not implied that these stocks would be sufficient for any specific time.

Judging by the number of enquiries received, it is apparent housewives want suggestions for quantities of canned food to be stored to provide meals over a given period.

These quantities must of necessity vary with the amount of everyday commodities available and as the extent of these supplies is at this time an unknown factor, it is difficult to suggest the amount of canned foods necessary to supplement the rations available in times of emergency.

Another consideration is whether it is desired to feed as in normal times or immediately to adopt emergency conditions.

Two alternatives are therefore suggested :—

(A) The following suggestion assumes :—

(1) That due to temporary dislocation of transport, the only supplies available are FLOUR, TEA, SUGAR and CEREALS.

(2) That meals of a standard comparable with normal times are desired.

(3) That supplies are needed for a family of four (two adults and two children).

(4) That sufficient food is required to provide **three full meals a day for a period of seven days.**

In these circumstances the following quantities should be ample :—

SOUPS. 6 Cans Thick Soups (large)

FISH.
2 Cans Herrings, large (or 4 small) or Kippers.
1 Can Herring or Cod's Roes, or 1 can Sausages
2 Cans Sardines or Brisling (small)
1 Can Salmon (1 lb.)

MEAT.
1 Can Meat Roll or Galantine (16 ozs.)
1 Can Tongue (1 lb.)
1 Can Corned Beef (12 ozs.)
1 Can Stewed Steak (1½ lbs.)
1 Can Bacon or Ham (1 lb.)

VEGETABLES.
2 Cans Baked Beans in Sauce (large size)
2 Cans Spaghetti in Sauce
3 Cans Peas (medium)
2 Cans Spinach (medium)
6 Cans Potatoes (medium)
2 Cans Carrots (medium)
2 Cans Tomatoes (medium)
1 Can Macedoine of Vegetables (medium)

8

FRUITS.
1 Can Plums or Apricots (large)
2 Cans Blackcurrants (medium)
2 Cans Prunes (16 oz.)

OTHER FOODS.
4 Cans Milk Pudding
1 Can Steamed Sponge Pudding
8 Cans Evaporated Milk (large, unsweetened)
2 Cans Cream (medium size)
1 Can Coffee or Cafe au Lait
2 Cans Jam or Marmalade
2 Cans Butter (1 lb.)
1 Can Cheese (1 lb.)
1 Can Suet or Dripping (1 lb.)
Also Biscuits ; Tea or Cocoa

(B) Alternatively assuming that the Nation would be immediately rationed with a limited supply of MEAT, BUTTER, CHEESE, MILK FLOUR, TEA, SUGAR, POTATOES and CEREALS, the quantities of canned foods necessary to supplement these rations are obviously less than those given in the previous suggestion.

Under these more favourable conditions, the following stores should be sufficient to assure a normal standard diet for a family of four (as above) with **three full meals a day for one week** :—

SOUPS. 4 Cans Thick Soups (large)

FISH.
1 Can Herrings or Kippers (large size)
1 Can Sardines or Brisling (small)
1 Can Salmon (1 lb.)
1 Can Herring or Cod's Roe, or 1 lb. Sausages

MEAT.
1 Can Meat Roll or Galantine (16 oz.)
1 Can Corned Beef (12 ozs.)

VEGETABLES.
2 Cans Baked Beans in Sauce (large size)
2 Cans Peas (medium)
1 Can Spinach (medium)
2 Cans Carrots (medium)
1 Can Tomatoes or Tomato Purée (medium)
1 Can Macedoine of Vegetables (medium)

FRUITS.
1 Can Plums or Apricots (large)
1 Can Blackcurrants (medium)
1 Can Prunes (16 oz.)

OTHER FOODS.
2 Cans Evaporated Milk (small)
1 Can Cooking Fat (lard, suet or dripping) (1 lb.)

WHILE CANNED FOODS WILL KEEP IN GOOD CONDITION FOR LONG PERIODS IT IS ADVISABLE THAT RESERVE STORES BE CONSUMED AND REPLACED AT REGULAR INTERVALS

9

Two pages from a Government leaflet describing the canned food available to a family.

room on the first floor of the Priory as a Food Office for which the Ministry of Food agreed to pay £2.00 per week inclusive of services, the Council also provided the staff to man the office.

Food rationing was not introduced immediately due to the considerable volume of paper work required before an effective system could operate, in the meanwhile the average housewife had to cope the best she could. Elsie Woodhouse noted in her diary on 15th September that food prices had started to rise, towards the end of the month she recorded that groceries were in short supply in the shops. Once the Identity Cards had been issued on the 2nd October work started in earnest on writing up individual ration books taking the details from the National Register and they were ready to issue by the end of October. The New Year arrived and it became common knowledge in the town that rationing was imminent since both the chairman of the Food Control Committee and the Food Executive Officer announced in Council that an additional female clerk would be needed to deal with 40,000 meat coupons under the meat rationing scheme soon to be introduced. Elsie Woodhouse wrote in her diary on 8th January " food rationing started" but was a little premature with her entry since there was more bureaucracy to go through. All food retailers had to be licensed and were subject to Food Office control in respect of the amounts they could sell and the prices charged before householders could register with the retailers of their choice.

Meat rationing started on 11th March 1940 with everyone being allowed meat to the value of 1s-10d (£0.09) and by September this figure had been halved plus 2 ounces (57 grams) of corned beef. Sausages (often with a high gristle and bread content!) and offal were not rationed and were often kept under "the counter" à la Corporal Jones of *Dad's Army*. What did a ration buy? Elizabeth Chivers of Vicarage Road writing to her daughter Ethel Brazier puts this into perspective without delving into the mathematical complications of old and new pennies, metric and imperial weights and inflation. One weekend Elizabeth's son Ted serving in the army was home for the weekend and to quote from her letter to Ethel "I managed to get a pound of sausages from Donaghues so Saturday with a slice of bacon, an onion and a couple of sausages I made a delicious pudding and didn't we enjoy it. I managed to get a piece of loin of lamb which cost 1s -9d (the week's ration for one person) for Sunday dinner, we just managed to cut into three." As a result of this weekend Elizabeth had several dinners made from a packet of soup thickened up with oatmeal. If a couple fancied a five ounce rump steak for a Sunday lunch the rest of the week was meatless.

Rationing was soon extended to bacon, sugar and preserves, tea, butter, margarine and cooking fat, cheese, milk, cereals, tinned goods, soup and sweets. Eggs were limited to one per week which could be exchanged for chicken feed if the household kept their own chicken, to encourage this the Council relaxed their rules and allowed their tenants to keep chickens (and rabbits) on council owned allotments although they did draw the line and clamp down on two tenants caught keeping chickens and rabbits in their council houses! Later in the war dried eggs from the USA made their appearance as did Spam which was either liked or hated but it did make excellent fritters! Fish was never rationed but always difficult to get as supplies ran out quickly.

Bread and potatoes were never rationed and together formed the staple diet. The national loaf was introduced in 1941 and had a grey chalky look since it was made from flour with an 82% extraction from grain instead of the pre-war 73%. Bakers were restricted to making three types of bread, viz. split tin, sandwich and Hovis. Cargoes of oranges which successfully eluded the U-boat packs and arrived in Ware were converted into concentrated orange juice and bottled by Allen & Hanburys as part of their war-time operations. An article in the *Mercury* in early January 1945 recorded that oranges were back in Ware's shops but were kept under the counter which was causing friction within the community. Bananas were none existent in the green grocers until the closing days of the war. It seems incredible that rationing continued with some items until 1953 – fourteen years after the outbreak of war.

The nation's health had gradually improved in the nineteen thirties and in spite of food rationing and shortages had continued to do so during the war, welfare food schemes for infants were operated though the Priory Food Office who supplied cod liver oil, concentrated orange juice and rose hip syrup which was also produced in Ware by Allen and Hanburys. Milk in 1/3rd pint bottles was made available at schools. Memories of war time food and the post war luxuries still linger, school diners of mashed potatoes and cold boiled herrings, stews mainly of dumplings and a few pieces of chewy greasy meat, the delight of eating bananas and ice cream again in 1945, of being violently sick after huge helpings of salad cream when it made its reappearance and cringing when Spam sandwiches turned up in the post war lunch box!

Dig for Victory

In September 1939 the Minister of Agriculture, Sir Reginald Dorman Smith, demanded that all available space in gardens should be given over to cultivating vegetables so that as many households as possible could become self supporting as far as fresh vegetables were concerned. This was quickly followed by several Dig for Victory campaigns launched by the Ministry in which councils were encouraged to

maximise the use of open spaces for growing vegetables. Ware Council operated allotments at Sandpits, the Brickfields, the rear of Trinity Road, Musley Lane, Tower Road and Warehouse Field at Widbury Hill. Those at Tower Road were extended in 1942 with the Council ploughing the land prior to letting.

Albert Evans, the headmaster of the Central School, was very keen to grow as much food as possible for the school diner club. So under the guidance of Mr A. Lawrence, the school cultivated part of Christ Church paddock and an acre of allotment in Musley Lane. The school also kept chickens. Evans suggested to Henry Vaughan at the Technical School in Priory Street that a strip of his playground was given over to cultivation and

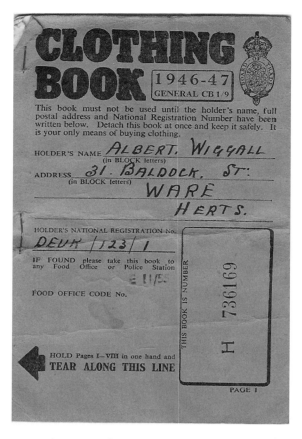

digging started that afternoon! Some of the evacuee boys from the Shelburne School helped with the garden at Widbury Hill then used as a children's nursery by the LCC. One war time activity which did not amuse Albert Evans was potato picking – in the school log book on 14th November 1941he wrote *"Attendance down last week of October has been adversely affected by the regulation which permits pupils to absent themselves from school for potato picking on farms. This regulation has been much abused"*. The wardens at the Waterworks cultivated the waste ground in front of their post for vegetables. The Council were not slow in letting other waste plots of land which could be cultivated, one piece at Caroline Court was let to Fred Baker of Century Road. Grapes and fruit grown in the Priory grounds were given to Western House, Hertford Isolation Hospital and Ware Park Sanatorium or sold off to local greengrocers such as Edward Timmons in Baldock Street.

Clothes rationing

An announcement in June 1941 which took Ware by surprise was the introduction of clothes rationing with no prior warning given. A spare page of sixty-six coupons in the food ration book was used and considered to be sufficient for one complete outfit a year. Women discovered that soft furnishings were not rationed and soon dresses made out of curtain material started to appear but in July 1942 this loophole was closed. A source of material for ladies underwear was parachute silk, one story which still circulates in Ware is that the silk from the land mine which fell in Ware Park on the 24th September 1940 was used for this purpose and that police proceedings followed some two years later! Although no record of a prosecution has been found there does appear to be a link, we have already seen that in the spring of 1942 when the storeman at the Priory Street gas cleansing centre left the Council's employ an audit revealed that thirty-two pairs of ladies silk knickers were missing from his stock. Since the Council had been actively involved with this mine did they, as a cost saving exercise, make the underwear from the parachute silk? Two "young ladies" who shall remain nameless since they are still living in the town confirm that the underwear made from parachute silk was a delight to wear!

This was an era of make-do-and-mend, ladies magazines and national advertisements gave practical hints on how to make use of materials and Ware's second handed clothes shops flourished. There was a thriving black market in clothing coupons where the poorer families sold theirs to the better off, the going rate was 10s-0d (£0.50) per page so Annie Wells of Vicarage Road definitely paid over the odds when she was caught buying eighteen for 10s-0d in April 1944 – she was fined £1-10s-0d (£1.50).

Advice to the public

With new regulations being introduced at regular intervals coupled with the absence of the head many families on active service in the armed forces it became increasingly clear that the public needed general advice and help coping with bureaucracy. To their credit Ware Town Council recognised the need and acted quickly. In November 1939 the Council suggested that a Citizens Advice Bureau should be set up in the town being run by voluntary donations, Councillor Arthur Swain responded by offering space at his Crane Mead works for such a purpose. The CAB offices opened in February 1940, the first to do so in East Hertfordshire with a member of Mr Swain's staff, Mr R C Joyce, as its first secretary. It was soon receiving enquires from the general public as far away as Saffron Walden. The office remained open throughout the war and continues today from offices in the library car park. Miss Joan Pamphilion, the senior typist to the Town Clerk, was appointed the town's Information Officer to give advice on day to day matters caused by the war. Much of her office work was associated with ARP duties so her weekly salary was recoverable from the Ministry of Home Security. She would have been responsible for the distribution and display of the many posters put out by the various Ministries many of which would not be out of place today.

Holidays at Home

With everyone working flat out on the war effort the Government realised in 1942 that people needed a holiday to recharge their batteries, with the usual holiday resorts "shut for the duration" it was suggested that all local authorities laid on entertainment so that people could take their "Holidays at Home" and have some form of escape from the drudgery and hardships of war. The same Councillors who begrudged spending money on immunising the town's children against diphtheria and civil defence matters objected strongly against this proposal on the grounds of cost and the whole idea appears to have been dropped. However common sense prevailed within the town and a series of events were staged over a three week period all of which were highly successful. The following advertisement appeared in the *Mercury* dated the 28th August:

HOLIDAYS AT HOME
RINGLANDS SUPERB CIRCUS
Amazing talent
The Royal Cream Horses
Ponderous Elephant
Comedy Sea Lions
Cowboys from Dakota
Delightful Tiny Ponies

Ware Football Field, Park Road
Monday and Tuesday Aug 31 and Sept 1 at 4.15 and 6.05pm

The circus was a huge success drawing crowds from the town and the surrounding district. Allen & Hanburys organised a concert in their sports pavilion followed by a dance on Saturday the 29th of August with Stan Bloomfield's Band providing the music. Another concert was held in the Priory grounds the following day as well as a bowls tournament. During the week a baby show drew ninety-two entrants with the winners receiving savings stamps as prizes. The following weekend St Mary's Church held a fete at the Priory, here twenty-two members of the recently reformed Ware Brass Band provided the music under Bandmaster E B Carter. Local children, the Scouts and the NFS put on displays, Madam Zeta was on hand to tell fortunes, there were sports and pony rides for the children and incredibly there was an ice cream stall. Who provided the ice cream remains a mystery, most of us who were children at the time have no recollections of having this luxury during the war years, maybe the American servicemen who had just arrived in the area were the providers. The final week saw a swimming gala organised by the local club, the Ware Choral Society put on a performance of "Merrie England", Allen & Hanburys held a huge whist drive at their sports pavilion and Ware Brass brought the three weeks festivities to a close with a band concert.

Although no other "holiday at home weeks " were held in the town the Council did back a scheme in April 1944 known as "Lend a hand on the Land Week" which invited people to spend their holidays on a farm camp "somewhere in Hertfordshire". The advert in the *Mercury* offered to pay takers £2-11s-0d (£2.52) per week less £1-8s-0d (£1.40) deducted for accommodation – hardly and incentive to spend forty-eight back breaking hours weeding and thinning sugar beet by hand!

National Days of Prayer

Apart from their normal and valuable role within the community the town's churches were to the first to organise canteens and recreational facilities for servicemen stationed in and around Ware. With the threat of invasion after the fall of France and in common with churches throughout the land St Mary's bells remained silent from the 13th June 1940 and could only be rung as a warning that German paratroops had landed in the immediate vicinity. The town's churches led the National Days of Prayer and Thanksgiving which were often held during the war. Generally on these special Sundays the services were preceded by a march past through the town by detachments from the Armed Forces, the Home Guard, The Civil Defence and Fire Services, the British legion and the various Youth Services. Among the special Sunday services were:

26th May 1940, for the safe evacuation from France (Dunkirk).

7th September 1941.

14th June 1942, United Nations Day.

15th November 1942, honouring the Civil Defence Services.

15th September 1943, Battle of Britain Sunday.

17th September 1944, Battle of Britain Sunday, and the two Victory Days.

Press, radio and entertainment

The *Mercury,* an invaluable source in researching this book, was published as usual in the early war days – advertising continued with Ware Garage offering a new Austin 12 for £225, alongside notices for stirrup pumps, buckets and corrugated roofing sheets for shelters. However as the war progressed the number of pages in each issue was reduced and to compensate for this the print size became smaller and smaller. Reporting conditions were imposed – when an air raid took place the town hit could not be named and photographs of bomb damage were rarely published. Advertising space was limited mainly to national and local government notices. The national press followed similar lines. Weather forecasts were banned as they were on the radio and the barometer which used to hang in most homes provided a good indication of the day to day weather prospects. The limited television service ceased; not that it was missed since so few had a set. On the radio, news readers for the first time identified themselves, and Alvar Lidell, Frank Phillips, Stuart Hiberd and Bruce Belfrage became household names. Probably the most popular programme after the news bulletins was Tommy Handley in *ITMA (It's That Man Again)*. The main sources of entertainment in Ware were the Astoria Cinema in Amwell End, dances at the Drill Hall with its then excellent dance floor, the local darts league and the never ending round of whist drives to raise money for good causes.

Chapter 12
THE WAR EFFORT

S oon after the outbreak of war the Ministry of Supply under the leadership of Lord Beaverbrook set up the Directorate of Salvage to co-ordinate the recovery of useful materials from household and industrial waste. Salvage collection was the responsibility of the various Local Authorities who were entitled to offset their expenses through the sale of the various materials to authorised dealers at prices controlled by the Directorate. Ware appointed the town's Engineer and Surveyor as its Salvage Officer and set up a "salvage committee" whose members for most of the war were Walter Thurgood and Mrs Walter Clark. The Directorate issued over one hundred circulars and directives covering every aspect of collection, storage, transport, prices and also set collection targets each area were expected to achieve. The targets were based on set figures per 1000 of the town's pre-war population. The bulk of the salvage was collected in trailers towed by the town's dustcarts, the materials were sorted and stored at the Council's town depot behind the present day Library until 1943 when the whole operation was transferred to the rubbish tip at Broadmeads.

To start with the main materials collected were ferrous and non-ferrous metals (including tin cans), paper, rags, bones and kitchen waste but once the German U-boats started to take its toll on our merchant shipping other items were added. With the onset of the Battle of Britain Lord Beaverbrook used his propaganda skills and appealed to housewives to give the Government as many aluminium utensils as possible for the production of Spitfires. In Ware these were collected by the Women's Voluntary Service. The sad thing is that the pots and pans were never used in aircraft production. Although strictly not a salvage item the armed forces required 150,000 pairs of binoculars so an appeal was made January 1941 asking people to donate or sell theirs to the Government, local opticians F W Blythe and George West acted as voluntary collectors in Ware.

To encourage people to save salvage a large coloured "indicator panel" measuring 14ft by 12 ft (4.3m by 3.7m) was painted by Fred Woodhouse and erected outside 87 High Street. The indicators moved to show how the people of Ware were supporting the war effort. In the central panel were 12 illustrations depicting bullets, shells, bren guns, field guns, naval guns, armoured cars, light tanks, heavy tanks, mine sweepers, submarines, destroyers and battleships. The centre represented Britannia and Old Father Time. In the corners were a Spitfire, field gun, army clothing and a pig looking out of a sty. The top indicator was for paper etc. The bottom depicted a hopper for food scraps, that on the right for rags etc., that on the left was for bones. A fifth indicator was added on the extreme left of the panel for waste rubber products.

Salvage operations probably peaked with the Battle of the Atlantic in 1942. A massive salvage drive lasting two weeks was organised by the County Council in July, in Ware the drive was run by the WVS who involved most of the town's organisations and schools. Posters were designed by the Grammar School girls, the ladies section of the British Legion volunteered to be salvage wardens, the Scouts agreed to collect paper throughout the town for which they were paid £1 a ton, a salvage exhibition was on display at the Priory, local schools took part in an essay writing competition on salvage with the winners being awarded savings stamps. The town was divided into four zones to encourage rivalry and a carnival atmosphere prevailed. In "C" zone, the Widbury end of the town, Walter Thurgood and Edward Collins preceded by a barrel organ canvassed the area one Wednesday evening armed with a loud speaker calling on householders to clear out every scrap of salvage for collection on the Friday. Collins indulged in good humoured banter with the housewives. A procession of lorries and wheel barrows headed by the Ware Town Band returned to "C" zone on Friday evening and a team of Army Cadets, Scouts and Guides gathered and sorted the harvest. A salvage dance run by the NFS was held on the 21st February – no the admission price was not a bag of bones! Everyone who had collected and handed in 1 cwt (50 kilos) of waste paper at the Council Yard was given a free ticket. The two week drive ended with a children's fancy dress parade and sports, a swimming gala, a comedy play in the Priory grounds and community singing. During the two weeks seventy-four tons of various salvage was collected and the money raised was given to "Tank for Attack" savings drive.

A similar drive in 1943 concentrated on scrap iron and based upon "heads of population". Ware headed the County list, this was mainly due to the superb effort by the boys of St Mary's School together with the evacuees from the Pakeman Street School collected some eight out of the town's total of thirty-three tons. In recognition of their effort the Town Council gave a percentage of the scrap's value to the two schools which they spent on books. Mr Collins, the head of St Mary's, spent his share on bibles while Mr Piper from the LCC. School purchased copies of "The amazing story of weapons made from waste" for his pupils.

In 1944 the main items targeted were books and magazines, these were the for the services and restocking Blitzed libraries with any unsuitable material received used for pulping. A collection target of 16,000 books was set. Mrs Edith Hunt with the help staff from the local schools scrutinised the 25,000 books handed in! 3,500 were sent to the armed forces, 200 donated to libraries, four and a half tons were sent for pulping.

Iron Railings

On 11th September 1941 Lord Beaverbrook issued a decree stating that all iron railings in public places, on private property or in churchyards were to be removed

Below: the notice issued by four local councils that "all unnecessary iron and steel railings, gates, posts, chains" etc. were to be requisitioned.   The railings at 67 New Road (above) survived because they protected a basement, but those next door were removed.

DEFENCE (GENERAL) REGULATION 1939

IRON AND STEEL RAILINGS, ETC.

NOTICE IS HEREBY GIVEN that the Minister of Supply, in exercise of his powers under the Defence (General) Regulations, 1939, has decided to requisition all unnecessary iron and steel railings, gates, posts, chains, bollards, and similar articles ; and in pursuance of a Direction issued by the Minister, the respective Councils of the undermentioned Local Authority Areas intend to carry out surveys and make and submit to the Minister Schedules of all such articles within their respective Districts.

No appeal from the decision of the appropriate Council to schedule particular railings, etc., will be entertained unless a claim is made by the owner that they are of special artistic merit or historic interest. Any owner who wishes to make any such claim is required to do so within fourteen days of the date of this Notice by letter addressed to the Clerk to the appropriate Council as set out below.

Dated this 19th day of September, 1941.

Local Authority Area.		*Address to which Appeals are to be Sent.*
Borough of Hertford .	.	H. BENTLEY, Town Clerk, The Castle, Hertford.
Hoddesdon Urban District		F. W. MUTTON, Clerk to the U.D.C., Council Offices, Hoddesdon.
Ware Urban District	.	L. G. SOUTHALL, Clerk to the U.D.C., The Priory, Ware.
Hertford Rural District	.	E. A. WILLIAMS, Acting Clerk Hertford R.D.C., 20 Castle Street, Hertford.
Ware Rural District .	.	H. M. GISBY, Clerk to the Ware R.D.C., 6 Baldock Street, Ware.

WARE URBAN DISTRICT	PUBLIC NOTICES

to help the war effort. This applied to all railings made after 1820 unless they were installed for safety reasons such as protecting basement areas or prevented cattle from straying. The idea had originated in Germany where the Germans had carried out a similar scheme and Beaverbrook, always a master of propaganda, sold the idea to the British Public by announcing that stocks of iron were low and that the railings were urgently needed for making tanks and guns. He knew full well that the railings were unsuitable for the production of high grade steel and the majority remained in stockpiles, gradually rotting away. Compensation was to be paid at the rate of twenty-five shillings (£1.25) per ton.

After the war the Government attempted to "cover up" this architectural vandalism by ordering the destruction of the detailed records, our Town Council appears to have acted on this instruction but the Council's minutes do record that by May 1943 the railings already taken down in the town weighed 62 tons 9 cwt.

It is still possible to see where the railings were removed and where they remained in position. New Road is a good example to show this. The mortises in which the railings were fixed to the coping can still be seen at Christ Church, on the opposite side of the road at number sixty-seven the original Victorian railings were left to prevent pedestrians falling down the steps leading to the basement while those to the adjacent properties were removed and replaced with a "hotch potch" of brick walls. St Mary's Church lost its railings too, here a pre-cast concrete coping has been placed on top of the original stone or brick walls. Our historic railings along the New River, made and erected by the Merton Abbey Foundry in 1824, were saved because they prevented pedestrians from falling into the river during the blackout.

Waste paper

Ware had a contract in 1937 with Bow Mills to clear the town's waste paper, which, unlike today, was not restricted to newspapers and magazines. The paper was hand sorted into categories, newspapers fetched £1.50/ton and general waste £1.00/ton when packed in bags. The incentives to save more rose with the outbreak of hostilities and as the volume of paper collected increased the Town Council purchased a bailer in April 1940 for £25. Two ladies, Mrs Grimstead and Mrs Ward, were employed at a weekly wage of forty-eight shillings (£2.40) to sort and grade the paper at the Council's town depot, later in July 1941 they were joined by fifteen year old W Sinclair. A little known regulation made it an offence to burn any form of paper unless it was to prevent spread of an infectious or contagious disease so every householder in the town probably broke the law whenever they lit a coal fire.

On the 25th October 1941 Lord Beaverbrook launched an appeal for the collection of 100,000 tons of waste paper. However it soon became clear that the targets would not be met so he resorted to more trickery and issued a circular on Boxing Day 1941 asking the Local Authorities to consider disposing of all their old records such as the poor law records, rate books prior to 1914-1915, rating lists etc. He knew full well that all the County Archivists would objected to this proposal which they duly did, Beaverbrook took the easy way out and allowed the Archivists to decided the fate of our historical documents Fortunately the majority of Ware's documents escaped this folly and survived for future generations of family and social historians. Storing waste paper prior to collection had its hazards. Baled paper waiting collection by Bow Mills Limited caught fire on the 23rd August 1943 causing damage amounting to £100, with the insurance money the Council purchased a new hut and transferred operations to the rubbish tip at Broadmeads where it continued for the remainder of the war.

Other items salvaged for the war effot were motor tyres, rags and bones, bottles, jars, shotgun cartridges, gramophone records and used HT and torch batteries.

Kitchen Waste

Towards the end of 1939 the Town Council started to keep pigs at Ryegate Farm which formed part of the town's sewage works at Rye Meads, from modest beginnings it grew into a thriving business with up to fifty pigs kept at any one time. Part of their diet was kitchen waste, more commonly known as pig's swill collected from some thirty or so bins placed around the town and taken to Ryegate Farm. To improve pig swill the Council purchased the grain husks from Ware Brewery at four pence a bushel. When mature the pigs were sold at Hertford cattle market and in February 1941 twelve fetched £76.4s.9d (£76.24). Some 61 acres of land at the farm were under cultivation by the farm bailiff, Mr W Creasy, who grew potatoes, greens, lettuces etc. The land was worked by several Land Army girls using two horses, an impressive range of horse drawn farm implements and a tractor.

Soon after the outbreak of the war John Hanbury rather than discard the waste food from the production lines at Allen & Hanburys set up a poultry and pig farm in an old gravel pit off Wengeo Lane which was run by a lady seconded from the Priory Street factory. As we have already seen a large number of the chickens kept there were killed by a flying bomb in September 1944.

Allen & Hanburys

Throughout the war years Allen & Hanburys continued to make their well known range of milk and baby food products, pastilles and lozenges at Ware. As the war progressed production expanded to embrace other products such as operating tables and surgical instruments. The ladies working on the pastille production line formed a blood donors group. Several of the then girls working on the pastille line laugh when they relate that they were paid eleven shillings (£0.55) per week as a starting wage which was a shilling a week more than a shop assistant received.

The ruins of the Allenburys Bethnal Green works in 1940, which led to the transfer of production to Ware.

Their Bethnal Green factory was hit by a parachute mine in September 1940 and severely damaged, the most serious loss was the destruction of the Insulin sterile rooms and apparatus. A fortuitous pre-war development at Ware allowed work to continue. E K (Ken) Samways had set up a laboratory and production facilities in the Priory Street works for "Sterivac" intravenous fluids and the equipment was readily adaptable for filling Insulin fluids. Within ten days the Insulin packing and filling department together with some key workers were transferred to Ware and production successfully restarted. The London workers were either billeted in Ware or travelled to the town daily. Four new nissen huts were built at Ware to house part of the packaged drugs department from Bethnal Green and as the new building were occupied and stocks replenished new work began to pour in. Orders from the Ministry of Food included packing household milk powder, concentrated orange juice and rose hip syrup coupled with the production of special medicines for the Ministry of Supply and the British Red Cross. These were the buildings gutted by fire on 16th September 1941.

With many more workers now at the factory the sports pavilion veranda was removed, the building enlarged and used as a works canteen. With increased production working space and storage facilities became a problem so a series of buildings in the town were leased for the duration of the war. These included malting buildings in Crib Street, Priory Street and Watton Road as well as miscellaneous workshops, stores and houses for offices and workers. Around 1943 a pilot plant set up at Ware to make penicillin on a limited commercial basis using the "bottle" method of production, the penicillin produced was used in "penicillin chewing gum" and field dressings for the services.

The Prime Minister Winston Churchill, sitting on a Wickham's No 17 gang trolley during the Second World War.

D. Wickham & Co.

Wickham's Engineering was engaged on various forms of military work throughout the war years including the manufacture of Mosquito aircraft parts, development work on the Piat anti-tank mortar which may have been tested out by the Standon Home Guard, also the design and production of a mobile jib crane for lifting engines from tanks and aircraft. Their expertise with light railways was put to use in designing and building target towing trolleys which ran on narrow gauge railways, six of these towing units complete with dummy tanks also made at Crane Mead were used on an artillery range near Milford Haven.

The company is probably best remembered in the town for the repair works they carried out on army tanks. The local workforce were augmented by workers drafted in from London and billeted in the town, among them were craftsmen from the London Passenger Transport Board Engineering Base who had considerable experience with AEC bus engines similar to those used in tanks. The first tanks to arrive were Valentines which, although obsolete as a fighting vehicle, were repaired, fitted with flail chains to explode land mines and tested in the old gravel pits at Foxholes before being shipped to Russia. The tanks generally arrived and left from the railway goods yard next to Ware station driven by seven soldiers billeted in the town. Covenanters, another lightly armoured and obsolete tank, made up the second batch which were similarly converted into flail tanks. The far superior American Sherman Mark IIIs and Sherman Medium M4A2s soon made an appearance at the Crane Mead site where they were repaired and overhauled by a team of eight men, normally eight to ten tanks were being worked on at anyone time. The far heavier Shermans moving to and from the Station and Crane Mead damaged the local roads especially the slope leading from the works to Viaduct Road. The County Council replaced this section in October 1943 with a concrete road the surface of which was grooved to give the tanks a better grip remnants of which road were exposed recently during the Crane Mead redevelopment.

Thurgood's coach works

We have already seen that Walter Thurgood's Coach Works in Park Road was actively engaged on the conversion of civilian vehicles to wartime use by the town's civil defence services. Their major contribution to the war effort was in the production of timber components for the most famous of de Havilland's wartime planes, the Mosquito.

The photograph of Thurgood's workforce on the opposite page clearly shows the wing spars packed ready to go to Hatfield for assembly – originally these were constructed from balsa wood from Equador though as supplies became scarce English ash and Canadian yellow birch were substituted. The majority of the men in the photo operated the woodworking machinery while the women, mainly housewives, undertook the finishing processes.

Walter Thurgood was one of the town's entrepreneurs, in 1927 he founded Ware's first bus service based in Church Street, the People's Motor Services. In 1933 he was the founder of Jersey Airways. Another of his enterprises was the coach building works in Park Road building coaches for Phoenix Coaches. He was inventive holding several patents for sliding roofs to coaches and the like. Warerite came under his domain as well as did the "Feathers" at Wadesmill, when his Park Road Coach works was damaged by a bomb in 1940 his first reaction was "lets clear up and start rebuilding." Walter was also a town Councillor.

Swain's Mill

Parts of Swains Mill were requisitioned during the war, the 1st floor was used to store parts made by small engineering companies within the town for the Mosquito aircraft assembled at Hatfield and Burnt Oak (Stag Lane).

The staff of Thurgood's coach works in about 1944. Walter Thurgood is seated in the third row to the right of the centre in the dark suit, others in the photo are Charlie Wikinson (Walter Thurgood's brother-in-law), Wilfie Wright the office cleaner, Winnie Gygax, Arthur Risby who worked in the sawmills and Fred Haywood.

Ware Homing Pigeon Club

Pigeons played an important part in the war, many a wood pigeon found its way to the cooking pot as a supplement to the meagre meat ration while the homing variety were extensively use by the armed forces to carry messages especially when radio silence was imperative, after the war it was revealed that three members of the Ware Homing Pigeon Club trained and supplied some of these birds. The following unusual news story appeared in the *Mercury* on the 25th December 1942:

S.O.S. by Pigeon: HOW RAF LIVES ARE SAVED

Mr A (Arthur) Goldstone of 48 Vicarage Road, Ware, who is the secretary of the Ware & District Homing Pigeon Society has been the local representative of the National Pigeon Service & Supply Officer to the district for the past two and half years. On Saturday last a pigeon entered Mr Goldstone's loft carrying an urgent RAF message. The bird had been released from an aeroplane in distress and because of bad weather was unable to find its home loft which was situated in Lincolnshire. Arthur went on to say that anyone finding a message carrying pigeon should contact him or the police.

Evacuee businesses

Stadium: Stadium were a north London company who moved their factory to Ware during the Battle of Britain in the summer of 1940, occupying premises behind Nos.77 and 79 High Street (Brown's the Grocers) and an old malting in Church Street. The company brought their key workers to Ware many of whom lived at 61 and 63 New Road, the two houses demolished by the bomb on 18th September 1940. In 1941 some 100 women were making high class goggles and similar products for the RAF at the Church Street works together with cycle motor car accessories.

Warerite: Warerite, originally with its Head Office in Birmingham and eventually became another of Walter Thurgood's enterprises, manufactured large quantities of Warerite and laminated plastic boarding used by the services throughout the war. Its sister company, Britannia Mouldings, took over premises in Crib Street soon after the outbreak of war and made plastic mouldings for the services.

Feugeson Radio: Feugeson relocated part of their north London factory in a Crib Street malting to make field radios for the army. Cosmos, one of their subsidiaries, rented space at Swains mill where they made radio valves for the services.

Timber Yards A common sight along the banks of the River Lee from Cheshunt through to Ware were huge stacks of building timber brought by horse drawn barges from ships unloading in London Docks. The Government Timber Controller rented some ten acres of land at Broadmeads owned by Mr H Ward which was used by Gliksten & Son Ltd for temporary office accommodation and timber storage. Timber was off loaded from the barges and moved around the site by four derricks sitting on large concrete bases, the bases were still there for many years after the war. Timber merchants M A Morris Ltd stored timber on the burnt out site of Star Street Joinery together with land at Crane Mead and London Road, James Latham of London used land at the Brickfields for the same purpose. The presence of large stocks of timber on the river frontage was a potential fire hazard so the Council repeated their request to the Ministry of Home Security for a fire float. Again this was rejected and the timber merchants had to provide and maintain the necessary fire fighting equipment to Arthur Brazier's satisfaction. Another timber dump was established just outside the town's boundary at Hardmead Lock where the remains of the concrete roads and buildings can still be seen amongst the undergrowth which now covers most of the area. Ware's concern over potential fire risk to these timber dumps was justified since a 50 kg German phosphorous oil bomb landed in a boggy ditch adjacent to the timber dump at Hardmead Lock on 19th February 1944. Fortunately no damage or casualties were caused.

Chapter 13
PAYING FOR THE WAR

Paying for the war required the sacrifice of many of our overseas investments and assets so the public were encouraged to invest in Government securities through the National Savings Movement. Savings committees were organised throughout the country with Ware UDC and RDCs combining as one area under the chairmanship of Councillor Charles Ward of Collett Road. Ward was typical of many of the World War I veterans who had experienced the horrors of war (he had served as a Lieutenant in the 3rd Battalion of the North Staffordshire Regiment) and gave much of their free time to both the town and the war effort. The committee encouraged people to form savings groups throughout the area and by the end of 1940 at least 65 such groups were collecting in schools, factories etc. and had invested £122,930 in savings certificates and defence bonds. Other people invested at the Post Office and through the town's banks. Towards the end of 1942 the WVS opened a National Savings Centre in their office at No.78 High Street.

The Spitfire Fund

The first savings campaign was called the Spitfire Fund and differed from the subsequent ones inasmuch that it was an open ended campaign with the money collected through fund raising events whereas in the "War Weapons Weeks" which followed the public invested directly into savings certificates etc. On the 28th August Ward and his committee set out to raise £5500 being the nominal cost of the fighter plane and in the midst of vapour trails from the Battle of Britain "dog fights" overhead which ensured a good start. Mr Sayers of the British Legion assisted by Mrs Wallis and members of the Ladies Branch organised a "trail of pennies" which began at the level crossing gates at Amwell End on Tuesday the 15th September reaching the Priory by the Saturday. The trail raised £54.1s.6d (£54.07). Other events such as whist drives and dances at the Drill Hall followed and the progress of the moneys raised recorded on a "thermometer" placed outside the Priory. By the end of October some £900 had been collected by various means including a barrel organ mounted by a model Spitfire and operated by members of the British Legion. Although the fund had crept up to £1470 by the end of January 1941 it was clear that the target was not going to be achieved quickly so Ware and Hertford amalgamated to ensure the sum raised would exceed £5500 by the end of February, with a final flourish of fund raising the target was reached with a total of £5538.

War Weapons Week

The next challenge Ward and his colleagues faced was the first of five War Weapons Weeks which was held during the week commencing the 25th March 1941. The committee set out to raise £50,000 without specifying any particular weapon as a target although a mine sweeper was suggested which might be called HMS "Ware". To ease the workload on post office and banks Robert Harradence made his shop and staff in the High Street available as a savings centre.

The inaugural ceremony was an inspection of a guard of honour formed by the Duke of Cornwall's Light Infantry who then marched through the town accompanied by the Beds and Herts Regimental Band. A fly past by RAF bombers had been planned but this was cancelled at the last moment. Reg Jennings was in charge of publicity and he printed War Weapon Week posters designed by the girls from the Grammar School advertising the various functions arranged for the week. Fred Weatherly was in charge of the events which included an exhibition at the Drill Hall where the exhibits included a 1,200lb bomb, incendiary bombs, a land mine, photographs of German P.O.Ws and model aircraft. The highlight of the show was a German Messerschmitt fighter showing signs that it had crash landed. Some 1,400 local and evacuee children from the district watched national savings films at the Ware Cinema while their parents had the opportunity to go to whist drives at the Priory or watch a review at the Drill Hall entitled "On Target". The week was rounded off by a grand dance at the Drill Hall attended by over 400 people. The incredible sum of £137,832 was invested during the week.

Warship Week and HMS Tulip

Following huge shipping loses in the Battle of the Atlantic the next major savings campaign was Warship Week held from the 31st January to the 7th February 1942, this time they set a target £55,000 being the cost of a hull for a corvette. The opening ceremony was held in the Drill Hall where the assembled crowd were addressed by Admiral C V Osbourne supported by the Under Secretary of State for War, Lord Croft. In his address the Admiral told his audience that the Lord Commissioners of the Admiralty had authorised the town to adopt the corvette HMS Tulip only if they could set their sights higher and raise the £120,000 it had cost to build her. Sunday saw a civic parade through the town in which the Home Guard, the Air Training Corps, the British Legion and the VAD took part and joined a large congregation at St Mary's Church for a Warships Week service.

During the ensuing week a series of events and displays were staged at the Drill Hall starting with the town's school children. Models of ships, aeroplanes and gardens together with posters made and drawn by the children were exhibited, entertainment was provided by pupils from St Mary's School, the boys from the Central School put on a physical training display while the girls from the same school performed country dances. Songs were sung by the evacuee girls from Hastings High School. A boxing tournament between the Army and the RAF was staged on Thursday evening Hall, the referee was the British world light heavy weight boxing champion Pilot Officer Len Harvey stationed at Hunsdon. A concert was held on the Friday evening and the week's events closed on the Saturday night with a grand dance arranged by the Ware's NFS social club and organised by Firemen E Devonshire, J Long and G Warby who acted as the M.C. A large crowd danced to music provided by Jay Dimmock's band. To the younger reader used to the comforts of central heating the major "spot prize" may seem unusual and even amusing, it was five hundredweight of coal won by Mr Starkiss of Tower Road whose family no doubt welcomed a little extra heat that winter.

WARE & DISTRICT WARSHIP WEEK

31st January to 7th February 1942

OUR TARGET

is

Corvette

H.M.S TULIP

ARE YOU A MEMBER OF A SAVINGS GROUP ?
IF NOT PLEASE CONSULT :—

Mrs L. THURGOOD

62, MUSLEY LANE.

ALL WE LEND WILL MAKE IT MORE—
SAY IT !   IT'S **MY** WAR.

An appeal leaflet for the HMS Tulip savings fund – this photo and that on page 100 kindly lent by Beryl Tyser.

By the end of the week £120,706 had been invested in various forms of savings certificates and bonds so the town was allowed to adopt the Tulip and provide her crew with a few home comforts. To mark the event plaques were exchanged, the town's crest carved in wood was sent to the Admiralty for onward transmission to the Tulip and in return the Commissioners presented Ware with a huge gunmetal plaque of the Tulip's badge suitably inscribed to record the town's efforts during Warship Week. Ware RDC received a pictorial reproduction of the badge.

The Tulip was a "Flower Class" corvette of some 1030 tons being laid down at Smith's Dock Company Ltd of Middlesborough in May 1940, launched in the September and commissioned on 5th November 1940. She was allocated to the Western Approaches Command based at Liverpool in January 1941 for escort duty with the Atlantic convoys. In July 1941 she proceeded to the U.S.A for a refit at Charleston and on completion two months later joined the American and West Indies Station escorting ships between Kingston, Jamaica, and Trinidad. Her stay here was brief since she was soon transferred to the South Atlantic Station at Durban. Shortly after her arrival she was allocated to the East Indies Command at Colombo (Sri Lanka) arriving there on 4th March 1942 – about the time that she was adopted by our town. The Tulip, affectionately nick-named the "Tidley T" or "The Terror of the Indian Ocean" by her mess decks, had a ship's complement of six officers and some eighty ratings. She remained in this theatre for the rest of the war.

An HMS Tulip Comforts Fund was set up run by Charles Ward and Fred Weatherly who was also heavily involved with the "Ware Boys at the Front Fund". Moneys were raised by various entertainments within the town and soon enough was in hand to purchase a wireless together with football kit, in Ware Town Football Club's colours of course. The actual purchases were made by HM Comforts Committee who were responsible for their despatch to the "Tidley T". It took many months for the gifts to reach her and finally Mr Weatherly received a letter of acknowledgement from her skipper, Lt. L H Harvey RNVR.

"Tanks for Attack"

Another campaign was run 1942 being held between the 20th July and the 25th September, this the Army were to benefit. The target set was £33,333 but with the amount raised for HMS Tulip earlier in the year it is not surprising that towards the end of the period the figure raised was some £7,000 short of the target. In a last ditch effort the Committee organised a march through the Ware by every organisation in the town to a fund raising rally in the Buryfield. Here, not only were people urged to invest more money, an additional appeal was made to all the young ladies present to join the armed forces. Of course by the time the savings drive closed the target was achieved, in fact the total raised was £38,666 was raised, sufficient for the purchase of two tanks which the savings committee suggested should be called Ware and Ware Rural.

Wings for Victory Week

With the thousand bomber raids over Germany becoming a regular feature in the news it is not surprising that the 1943 savings week was billed as Wings for Victory Week which was scheduled to start on 15th May. The savings committee were confident that they could raise £80,000 which was enough to fund a Lancaster bomber and eight Typhoon escort fighters. The proceedings were opened on the Saturday by Air Chief Marshall Sir W G S Mitchell at Allenburys sports ground with a march past by detachments from the RAF, the RAF Regiment, the WAAF and the ATC headed by the Worcestershire Regiment and Haileybury College Cadet bands. On Sunday a drum head service was held in the Buryfield attended by detachments from every organisation in the town as well as representatives from military units stationed in the area, this time Salvation Army band provided the music. Amwell End was decorated in keeping with an exhibition held in the Drill Hall featuring RAF equipment such as parachutes, guns, flying suits and model aircraft, the ATC organised a boxing tournament there as well. Lesley Southall reviewed the state of the Council's finances and suggested that £1600 of the town's money could be invested in 3% Savings Bonds during the Wings for Victory Week, this was readily agreed to by the full Council. By the end of the week the staggering sum of £182,255 had been invested.

Salute the Soldier Week

The next savings drive was to take place nationally between the 25th March and the 1st July 1944 being known as Salute the Soldier Week. Ware had selected the 10th June as the start of their week and they could not have picked a better

time as the whole country was buzzing with excitement of the D-Day landings in France, the target was set at £111,111 using the slogan "Sufficient to send a Division to Berlin". The week's events followed on similar lines to successfully used in previous savings drives. Starting with a march past of service units headed by the Royston Home Guard band followed by sports and parades at the Buryfield, a drumhead service on the Sunday and a whole host of events during the week. The target was comfortably beaten with a final total of £160,050.

Thanksgiving Week – "Peace through Savings"

The final savings drive was set for 1945, the last year of the war, with a target of £50,000 for Ware UDC and RDC to be raised between the 3rd and 10th of November. However with the war over most of the enthusiasm for National Savings had gone and the town's fund raising activities were directed to the War Memorial Fund, in spite of this the target was met.

Chapter 14
WOMEN AT WAR

This chapter is devoted to activities not mentioned elsewhere of the Ware ladies during the war. Not only did many run the home while their men folk away on active service, coped with rationing and queuing, often evacuees expanded their family yet they still managed undertake welfare, charity and warwork. Nationally one in twelve jobs previously done by men were now carried by women, conductresses became a common sight on the buses, postwomen and delivery women became part of the street scene. Miss Pike drove one of the Ware Council's lorries and Josephine Carr of Hoddesdon operated the railway level crossing gates at Amwell End. Others from Ware either volunteered or were directed to work at the Murphy Radio factory at Welwyn Garden City where they made radios and radar sets for the forces, they left the town by bus at 6.50 am for Hertford from where they caught a train on the now defunct line to Welwyn. The ladies were unstinting in their efforts when it came to providing comforts for the services and prisoners of war.

The Women's Voluntary Service (WVS)

The WVS was founded in 1938 by the Dowager Marchioness of Reading to encourage women to join and take part in the ARP's activities. The service was mainly middle class with its uniform of a grey-green tweed suit, beetroot-red jumper and felt hat, often they jocularly called themselves "widows, virgins and spinsters" although to the public and servicemen they were often referred to as "the women in green". The service was modestly funded by central government. Throughout the war they served the country magnificently on the home front helping with evacuees and air raid victims, working in conjunction with the ARP, running canteens and distributing clothing just to name but a few of their activities. The ladies of Ware were no exception, Mrs G E May of 95 New Road (wife of Doctor May Senior) formed the Ware branch and immediately offered their services to the Town Council who gratefully accepted.

Their first task for the Council was to undertake the survey to see how many evacuees could be accommodated should war occur and has already been described in chapter No.2. To assist the ladies the Council set aside a room at their offices at 87 High Street for their use, provided stationary, arm bands and badges knowing full well that they would recoup the rent and all expenses from the government. The survey was undertaken in January 1939 and one of the enumerators, Barbara Haworth (now Mrs F Morris), recalls that the weather was extremely cold with snow on the ground. Two members of the WVS team who carried out the accommodation survey, Miss Cavell of Walton Road and Miss Gibbs of Hunsdon Hill, were appointed as the town's unpaid billeting officers. They had an unenviable task which they carried out until October 1941 when they both resigned.

During the early days of the war the ladies played a leading role with the welfare of the evacuee children and bombed out families who had found refuge in the town to whom they gave clothing donated locally and from the Colonies. In the event of mass bombing they were to man the various rest centres established in the town and eventually ran this operation in its entirety. In conjunction with the Salvation Army they organised Christmas parties for the evacuee children at the Citadel in Baldock Street. By January 1941 were running the Women's Voluntary Services Canteen, later renamed the United Services Club, at the Masonic Hall in Church Street.

Gradually their role within the town expanded, besides their on going welfare services they delivered leaflets concerning Civil Defence matters for the Council, collected vegetables which were sent to mine sweepers operating out of Great Yarmouth, spearheaded several of the town's salvage drives, organised the collection of "conkers" and acorns which were milled for pig feed and collected rose hips for "rose hip syrup" – an evil tasting liquid which was supposed to be beneficial to us war time kids! A close liaison was formed with the Red Cross ladies helping with sales of works in aid of the Red Cross Prisoner of War Fund and led an appeal for blood donors. In June 1942 the ladies absorbed the members of the Priory Comforts Fund within their organisation and co-ordinated activities of all the knitting circles in the town such as the Allenburys social club and the local schools.

Sometime in the latter part of 1942 their offices were moved to and shared premises with James Walker at 78 High Street, now Ian Keith the Estate Agent's office. Their offices were unheated and the Council graciously consented to spent £10 installing electric fires. Around this time Mrs May handed over her role as the local organiser to Mrs L A Galloway of Chadwell. From their new offices the ladies ran a National Savings centre and by August 1943 they operated a typing service for the relatives of prisoners war held by the Japanese who would only permit typed letters to be sent.

The ladies played their part with the ARP services. In 1942 they were given a series of lectures by William Ward and to assist the wardens they kept a register of people who normally occupied houses within the town and noted when there were absentees. The register was kept so that in the event of a house being damaged by bombs time could be saved looking non-existent casualties. Later in the war the WVS training intensified so that the ladies could set up and run Incident Enquiry Posts at bombed sites. The role of the posts were to :

    (a)   To relieve the Incident Officer of enquires from the general public.

    (b)   To pass to the Incident Officer information such as who occupied the bombed property.

    (c)   To pass information to the general public.

Their last wartime role was in June 1945 when Mrs Galloway reported that all the rest centres set up in the town had been cleared of food, clothing and equipment and closed down by the WVS. As the war drew to a close the Government asked the service to continue with its welfare work for another two years, in the event their "stand down" came at the end of the "Cold War" in 1994 when state funding ended.

Priory Comforts Fund

In November 1939 a group of the town's ladies formed the Priory Comforts for the Forces Fund with the objective of knitting items of warm winter clothing for the armed forces. Among the seventy or so who met at the Priory for a couple of hours every Friday afternoon to knit balaclava helmets, mittens, gloves, scarves and body warmers was 91 year old Mrs Bryant of Musley Hill. In the early days of the war their completed garments were handed over to the "Ware Boys at the Front Fund" for onward transmission to the Ware men serving overseas. After the fall of Dunkirk, their garments were handed over to the services themselves for distribution. The following report appeared in the *Mercury* on 12th January 1940:-

The third parcel of knitted garments made by the helpers attached to Ware Priory Comforts Committee was despatched on Friday to men on active service. It comprised of 80 garments, making a total of 381 sent to the forces since the beginning of December. The clothing most urgently needed are helmets, socks, mittens and body belts.

Many organisations within the town raised money for the Priory ladies including the elderly patients at Western House who held sales of work of articles they had made such as work bags, tea cosies, tray cloths, milk jug covers, needle cases and pin cushions from oddments of material received from their friends and relatives. Through their efforts they handed over some £15 to the Priory Comforts Fund – who said occupational therapy was a new thing? By the time the war in Europe ended in May 1945 the Ware ladies and girls – and may be a few boys as well – had worked their way through 16,000 lbs of wool.

The Red Cross and Prisoner of War Fund

The war work of the Red Cross ladies and their colleagues in the St. John Ambulance Brigade at the Priory Street First Aid post has been described in chapter 6. Together with the WVS, they started a blood donor scheme in 1942, the drive for donors was organised by the WVS – who could resist the charms of this formidable band of ladies – while the Red Cross ladies saw to the "technical works". Blood donor groups were formed including one in the pastille packing department at Allen & Hanburys.

In their off duty spells the Red Cross and St. John ladies raised money for their general funds and in particular for the International Red Cross Prisoner of War Fund which sent food parcels monthly to our prisoners of war. Fund raising was through flag days, a penny-a-week fund and sales in a shop they opened within the Northmet Power Company offices and showrooms at Bridgefoot (now The Bridge pub) to sell toys made or donated by people in the town.

Fund raising reached a climax in the summer of 1943 when the notification of prisoners held by the Japanese started to filter through and independent observers sent back reports of the horrendous conditions the P.O.Ws were living in and ill treatment they received. At least ten men from or associated with the town were held in prison camps in Malaya and Thailand. On August Bank holiday a large fete was held

*Mrs Margaret Ling
in Red Cross uniform.*

in the Priory grounds and over £200 was raised. A swimming gala at the Priory Street baths added to the total. Practically every organisation and pub in Ware collected money for this well deserving fund at some stage during the war.

The Woman's Land Army

The Women's Land Army (WLA) was founded in the first World War and revived by Lady Gertrude Denman in June 1939. The girls, mostly volunteers, wore brown cord breeches, brown shoes, cream shirts, green jersey and wide brimmed felt hats and were numbered in the same way as service personnel with their wages set by the National Wages Council. At the end of the war this went against the girls as the government refused to pay them a war gratuity servicemen received arguing that they had paid the rate for the job. In 1939 their basic weekly wage was thirty-seven shillings and six pence rising to forty-eight shillings later in the war (£1.87 rising to £2.40). They had to pay for their board and keep in the hostels or farms where they stayed. Their war effort for their country were not fully recognised until the year 2000 when they were allowed to take part in the Remembrance Day march past at the Cenotaph for the first time.

The girls carried out a multitude of jobs and apart from general farming and horticultural work others were employed in forestry and some were even employed as rat catchers! Several Land Army girls were employed by Ware Council at their

Ryegate Farm, these girls probably came from the hostel in North Street at Nazeing while those working on the farms to the north of Ware were billeted at Rowney Priory at Sacombe Green. Other girls were billeted with families in the town.

Win Stalley (née Long) in WVS uniform

When Win Long (now Mrs Stalley) of Bowling Road joined the WLA in 1942 she was posted to Aston Bury (between Watton-at-Stone and Stevenage) without any prior training in the horticultural work she was expected to undertake. It was a lonely posting since she was the only girl there and for the first week her billet was an estate cottage complete with an earth privy and well over a mile from the nearest main road, in Win's words "it was a cultural shock after my comfortable home in Bowling Road." Fortunately conditions improved when she was given a room in the "big house."

From Aston Win was transferred to Bengeo Lodge where she helped the gardener produce vegetables for the local hospital and was now able to live at home. Bengeo Lodge belonged to Major Robert Pyers and was used as a lodging house by the circuit judges together with their entourage. When the County Court was in session and the judge in residence at the Lodge Win helped out in the Lodge as well for which she received extra wages. On 15th January 1945 a V2 rocket fell in Bengeo not far from the Lodge garden where Win and the gardener were working, they rushed to the scene since they concerned about a lady living in a nearby cottage, their fears where groundless as the lady's only worry was for the safety of her dog! Win was demobbed from the WLA in 1946.

In complete contrast to Win Long's experiences when Pat Kemp joined the WLA in June 1943 she stayed at Totteridge for a short while before going on a four week basic training course at the Hertfordshire Training Centre at "Oaklands" near St. Albans. In Pat's case she stayed an extra week as the Duchess of Gloucester was due to visit the new recruits and she was selected to demonstrate her skills on a Caterpillar tractor to the Duchess. From "Oaklands" Pat went to Rowney Priory where she joined some fifty other girls. Every morning groups of girls were taken by lorries driven by a forewoman to whichever local farms required labour. Among the tasks they undertook were milking and mucking out the cowsheds, hoeing sugar beet, potato picking, tractor driving and ploughing together with the two most hated jobs – picking brussel sprouts on a cold, frosty morning and threshing which was a dirty dusty operation. It was not all work and play – the Yanks had arrived in Hertfordshire and the fifty girls at Rowney Priory were in much demand! The G.Is sent transport to take them to dances Nuthampstead, others from Colliers End took Pat and her friends Elsie Bell, Eileen Parker, Mary Doyle, May Robinson, Sandy Henshaw and Margaret Calligahan to the weekly dances held at the Drill Hall in Amwell End. Strict discipline was maintained at the Priory as everyone had to be back by 10.30 pm during the week with an hours extension on Wednesday and Saturday nights.

Life on the farm had its funny side for Pat and her friends, a farmer was selling some of his pigs so they had to be a good scrubbing before going to market. Pat and another girl had to take an immaculate looking pig which had been sold to its new owner. On the way it began to rain so Pat said to her friend "if this pig gets wet the farmer will be angry and we will have to take it back so you had better put your coat over it" which she did. By the time they arrived at the farm she was soaking wet and when the men there saw what she had done there was raucous laughter! The girl was not amused but cheered up when the farmer gave Pat a tip which was handed to her.

Nona Poyser (now Mrs A Wallis) from Cross Street was a nurse at Western House from March 1941 to February 1945, Nona married Pilot Officer Alan Wallis DFC of Vicarage Road.

Western House and the nurses

In broad terms Western House comprised of two separate units, the infirmary based in the old Octagon building and the much newer hospital unit built in 1936. Both came under the control of the Master and Matron, Hubert and Myrtle Martin although the hospital was run by Sister Maunders who was a trained and qualified nurse. Many of the nurses at Western House such as Emily Hunt, Mina Sell, Nona Poyser, Nina Lond, Kath Brazier and Mrs Bob Cruse were local girls, others such as Ginger and Betty Kirston came from Ireland and their numbers swelled with the arrival of their evacuee guests from Paddington and Barnet. Ladies from the Red Cross assisted throughout the war and we have already seen that full-time Civil Defence members were seconded there towards the later war years.

Western House was a secure unit surrounded by high walls or railings at the front and staff discipline was strict, however this did not pose too many problems for the girls! Mina Sell and her father George, the electrician there, lived in High Oak Road with their garden backing onto the hospital grounds and when cutting it fine for work they scaled the wall by means of a short ladder. The main front gates were locked in the evening which restricted the live-in nurses social life, one nurse still living in Ware recalls that if they went to one of the many dances at the Drill Hall and returned after the "curfew hour" they gained entrance by the same route as Mina often took to work. They were puzzled how Sister Maunders knew that they had returned late until she let slip that she could hear the toilet flushing frequently on such occasion! The story stops there! Besides their nursing duties they contributed to little known fund called The British Nurses Fund for Invalid P.O.Ws.

NAAFI Girls

Everyone who served in the forces during the war or post-war era appreciated the services provided by the Naafi, and of course by Red Shield Clubs and "Sally Ann" vans run by the Salvation Army. Who can forget their rock cakes, buns and weak tea with its distinctive taste of tinned milk!

At least four girls from Ware volunteered their services to the Naafi including Maisie Kent (now Mrs Webb), Audrey Turner (now Mrs Campkin) and the sisters Dora and Peggy North. The girls volunteered for various reasons. Audrey, then a waitress at Christine's charming "olde world" tea rooms in Hertford, liked meeting and serving people and preferred to continue with this sort of work; Maisie, who liked her food, admitted that piles of jam tarts and doughnuts was an attraction and thought that the discipline would be less strict than in the services! However life was not that easy and barrack room conditions were a revelation after the relative comfort of their Ware homes, the day was long starting with lighting the coal fires in the canteens early in the morning and serving the forces until late evening for six days a week. All four girls went to RAF Hunsdon, Maisie and Audrey also served in an isolated army camp at Aston End (Stevenage) before Maisie went to the combined RAF and American installations at Chicksands (Bedford). With the end of the war in Europe the Naafi set up a tented camp in Hyde Park to provide refreshments to the British and Commonwealth Forces taking part in the Victory Parade through London. Both Dora and Maisie were posted there and took part in the celebrations along with thousands of others.

Children's Clinic, the War-time Nursery and British Restaurant

Soon after the outbreak of war the County Education Committee proposed to set up a war-time day nursery to care for young children while their mothers were engaged on war work, but it is clear some of the Town Councillors were against the idea from the start. About twelve sites were proposed either by the County or the Ware Town Council and with no agreement forthcoming they agreed that the nursery was not needed anyway. However there was a complete U-turn in May 1943 when Hertfordshire County Council built and ran a nursery in Bowling Road, now used as the Ware Health Clinic. Places were available for fifty children between the ages of two and five who were provided with breakfast, dinner and tea for the princely sum of one shilling (five pence). The nursery was run by Majorie Bradshaw, a children's nurse from Cambridgeshire billeted with the Bouttell family in Musley Lane.

The uncaring side of Ware Town Council again manifested itself over the provision

Children and staff at the Bowling Road Day Nursery (now the Health Clinic) in 1943-44. Zillah Bunten (fifth from the right) came to Ware from Cambridgeshire and was billeted with Mr & Mrs Wilf Barker at 10 Cromwell Road.

of a British Restaurant, these were to be run on a non-profit basis by councils and had their origins as emergency feeding centres after the heavy air raids during the winter of 1940/41. The Ministry of Food wanted to adapt these centres to provided a simple nourishing three course meal at a modest price of 11d (about £1.50 at today's prices) for workers who did not have access to a works canteen and also by housewives. Late in 1941 the Town Clerk, Leslie Southall, attended an interview with the Ministry and pointed out that there was no suitable premises within the town and suggested that the Ministry might be able to supply nissen huts for the purpose. What Southall did not reveal was that main emergency centre set up at the Congregational Hall was already being used by the County Authorities as a school canteen. With a little co-operation with the County and at virtually no cost to the town it would have been possible to go along with the Ministry's proposals. The Town Clerk received the backing of his Council who resolved in December 1941 that there was no need for a British Restaurant in Ware and so those townsfolk and housewives who did not have access to works canteens were denied the chance to supplement their meagre war time rations. Other towns in the area took a more enlightened view, British Restaurants were set up in Hertford, Hoddesdon and even in Roydon village.

Chapter 15
SCHOOLS AND YOUTH SERVICES

The months of uncertainty leading up to the outbreak of war had little effect on Ware's school children, their education continued in the time honoured way. Their first hint of how serious the situation was came on 4th July 1939 when they had to take their gas masks to school for fitting and inspection by the town's air raid wardens, no doubt there were scenes of merriment and laughter within the class rooms. Meanwhile behind the scenes the County Education Authority made arrangements to construct air raid shelters at the schools and to receive evacuees from London.

A few days before the outbreak of war the County Authorities instructed Ware Town Council to commence work on trench type air raid shelters at the town's schools to give protection to an estimated 1068 children. The specification was that the trench should be lined and roofed with concrete or steel with sandbagged entrances, 4ft 8inches wide and partially or wholly buried dependent upon ground conditions. A simple floor drainage system was to keep the shelters dry but appeared to be ineffective in those built in New Road since Mr Evans noted in his school logbook on the 2nd February 1940 "two of the shelters were unusable due to flooding". Conditions within the shelters were primitive with simple bench seating and no lighting, my own recollections are that they were cold, dank and smelt awful. The work was undertaken by the Council's labour force assisted by some of the people appointed for full-time civil defence work. The shelters built at a cost of £1,700 were at the following schools:

Ware Girls Grammar School for 300 pupils.
Musley Hill Infants School for 124 pupils.
St Mary's Junior Boys, Girls School and Infants for 520 pupils.
Central School New Road for 124 pupils (built in the Vicarage Paddock).

On Friday 1st September, teachers in Ware were recalled from their summer holidays to receive the London evacuees and help with the billeting arrangements. The schools were due to start their autumn term on 4th September but entries in the various school log books state: "School to be closed until further notice owing to war being declared". They remained closed until 18th September. The St Mary's Schools were the receiving school for Mr Piper and his children from the Pakeman Street School of Holloway while their sister school, Shelburne Senior School, were hosted by the Central School in New Road. Girls from the Lady of Sion Convent School under Mother Gerard Majella shared Ware Grammar School for Girls with whom they virtually integrated. More evacuees arrived at the Grammar School in July 1940 from Hastings High School for Girls.

The delay in opening the schools for the new term gave time not only to arrange for additional accommodation and to reorganise the timetables but also to install air raid precautions. Those taken at the Technical School in Priory Street were typical of other schools in the town. The entry made by Henry Vaughan, the headmaster, in his log book for the 25th September 1939 reads "Commenced protecting building against air raid damage, ceilings shored up, windows covered with wire netting and curtains to all doors and windows except front windows which have plywood shutters". This was fine except that the wire netting was fixed to the outside of the windows and would not have protected the students against inward flying glass. It wasn't until the following May that this serious error was recognised and rectified. Stirrup pumps were not made available until June of the following year. The school often closed early to allow civil defence First Aid lectures to take place on the premises.

In her school log Miss Metcalf, headmistress of St. Mary's Junior Girls School, describes the split shift rotating system which was to be operated so that pupils from both schools could continue their education. In the first week the Ware girls used the school from 9.00 am until 12.30 pm and, after lunch, occupied the Wesleyan Hall, the Buryfield or went on nature walks, while the Pakeman School girls had use of the school from 1.30 until 4.30 pm. Similar arrangements were operated in St. Mary's Junior Boys School and indeed throughout the country wherever evacuees were billeted. The following week the roles were reversed. As winter approached the outside activities were curtailed and the Congregational Church facilities were used as classrooms. Miss Metcalf also noted that the Wesleyan Hall was dark and cold with only broken pews as seats and only had one office. Conditions improved when St. Mary's and the Pakeman Street schools virtually amalgamated in the spring of 1940.

The children from the Shelburne Road School Senior School arrived in two batches, 151 children on 1st September followed by a further 71 the next day. Both groups were met and welcomed by Mr W S Braybrooke and Miss G Eeal, the senior master and mistress from the Central School, and the headmaster, Albert Evans, immediately placed Christ Church Memorial Hall at the disposal of the London headmaster, Mr A E French. Mr Evans was obviously a good organiser since towards the end of September he suggested to Mr French that full-time education could be achieved if the two schools integrated, shared resources and also utilised space available at the Technical School. Two more classes would be needed but there were sufficient teachers available to make his idea work. Although there was some opposition from the London teachers, the proposal went ahead in October and ensured that both schools received full-time education.

Obviously the air raid shelters were incomplete when the schools reopened and Miss Metcalf wrote in her log: "School reopened. Until adequate protection is provided for air raids attendance is voluntary, trenches are being prepared, ready in three to four weeks". Miss Metcalf noted that seven of her girls would not be coming to school. Miss Want at Musley Infants school noted in her log book on 8th December:

"The playground is occupied by workmen building the air raid shelter so no games can be taken out of doors and the children have short breaks in school."

Gradually both teachers and pupils settled into their new routines, often under cramped conditions, and normal school activities resumed for the first year of the war. However the start of the new school year on 3rd September 1940 saw the school shelters used for the first time for children had returned to school at the height of the Battle of Britain and the almost nightly bombing raids on London. On 13th September Miss Metcalf noted in her school log book: "The children are coming in at anytime during the morning owing to the air raid warnings lasting from 9 pm or 10 pm to 5 am each day". Again on the 25th September she noted: "The morning session for the rest of this week will commence at 10 am to give the children a little extra rest after very disturbed nights". It was not until February 1941 that the raids started to abate.

With the arrival of the Hastings girls at the Grammar School some four hundred children were crammed into a relatively small school, to relieve the pressure the younger girls (the preparatory school) were accommodated in three large ground floor rooms at "Presdales" while the remaindered of the girls were educated at Amwell House and Millbrook. The Sion Convent girls returned to London in 1942.

In February 1941 the St Mary's Schools had set up their fire watching scheme, Miss Metcalf recorded in her log book: "The staff commenced fire watching duties from dusk to dawn – duty will be every eighth night with three people on duty at a time". A similar scheme was operated by staff and six formers at the Girls Grammar School where they slept on camp beds in the staff common room. The ATC cadets played a similar role at the Central School. The schools helped the war effort in other ways too, each operated a National Savings Centre and the pupils took part in the activities organised during the various War Savings Weeks. The children, both collectively and individually, "Dug for Victory" on school allotments, took part in the many salvage drives and raised moneys for many charitable and service organisations.

A canteen was opened by the County Council at the Congregational Hall on the 24th September 1941 to serve hot lunches for children from the St Mary's Schools as well as the evacuee schools, other children unable to get home for a hot lunch could attend too. The canteen, supervised by Mr S B Piper and his wife, proved to be extremely popular serving 840 meals in the first week. Staff and senior girls from St Mary's School acted as supervisors and dinner monitors.

Apart from a flurry of short air raid warnings in the summer of 1944 when Ware was on the fringe of the "Doodle Bug" (the VI rockets) range Ware's schools were little affected for the remainder of the war. All schools were closed on 8th and 9th May 1945 which were declared as public holidays when VE Day finally came.

It is worth while noting the contribution to the war effort made by the pupils from the St Mary's School. Edward Collins, their headmaster, recorded in July 1945 that the various branches of the school had raised nearly £100 for the Merchant Navy

Fund with another £443 for other charities. They also sent one ton of vegetables to the merchant seamen and in September 1944 St Mary's Girls School held a Harvest Thanksgiving service at their school, the children brought gifts of fruit and vegetables which were despatched at once to the Navy mine sweepers based at Lowestoft. Their war effort didn't end here either since the children collected eight tons of salvage and invested £7029.12s.9d in War Savings. Collins said that these activities were not "just a stunt" but were part of the school's education system to teach the children the value of public service.

The Merchant Navy Fund

The town always considered that Ware men serving in the Merchant Navy should be treated "on par" with those in Royal Navy and the other armed services in receiving comforts from the Boys at the Front Fund. Consequently few, if any, events took place in the town to raise money for Merchant Navy funds until Christmas 1943 when the St. Mary's schools donated part of the proceeds of a carol service and sale of toys made by the children and their parents to the "Merchant Navy Fund". St Mary's Boys, Girls and Infants schools continued their association with the sailors serving under the Red Duster until the end of the war, through regular sales of articles made by the children raised nearly £100. The sailors did not forget the children's efforts and on 10th July 1945 the secretary of this fund, Mr Kirkland Bridge, presented the St Mary's schools with a battered Red Ensign flown by the merchant ship "Beaconsfield" throughout the war. For a while the flag flew on flag pole in the school's playing ground.

Mrs Churchill's Red Cross Aid to Russia Fund

The main contributors to this little known fund were the town's school children although the Priory Comforts Ladies donated a selection of their knitted garments. To quote a couple of examples of the children's efforts, Dawn Devonshire of 12 Musley Hill saved 12s.0d (£0.60) in silver three penny pieces while Doris Trott, a ten-year-old evacuee from the Pakeman School billeted with Charles Adams of 4 Park Road, made 70 kettle holders which she had sold for twenty-one shillings. Both girls were delighted to receive a personal letters of thanks from Clemantine Churchill.

The Youth Services

In common with the rest of the country organisations were formed in Ware to give youngsters some pre-service training before they were called up for the armed forces although it did not guarantee that they would be allocated to the service of their choice. They ran in parallel with the traditional organisations such as the Scouts and Guides who both played their part in the war effort.

The Army Cadet Force (ACF)

It was proposed to form a Cadet Corps for lads between the ages of fifteen and eighteen after the fall of France in 1940 but the practicalities of finding suitable meeting places coupled with the lack of instructors meant that the fifty or so Ware youngsters who wanted don khaki uniforms could not do so until 1942 when the Hertfordshire Army Cadet Force was formed. The cadets were affiliated with the Home Guard and were organised in Battalions and Companies which generally followed the boundaries set for their seniors. The cadets in Ware formed the 20th Hertfordshire (Ware) Company of the Hertfordshire Cadets (later to become "C" Company 1st Battalion Hertfordshire ACF) based at the Drill Hall under the command of Captain Edward Collins, the headmaster of St Mary's School. Their Adjutant was Lieutenant C J Marks, Lieutenants Horace Skipp and Fred Weatherly were the two Platoon Commanders. Archie Baker of Cross Street was appointed as the Regimental Sergeant Major and added experience to the team. Archie, a W.W.I veteran, had served as a Sergeant Instructor with the Royal Engineers in the British Expeditionary Force in W.W.II until he was invalided out of the army having received a leg wound during the withdrawal from St. Nazaire in June 1940. Their N.C.Os were appointed and trained from the ranks.

Once the cadets had mastered foot drill they studied machine guns, map reading, aircraft recognition and automatic weapons in a series of courses run by Lt. Beard and others from the Ware Home Guard. Signalling and the use of trench mortars were added to the syllabus, the cadets were aiming to gain their War Certificate "A" which signified a level of proficiency, which in theory, would advance their careers when called up for military service. Visits were made to various army establishments and in August some twenty lads from Ware joined other cadets from the county under canvas at a camp run by the regular army "somewhere in Hertfordshire". Here they received their first "taste" of army life, there were complaints that the food was not up to "Mum's cooking", no doubt they had two courses and tea in a pair of mess tins – did anyone ever come to terms with this?!

Edward Collins resigned as their CO. in November 1942 on health grounds and Horace Skipp of Ware Garage took over command, Horace, as might be expected, was a WWI veteran having served in the Herts Yeomanry. The cadets held regular field exercises with the Home Guard and with other cadets in the area. For example in March 1943 the Ware Cadets attacked Hertford Sewage Works which was defended by Hertford's Cadets, Ware's "suicide squad" of hand grenade bombers won the day for our town. At other times they, together with the Air Training Corps cadets, acted as messengers in combined Army, Home Guard and Civil Defence exercises.

The social side of life played its part too, Under-Officer L G Allen, Sergeant R Adams, Sergeant D Clemo, Corporal G Lister together with L/Corporals E Hunt & W Campbell organised a Christmas social in 1942 at the Congregational Church to which the Girls Training Corps were invited. Cadets Ron Page on the piano and Alan Coombes on the drums provided the music. The lads obviously enjoyed the social side of life as they decided to form their own social club, although the Government provided all the military equipment the cadets had to raise their own money for any extras they required. This they did through a series of dances held at their Drill Hall headquarters where their club was soon to open every weekday evening.

The cadets were reorganised following the Home Guard's "stand-down" in November 1944, Lt. Beard become the new CO assisted by existing ACF officers and others from the Home Guard. Platoons were now based in Ware, Wadesmill and Dane End. A detachment of cadets is still based in Ware today.

936 Squadron, Air Training Corps (ATC)

936 Squadron of the Air Training Corps was formed at Ware's Central School on Tuesday the 11th February 1941 when its Executive Committee received permission from the Air Ministry to form a squadron. The main instigator behind the scenes was Albert Evans, the Central School's headmaster. Albert, affectionately known as Taffy or Snave (Evans spelt backwards!), had written to former Central School pupils suggesting that they formed a Squadron at the school. On the Thursday 27th February 67 young men enrolled at their first parade and were addressed by Group-Captain I J Rodway of the RAF who outlined the objectives of the Corps and showed several Air Ministry films depicting life in the Air Force. Rodway was elected as the Squadron's first President and the school served as the Squadron's headquarters

The ATC at Allenburys football ground, probably in summer 1941. Standing: R Davis, F Prior, R O'Smotherly, F Church 'Ginger' Smith, A Hollands, A Beale, K Sheppard, R Wilkins, T Dennet, — , — and A Risby. Seated: D Taylor, R Skeeles, Pilot Officers DG White and HS Vaughan, Mr H Campkin, A Davis, A North, W Cockman and N Murphy.

throughout the war years. Within a month their numbers had risen to over eighty and they were measured for their uniforms some of which an ex-cadet described as "relics from the 1914-18 war." The squadron consisted of four flights under Squadron Leader RJ Overton; Mr DG White (headmaster of Thundridge School) Mr HS Vaughan (headmaster of Ware Art & Technical School) and Mr WS Braybrooke were made Pilot Officers while Lt Wood of the Royal Navy was appointed as the adjutant on a temporary basis. Cadets Bert Goldstone, Bert Ling, Frank Prior, Norman "Spud" Murphy, Bob Smith, Richard Bush and King were promoted as non-commissioned officers.

Parades were held on Monday, Wednesday and Friday evenings. Basic foot drill was conducted on the school playground under Warrant Officer H G Campkin and the officers, who were all schoolmasters, held classes in maths, electricity and magnetism which were necessary to grasp the principles of navigation. In spite of the fact that there were no training manuals to start with the cadets soon learnt the basic skills of plotting aircraft courses incorporating the effects of wind speeds, signalling and sending messages in Morse code with an Aldis signalling lamp. Lt. Ken Samways of the Ware Home Guard gave lectures on gas attacks and aircraft recognition. The cadets visited various RAF stations in the area such as Hunsdon and Sawbridgeworth to get an insight of service life, others went to an airstrip at Allens Green where the highlight was a flight in a Tiger Moth. Rifle shooting was undertaken at the RAF stations.

The lads played their part in Ware's defence schemes against aerial attack and in the invasion plan. They acted as casualties and messengers in Civil Defence exercises – described as "so called manoeuvres" by one cadet. They also undertook fire watching duties at the Central School. Every night one NCO and two cadets put up camp beds in the male teacher's staff room, Arthur North recalls: "one night a cadet named Tom Blayden shouted out that there was a mouse in his bed. The corporal switched on the light and as Tom threw back the bed clothes there was a mouse running down his leg, I threw a boot at it but did more damage to Tom's leg than the mouse! None of us could get back to sleep so we went and played football in the main assembly hall." Others played a part in some of the Home Guard more bizarre plans. For example a few cadets learnt how to handle homing pigeons probably trained by Arthur Goldstone of Vicarage Road whose son Denis was a cadet and became a Pilot Officer in the RAF. The idea was that should the Germans be in the area then the cadets and their pigeons would be stationed in St Mary's Church tower and as soon as the enemy was spotted coming down Pepper Hill at Great Amwell the birds would be released carrying messages to warn the Puckeridge and Standon Home Guard of an attack. However the cadets were not too keen on this idea when they realised that the first target for a German tank entering the town would be the church tower! Another group who had learnt to use the Aldis signalling lamp were to rush to the water towers at Tower Road, Moles Farm and Old Hall Green when the church bells rang

Gathering of the founder cadets at their 60th Anniversary. The propeller in the photograph dates from W.W.I and was given to the Squadron by Fred Smith of Park Road whose son Bob was a cadet. Originally it was hung in the assembly Hall at the Central School and is now proudly displayed at the Squadron's Headquarters at Broadmeads. Standing: Christopher Trevenna, Alan Risby, Ron Saunders (squadron padre), Don Allum, Ron Cakebread, Bill Cockman, – Lancaster, Bob Acres, Frank Prior, Ken Rowley, Eric Clibbon, Reg Rand, John Carter, Jeff Chandler, Peter Leigh, John Change and Flt Lt. Tony Fleetwood. Seated: Ron Papper, Arthur North and Fred Church.

out to signify that German troops were in the area. The towers formed a three ways signalling system from which they were able to relay messages on enemy troop movements to the Home Guard. Others were to act as foot runners carrying messages.

Sporting activities featured strongly in the Squadron's activities, the cadets took part in soccer and boxing tournaments in which they were particularly successful, an annual athletics day was also held at Allenburys sports ground. However unlike their brothers in the Army Cadets there was little or no socialising with the Girls Training Corps. The cadets training stood them in good stead when they joined the Royal Air Force, Alan Hollands made the ultimate sacrifice and several were to gain medals for conspicuous service. The squadron was always well turned out for all the National Thanksgiving services and Armistice Day parades as indeed they are today operating from their headquarters at Broadmeads under the leadership of Flight Lieutenant Tony Fleetwood.

Their comradeship has passed the test of time. The original members met up for a fiftieth anniversary dinner and get together in 1991 arranged by Spud Murphy at the Age of Concern Centre in Priory Street and again on the 21st February 2001 at Vintage Corner, Puckeridge organised by Fred Church – see photograph.

73 Company of the Girls Training Corps at the Grammar School. Back row: Olive Lambert, Doreen English, Jean Springham, Connie Whitmill, Joan Page, Yvonne Turner and Cynthia Menzies. Front row: —, Mary Murton, Marion Wheeler, Beryl Boutell, Miss E. Millard, Elsie Hills, Marjorie Blake, Peggy Millar and Daphne Blake.

No. 73 Girl's Training Corps (GTC)

The first unit to provide pre-service training for girls was formed at Dartford in September 1939 and was known as the Girl's Emergency Ministration Service. Subsequent units followed, in many cases with the simple title of the Girls Training Corps. Discussions were held between the three Service Departments, the Board of Education and the Ministry of Labour who all agreed that general pre-service training requirements for girls, unlike that for boys, was the same for all three services – henceforth all units bore the name GTC and were sponsored by the Ministry of Education.

No. 73 Company (Ware) Girl's Training Corps was probably formed at the Girls Grammar school in May 1943 under Acting Commandant Lieutenant Miss C Evans and Quartermaster Lieutenant Miss M Jones. The Company was open to all girls in the town. Their section officers were Miss G Seal, Miss C V Bolton, Miss E Millard and Sub-Section Leader Miss Margaret Marques. Later the Company was expanded to four companies. Their dress was a white blouse with a navy blue skirts. Their basic training programme included hygiene, PT and foot drill with Corporal Monica Skipp (now Mrs G Hale) and her friend Joyce Wren often taking the parades. They had a choice of specialist subjects which included air raid precautions run by the St. John Ambulance Brigade, aircraft recognition given by Lt. Ken Samways of the Home Guard, handywomens classes run by Archie Baker of the ACF and First Aid classes run by the Red Cross. The girls visited ATS gun sites and a RAF station where they saw WAAFs packing parachutes. They also took part in an exercise run by the Home Guard when they were told to wear trousers, this posed a problem for one young lady whose father was away at work and she didn't have a brother. However her mother was enterprising and made her a pair from a hop sack and promptly told her daughter that "trousers didn't suit her. The young lady in question who shall remain nameless to spare her any embarrassment has never worn trousers since! Like their counterparts in the ACF they enjoyed a good social evening several of which were held at the school with the Army Cadets.

On 12th May 1945 Chief Section Leader Beryl Bouttell (now Mrs Tyser) from the Ware Company was one of two girls to represent Hertfordshire at a national GTC gathering held at Thorton Heath in Cheshire. Their billet had been used as a wartime hospital and the girls soon discovered that the basement area was full of empty coffins. Dressed in their white blouses and navy blue skirts the girls were transported to the rally in the back of a coal lorry!

Boy Scouts

At the outbreak of war Ware had two Scout Troops, the 2nd Ware (St. Mary's) under group scoutmaster Fred Beazley and the 3rd Ware (Christ Church) under group scoutmaster Jack Taylor. Both scout groups made their contribution to the war effort in many diverse ways, they acted as messengers to the ARP wardens, the Police and Home Guard, they were aircraft spotters at church services, acted as casualties at First Aid lectures and civil defence exercises and helped to raise money for the troops comforts fund and savings campaigns. In their "spare time" they salvaged waste paper etc. for their own funds. The scouts used various modes of transport for their paper collecting and probably the most bizarre was that used by Norman "Spud" Murphy, his father ran a rustic furniture business next to the Victoria pub in Star Street and included in his stock was a three wheel wicker Bath chair complete with steering handle which "Spud" and his mates converted into a paper collecting trolley. One of their favourite calls was the Canons Hotel part of which was used by an American gold company, the paper from here was carefully sorted by the lads for envelopes bearing foreign postage stamps.

Jack Taylor, a foreman at French's Mill, was attached to the Home Guard and one of his ideas for a training scheme was that three of the scouts were to act as three German parachutists and be tracked down and captured by "Dad's Army". Fred Church recalls that they set out from Dane End armed with paper bombs to "bomb" Woodall Park, not only did they evade capture but succeeded in attacking their target as well.

Their presence was always to be seen at the Services of Remembrance at the War Memorial and at national days of prayer. A problem the scouts shared with their sisters in the Guides was their parent's fear of an air raid taking place in the blackout when they attended their weekly meetings and so it was arranged that they could use the school's shelters.

Girl Guides

There were two Guide Companies in Ware, the 1st and 2nd Companies, a Guide Ranger Company was formed for the older girls in November 1939. When the Hastings High School were evacuated to the town the Guides among them amalgamated with the 2nd Ware company based at the Girls Grammar School. The Ware Rangers and Guides helped out at Western House and at the Cheyne Hospital for Children evacuated to Fanhams Hall in 1942 for which the girls were especially commended at national level. The younger girls in the Brownie packs collected silver paper for the Lord Mayor of London's Red Cross Fund and for local hospitals. Their elder sisters acted as casualties for the Red Cross ladies – the sexes did not mix in the early days of the war! The Hastings Ranger Company trained as firewomen and formed a team at Ware fire station The girls also knitted for the Forces Comforts Fund as well as collecting and sorting 28 tons of waste paper in 1940- double the amounted their brothers in the scouts achieved in the same period.

Chapter 16
THE ARMED FORCES AND DEFENCE OF WARE

Ware was never a regular posting for the military during the war although army units were quartered in the town for relatively short periods with several buildings requisitioned for their use. The largest influx of troops took place following the British Expeditionary Force's evacuation from France between the 27th May and the 4th June 1940. They were concentrated along Walnut Tree Walk from the present day entrance to Presdales recreation ground through to Pepper Hill. Walnut Tree Walk was tarmaced by the army and a series of hard standings constructed either side of the road to accommodate army vehicles either in the open or under nissen hut type blisters, short lengths of the surfacing and the location of some of the hard standings can still be seen today. More vehicles were parked on the north side of Post Wood roughly from where the footpath from Lower Road enters the wood back towards Post Wood Road. The troops remained here for some six to nine months.

With the presence of a large number of troops on the outskirts of the town it was not long before Mr Reynolds, the proprietor of the Ware Cinema, was asked to open his cinema on a Sunday. Armed with a certificate from the military authorities saying that such a move would be beneficial to the troops in the area he approached the Council for permission to do so. The request was sympathetically received by most of the members who agreed to place an advertisement in the *Mercury* giving members of the public a chance to object. The request was granted, with the reservation that no children under the age of sixteen be admitted. The gas lights in the cinema dimmed on Sunday the 9th March to show *Calling All Stars* featuring Ambrose and his Orchestra.

The Council allowed the troops stationed in and around the town free use the swimming pool, tennis courts and the football pitch at Buryfield for tournaments. The RAF from Hunsdon also used the swimming pool for life saving exercises from rubber dinghies, since this did not rank as recreational purposes in the view of the councillors the RAF were charged 30s.0d (£1.50) per visit; the RAF did not take kindly to this so they transferred their dinghy drills to the pool at Haileybury College who readily agreed to make their facilities available free of charge.

At the outbreak of war an anti-aircraft battery was set up at Colliers End. Subsequently this was replaced by 331 and then 334 Searchlight Batteries Royal Artillery, with satellite stations at Allens Green, Westmill, Blakesware and at London Road in Ware. Fifteen men manned the London Road searchlight together with its associated direction and range finding equipment. The concrete bases of the huts can still be seen on the left hand side of the footpath leading from Lower Road to Post Wood – the searchlight and its ancillary equipment were some hundred yards away towards the town while the generator together with a small hut were located inside Post Wood. Another searchlight was located in the grounds of Poles for a short time.

A large barn beside the Red House Pub in London Road was used as an army meat distribution point, vehicles called daily to collect the troops rations for units such as the Eastern Command's Military Police Headquarters at Frogmore Hall (Watton-at-Stone) and the Pioneer's Training School at Burford House in Hoddesdon. Bread was issued daily from an army lorry parked in nearby Post Wood Road. Other buildings requisition by the army were Chadwell Country Club (to the East of the Golf Club) and a large timber malting building which stood on the south side of the road to the west of the present day John Gilpin pub. During 1940/1941 "D" Company of the 9th Battalion of the Suffolk Regiment used Alpha Cottage at the end of Francis Road together with the timber parish hall in the grounds of the Catholic Church. Ernie Whybrew who had served in the First World War lived in King Edward's Road appreciated the lack bathing facilities available to the troops billeted nearby and made his own bathroom readily available to them. The Suffolks left the town in the summer of 1941 and the hall was then designated as an emergency rest centre for bombed out people before it was returned to the parishioners in December 1944. The army also had a petrol pump at Grange Garage in London Road. Other troops collected tanks which had been repaired or overhauled at Wickham's Engineering Works at Crane Mead.

Although Lady Anne Brocket was in residence at Fanhams Hall throughout the war for a while the Great Hall and one wing were occupied by evacuee children from the Cheyne Hospital for Children and by the RASC as a Reserve Supply Depot Headquarters. It is thought that the Army used the basements as Richard Prior who was employed by Lady Brocket as a garden boy recalls that there was a door leading from the grounds into the basement area which was out of bounds to the staff. Jim Myers now living on the Herts/Essex borders was a five year old when he came to Fanhams with the Cheyne Hospital. He recalls arriving there from Canning Town by bus, of sleeping in a cot in the long gallery, the grandeur place and of the kindness of the staff. He also recalls that now and again he and other children were given afternoon tea and lemonade by the high ranking army officers living there and is adamant that the Lord Gort was one of them. As a young lad he probably didn't realise that Lady Brocket's brother, Lord Croft, was a joint Under Secretary of State for War and often returned to the family home at weekends accompanied by high ranking military personnel so he could well have seen Lord Gort there.

The RAF had a presence in the town too, they had three paraffin bucket flares in Thrift Field, London Road. These acted as a turning point for homing night fighters approaching the east-west runway at Hunsdon opened as a night fighter station in 1941. Other times RAF personnel would fire Very lights for the same purpose and

Michael Ottley recalls collecting the empty cartridge cases after the airmen had left the field – collecting spent bullet cases, bomb splinters and other service paraphernalia was a popular hobby of most boys during the war. On one occasion the nearby searchlight came to the rescue of two RAF Mustang fighters trying to locate Hunsdon in inclement weather by switching its light on and pointing the beam in the direction of the flight path, one landed safely at Sawbridgeworth but unfortunately the second hit trees near Wareside. One of Sir Winston Churchill's "hush-hush" operations known as Turbinlite was developed at Hunsdon, American Bostons DB7 (renamed Havocs by the RAF) were fitted with radar and Helmore searchlights to seek out and illuminate enemy aircraft so that the two accompanying night fighter aircraft could launch an attack on enemy bombers. These flights, although not judged successful and the project abandoned, were often seen over Ware where one night the firewatchers had a first class view of one German bomber caught in the beam over the town. It was attacked by the night fighters and crashed near Epping. The conditions during the early days at Hunsdon were pretty primitive, the accommodation for the ground crews was without water or heating so transport was laid on every Friday night to take the airmen to Allenburys sports ground where they had a hot bath or shower. Many of the Squadrons based at Hunsdon used the Amwell End Drill Hall for their Squadron dances, this was particularly so with 85 Squadron.

United Services Canteen

At the outbreak of war various canteens which were set up in Ware to give the troops stationed in and around the town somewhere to get away from their sparse billets and to enjoy a few home comforts. The first one to open was organised by the Free Churches who, at a meeting held at Congregational Church, agreed that their canteen should open on 30th September 1940 serving refreshments between 6.00 pm to 10.00 pm every evening of the week. Another opened at St. Mary's but it wasn't long before it was realised that the troops would be better served if all the resources were concentrated under one roof. So, in January 1941, a new canteen was opened at the Masonic Hall in Church Street and was known as the Women's Voluntary Service Canteen, as its name implies it was run by the "Ladies in Green". Apart from the usual "wad and cuppa" recreational facilities were available. Although the WVS continued to run the catering side the canteen soon changed its name to the United Services Club, James Cooper was elected as President, Ernie Whybrew as the Chairman while Richard Trundle acted as the Secretary. Airmen from Hunsdon regularly used the Club coming to Ware in the back of Bedford 3ton trucks. One airman who didn't use the facilities when he came to the town was Ware born and bred John Storey who, for a short while, was stationed at Hunsdon! The club remained open throughout the war but with few servicemen in the town it was frequently used by the British Legion who staged darts tournaments there.

G I and Canadian Brides

At the later stage of the war American servicemen were stationed at Colliers End and often came into the town for the Saturday dances at the Drill Hall as did the airmen from Hunsdon, several of the local girls became G I and Canadian Brides. Whether the bridegrooms came from Colliers End and Hunsdon is not known.

Eileen Bailey of 6 Cromwell Road married Corporal Sidney Titus of Massachusetts serving with the U.S.A.A.F. Phyliss Carter of 48 King George's Road married Sergeant Thomas Avansato from Garfield in New Jersey serving with the U.S Army. Pamela Riley of 58 Trinity Road married Private Salvatore Guarino from New York serving with the U.S Army. Hilda Chapman of 55 Canons Road married LAC Harold Townsend from Saskatchewen serving with the Canadian Air Force.

The military's defences in Ware

With the fall of France in June 1940 the threat of invasion became a reality strange looking objects began to appear on the Ware landscape. Flat farmland in the surrounding countryside was obstructed with steel scaffold poles with wire cables suspended between them to foil gliders carrying German airborne troops from landing. Novel anti-glider precautions were constructed on the Hoe Lane rugby pitches, here two large vertical pylons some eight feet high were built from large concrete pipes partially set in the ground. Odd shaped brick or concrete structures sometimes disguised as buildings to blend in with the adjoining landscape were built by local contractors under the supervision of the Royal Engineers, these of course were defensive positions affectionately known as "pillboxes". Large concrete road blocks and "dragons teeth" made their appearance at the roadsides, their objective was to halt German tanks and armoured vehicles. Ware had its share of "pillboxes" and "dragons teeth". On 30th May 1940 the Home Office ordered that all road signs were to be removed to "disorientate the enemy should he land in our country," the same instruction applied to place names on railway stations, post offices, police stations and other buildings. The signs were restored in February 1944.

Pillboxes

The War Office built three pillboxes in Ware which were to form local fixed defensive points in conjunction with road blocks and did not form part of the main "stop lines" to hold back a German advance in the event of their invasion. Two remain in Ware today. One can still be seen under a mass of brambles is a few yards south of Thieves Lane at its junction with Hoe Lane. The walls of this particular pillbox are brick faced on both the external and internal faces and is known as a type 24, it could be garrisoned by eight men with a maximum of five light machine guns

(Bren guns). A second one at The Ridgeway was built on the high ground overlooking the Wadesmill Road in either direction, the pillbox was practically buried with builder's debris when the Kings Hill estate was developed. From the external walls still visible it would appear that this was a type 24 as well. The third one was in the field more or less opposite the old John Gilpin pub (Amwell Terrace) in London Road covering the town's southern approach, it was demolished in the 1950s.

Road Blocks

Road blocks to obstruct enemy tanks were constructed at various points in the town by the County Council and paid for by the Ministry of Transport. They consisted of large concrete blocks some four feet square and five foot high finished with a pyramidal top section set on the kerb line, the gap between could be closed by manhandling concrete "Crocodile" or "Dragons Teeth" into position. Road blocks were constructed in Star Street, Baldock Street, Bridgefoot, Cannons Hotel, The Bourne, New Road and Musley Lane cross-roads, the junction of New Road and King Edward's Road and finally at London Road. They caused endless problems for traffic and in March 1941 the County Surveyor instructed the Town Surveyor that they should be removed and the key ones replaced with anti-tank traps consisting of bent steel rails which fitted into concrete slots when required. Those in New Road

were removed altogether and not replaced and the presence of gas and water mains made it impossible to install the new type at Bridgefoot. Additional anti-tank traps were built in Amwell End and Viaduct Road. Their removal started in May 1945.

Left: the remains of the Home Guard checkpoint is stillvisible in Hoe Lane – in the hedgerow opposite South Lodge. A chain was suspended from the hook to a similar one on the other side of the road. The army's pill box is nearby. (photo by Michael Ottley).

Chapter 17
'DAD'S ARMY' – The Local Defence
Volunteers and the Home Guard

The Germans started their major offensive against the Allies on 10th May 1940 and the threat of invasion was now a reality, so much so that individuals began to arm themselves. The War Office wanted to form a small force of armed civilians to watch out for parachutists while the Government envisaged a much larger force to combat a seaborne invasion. The Government won the day, on 13th May four army officers sat down to formulate the rules under which the Local Defence Volunteers would operate. Much to the chagrin of the Civil Service they completed their task in twenty-four hours! The next day the Secretary of State for War, Mr Anthony Eden, broadcast an appeal on 9 o'clock evening news for all able bodied men between the ages of 18 and 65 not already engaged on National Service to enrol in the LDV and stated that every volunteer would be provided with a uniform and armed to defend the locality in which they lived. "Dad's Army" had been born. By the end of June 1.5 million men had enlisted nationally including some 6,000 in Hertfordshire where it was envisaged that there would be one Battalion of twenty companies based in the major centres of population. For a while Colonel Richard Page Croft was appointed to command No 3 (Ware) Company but was soon succeeded by Major Ian Buxton DSO of Stanstead Lodge.

In the early days their uniform were denims, a fatigue dress which were always shapeless and baggy, a forage cap and a LDV armband. There were few rifles and virtually no ammunition but plenty of enthusiasm. Enemy paratroops were a real threat so the volunteers were nicknamed the "Parashooters" or the less flattering titles of the "Last Ditch Volunteers" and the "Look, Duck and Vanish" volunteers. One of their first duties was to set up and man road blocks on the roads leading into towns

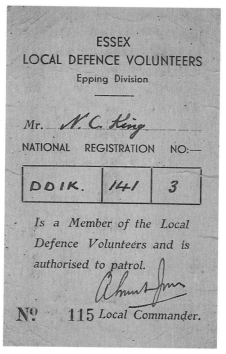

LDV authority to patrol for Mr N.C. King, the author's uncle

and villages, here travellers were to be stopped and required to produce their identity cards. At least three check points existed in Ware at London Road, Hoe Lane (part of which can still be seen today) and on the Wadesmill Road. John Fletcher, the late Town Clerk, recorded some of Maurice Wiggall's reminiscences of his days with the LDV before he was called up for active service, one story shows that Ware operated a slightly different system – they checked people leaving the town!

'Some Tales of Ware's Dad's Army' by John Fletcher

Maurice Wiggall of Crib Street was a young member of Ware's Home Guard before being called up for the Army. His platoon had a defence post in Wadesmill Road near to where Heath Drive junction is now. There they had a wire rope which in the event of an invasion they were going to pull across the road to stop enemy tanks etc. Later they even had rifles and ammunition.

One of their duties was to stop vehicles and check people for their identity cards and one of their pleasures was to stop the last bus out of Ware at night taking the late night drinkers home from Ware's pubs to the nearby villages. They took great delight in marching anyone without an Identity Card round to the Ware Police Station even though they probably knew most of them personally by name. Another of their duties was to go out on a patrol i.e. walk up to Poles (where there was a searchlight) and back again – not really knowing what they were looking for. One night Maurice was in such a patrol with a Mr Walters and they were accompanied by a young lad not really old enough to join the Home Guard officially but he went along for the walk!

It was a dark night and planes could be heard overhead when suddenly they saw a light flashing in the bushes. They thought it must be a spy signalling to the planes above and after a discussion decided they ought to do something. Mr Walters being the eldest took charge and told all of them to get in a line (there were only three of them) and walk slowly forward but the light kept moving. Mr Walters decided he was going to challenge whoever was there and Maurice said "go on then." Mr Walters the called out "halt who goes there or I will fire" and immediately fired his rifle.

The light went out straight away and all was quiet but after searching the area they could find nothing and reported back that they had probably disturbed a spy. The next day the Police visited the area and had a look round in daylight and found a pile of snares used for catching rabbits so instead of shooting a spy they had probably given a fright to a well known local poacher.

The Home Guard

Winston Churchill disliked the term LDV and as from the 23rd June 1940 the volunteers became known as the Home Guard although they wore their original arm bands well into 1941. Arms and ammunition became more readily available in the summer of 1940 following the lease of our naval bases in the West Indies to the United States in return for armaments. The rifles Ware's Home Guard received were American P14s, P17s and P14 EY rifle cup grenade launchers which were all vintage models made in 1914 and 1917 but as Jack Bowman told the author "they were better than nothing". These rifles had a slightly smaller bore than the standard British Army Lee-Enfield .303s and to avoid jamming through the use of incorrect ammunition the stocks of both the P14s and P17s were painted with a red band and the base of the cartridges marked in red. With regular drills, lectures and training on Wednesday evenings and Sunday mornings coupled with the discipline and experience of the "old sweats" from the 1914-18 war they rapidly became an enthusiastic force to be reckoned with. "Dads Army" were ready for the enemy.

Between July and September 1942 the cumbersome organisation set up for the LDV was rationalised, the county was split into three sectors with Ware forming part of the Eastern Sector and designated as "C" Company of the 1st Battalion of the Hertfordshire Regiment, Home Guard – the same Company as many of its older members went to France with in 1914. "C" Company Headquarters remained at the Drill Hall under the command of Major Ian Buxton. Platoons No 1, 2 and 3 were based at Dane End, Thundridge and Wareside; Platoons No. 4 , 5, 6, 7 and 8 were all based in Ware.

Number 4 platoon held training sessions in the grounds of Presdales House where one of their sergeants was the groundsman but they had strict instructions not to go near the house as the McMullen family were still in residence. They also drilled in the grounds of Chadwell House near the golf course. Hand grenade training etc. was occasionally undertaken on a Sunday morning at the Battalion's Weapons Training School established and run by Captain C A Marques MBE behind his family business, Concrete Utilities Ltd, in Lower Road Great Amwell. Besides running the training school Marques was the author of several Home Guard training manuals. At the end of a training session they marched back and "fell out" near the Red House pub where no doubt some "fell in" again! Ralph Parker, the youngest member of No.4 platoon talked of the great rivalry between the platoons and that the machine gunners were an aloof bunch. No.5 platoon met at the Angel pub in Star Street and used an adjoining orchard for part of their training. No.6 Platoon met in a malting building at the junction of Park Road and Watton Road, very convenient for the New Rose and Crown (now The Worpell) and the Star Brewery Tap opposite (now demolished), they used Brazier's gravel pit in Wengeo Lane as a training area and a small bore rifle range on the way to Fanhams Hall. No. 7 Platoon, the mobile reserve, was based at the Drill Hall. No. 8 platoon, the machine gunners, under Percy Beard not only had machine guns but a locally made mortar which is now in the Imperial War Museum's collection at Duxford and later two Smith guns. The platoon used the ranges on the Easneye Estate or at Cold Christmas. The various platoons provided a NCO and three or four men each night to man the Drill Hall HQ telephone, apparently

at the first sign of trouble at the Saturday night dances it is said they doubled up as 'bouncers'!

This home-made mortar was donated to the Imperial War Museum by Percy Beard on the 28th November 1945 together with two practice mortar bombs. Jack Bowman who served under Lt. Beard, believes it was designed by Roy Smouton who had worked at Wickhams as an engineer before the war – since many of the platoon were Wickham men it is probable that the mortar was made in their workshops. It was lightweight and easy to handle, its construction is basic consisting mainly of standard pipe sections, its bombs were made from tin canisters complete with a fuse. The mode of firing was a little hair raising to say the least; a bag of black powder was placed in the barrel followed by the mortar bomb with its fuse lit, the charge was probably detonated with a shotgun cartridge. In reality it was probably a moral boosting weapon rather than a war weapon but it was fired, Jack Bowman recalls that it was set up on the Buxton estate at Easneye and fired with much trepidation and wariness towards the River Ash scoring a direct hit more by luck than judgement. The barrel bears a brass plate stating that it had belonged to No.8 (MG) Platoon of the 1st Bn Herts (HG) Regt. The mortar is now at Duxford.

Shortly after the reorganisation an Eastern Sector Mobile Reserve Company under the command of Captain Marques was formed by drawing one platoon from the four companies within the Battalion with its headquarters at Concrete Utilities. No.7 platoon was transferred from Ware to the new company where they designated as No.1 Rifle Platoon. They made their local headquarters in the old White Swan Pub in West Street. The objective of the Mobile Reserve was to rush reserves to protect strategic positions and to achieve this in Ware vehicles belonging to G Bell of Baldock Street, Allan & Hanburys, W Page & Son and Neave & Son both from the High Street and The Enfield Co-op in Star Street had been earmarked for transport. In the event of "action stations" the platoon was to assemble outside Swain & Nicholls grocery shop in the High Street and dash off in their requisitioned vehicles to their allotted defensive position which was Hunsdon airfield. In 1944 the platoon was commanded by Lt F Cavandish of Cannons Road who led 36 other ranks. A nominal roll of the platoon members in 1942 appears as Appendix No.11.

The age limit for joining was lowered to seventeen to enable young men to gain some military experience before being called up for active service, it is known that some under aged lads in Ware signed on one of whom died as a result of an accident in November 1943. Ralph Chapman, a school boy at the Richard Hale Grammar School and the son of the Ware Postmaster, died through a tragic accident with a sten gun at his parent's Chadwell home. Ralph who was nearly seventeen had joined the Home Guard some twelve months previously giving his age as seventeen and served with the machine gun platoon. The Coroner's Court reached an open verdict, only one spent cartridge case was found and since the sten was an unreliable weapon prone to fire with the safety catch on it would appear that one round had been left in the breach or magazine. Ralph is buried at Great Amwell. Tragedy was to hit the family again when his elder brother Peter was killed serving with the RAF. Another under aged member was Ron Wall of Canons Road who at the age of sixteen joined his father Albert in No.6 platoon. He was issued with a rifle and ammunition but soon after Ralph Chapman's death the police called on Ron's mother while he was at work at Allen & Hanburys and took away his rifle. Ron was allowed to stay in the Home Guard but was transferred to the Intelligence Section as a runner before he volunteered for the Royal Army Service Corps. John Storey was another who served with "Dad's Army" before joining the RAF.

Ware Home Guard played its part it the preparations for Allies landings in Europe, the machine gun platoon participated in an exercise held in a wood near Barwick Ford with American troops training for D-Day. The recorded strength of "C" Company on the 26th July 1944 was 11 Officers and 324 N.C.Os and men. They were well armed with 181 No. P14 and P17 Rifles with 26,300 rounds of ammunition, 18 No. E.Y. Rifles, 66 No. Sten Guns with 22,500 rounds of 9mm ammunition, 4 No. Light Machine Guns with 40,000 rounds of ammunition (these were 1914-1918 vintage water cooled Vickers machine guns), 6 No. Spigot Mortars with 194 No. 20 lb. bombs and 137 number anti-personnel bombs and 2 No. Smith Guns.

The Smith was another "Heath Robinson" weapon being a light gun which could be towed behind a car. Its unrifled barrel was mounted on mushroom shaped wheels which were detachable; when set up one wheel formed the gun's base and the other a shield. Charlie Stockwell who joined the machine gun platoon at the age of sixteen before becoming a Bevin Boy recalls seeing a Smith gun in action. The platoon was on a training exercise at Easneye and it was proposed to fire a dummy shell from the gun across the valley. Percy Beard told Charlie to take up a position where he could see the shell land and he clearly remembers seeing it cartwheeling in flight!

With the threat of invasion gone the Home Guard's role was almost over, a fact readily appreciated by the men themselves since they organised their "farewell dance" at the Drill Hall at the end of September. The Home Guard was officially stood down on 1st November 1944. After four and a half years of valuable service during which they progressed from shotguns to machine-guns the Ware Home Guard, in common with every other unit in the country, held their final parade on Sunday the 3rd December.

Above: No 4 Platoon photographed at Presdales House in January 1945 with 2Lt. EG Morgan and Lt. EJC Parker. Below: members of No 6 Platoon at Allenburys in 1942 – back row: Tom Pritlove, Ernie Reynolds, —, Sam Skipp, Buck Hutchinson, Alf Blows and Fred Hillier; front row: Fred Hitch, Bob (Wag) Castle, Michael Light, the Revd. Charles Kingston and Alf Wallis.

Chapter 18
WARE'S WAR BOOK or
THE PARISH INVASION PLAN

The threat of invasion still persisted in the early summer months of 1941 and the Government realised that contingency plans had to be made to deal with the invaders and the ensuing chaos so a series of meetings were called for and held in Regional Administration Centres. Representatives from Ware attended one such meeting at Cambridge on 30th May 1941 where they were told to formulate a "War Book" or "Parish Invasion Plan" which would be put into action should the Germans invade. The plan was to include the defence of the town should the army be engaged elsewhere and to provide the basic facilities needed by the civilian population. It was recognised that in event of an invasion London would come under heavy attack and that many people would trek out into the country. One of the main exit routes from the capital, the A10, came through Ware so the town had to make arrangements to accommodate, fed and look after the welfare of the anticipated refugees as well as the 9000 residents and evacuees already in the town. Contingency measures had to be made to deal with disrupted communications, food and water supplies.

To formulate the plan of action the town set up a small Emergency Committee under the chairmanship of Dr Walter Stewart backed up by officials charged with executive duties, in December 1941 the committee members were: Tom Burgess the Deputy ARP Controller; Leslie Southall, Town Clerk who was also the ARP Officer and Food Controller; Eric Cullin the Engineer and Surveyor; Norman Daker the Deputy Town Clerk; William Reid the Deputy ARP Officer; Charles Lucas the Sanitary Inspector; Major Ian Buxton of Ware Home Guard; Inspector Charles Hollands of Ware Police; Arthur Brazier of the NFS and Mrs May of the WVS.

Major Buxton was responsible for preparing the drawing up the town's military defences and he completed his plan by December 1941. The civilian plan of action took a little longer to put together. Copies of the "Invasion Plan" were published in leaflet form on 27th March 1942 and delivered by the WVS to every household in the town advising of the arrangements in the event of a "Major Emergency."

Home Guard Defence Scheme

A copy of Major Buxton's plan is now kept in the County Archives at Hertford, it opens with the patriotic words *"the enemy shall not be allowed to occupy the town of Ware, nor use the roads passing through it which were to be kept open for the use of our own troops"*. It goes on to detail the strength of the Ware platoons in the summer of 1941 as:

No.4 platoon (Amwell House) 38 men   No.5 platoon (Widbury Mount) 38 men
No.6 platoon (Wadesmill Road) 66 men   No.7 platoon (Mobile Reserve) 20 men

The detailed plan is rather sketchy but shows that there were to be two defensive lines within the town with the mobile reserve patrolling the outskirts. No.1 line was to be at the junction of the High Street and Star Street manned by 70 men with its headquarters in either the Co-op Building (Bridge Carpets) or Northmet House (the Bridge House pub), the second line was to be in the vicinity of the Amwell End and manned by 50 men with its headquarters at Amwell House. The Mobile Reserve consisting of 40 men was to patrol the outlying areas.

Major Buxton updated his plan in November 1942 a copy of which (minus its sketch map) is in the Ware Museum's archives. His objective was still to prevent the attacker from using the approach roads into the town but the defence lines were now moved to the outskirts and incorporated the military pillboxes and road blocks. He also clearly heeded the advice given in the Military and Home Guard training manuals of 1941 which warned that although pillboxes and road blocks had their uses they must not make the defenders "village Maginot-line minded". The manuals stated that although pillboxes gave protection against bullets, shell splinters and weather they were vulnerable against a direct hit from a bomb or shell and recommended that they formed part of a defensive system with supporting fire and barbed wire to prevent infiltration by the enemy using grenades and flame throwers. In the event of "action stations" being sounded the defence lines were to be manned by Nos.4, 5 and 6 platoons co-ordinated from the Home Guard's headquarters at the Drill Hall. The machine gun platoon would be held in reserve at HQ and would be responsible for immobilising the town's petrol stations. Every man would be to issued with 50 rounds, one blanket between two men; 48 hour ration packs would be delivered to the defence lines and First Aid posts set up in the defence line headquarters. Although not mentioned in the plan several of the ATC cadets were to act as signallers and their rather bizarre roll has already been described.

The southern defence line was to be manned by No.4 platoon under the command of Lt. C T Brooker with his headquarters at Ware Grammar School for Girls (Amwell House). Brooker's main defensive position was in London Road where considerable protection had been given to the pillbox with barbed wire entanglements. Another strong point was built where the Scouts' complex now stands, near Post Wood Road. Covering fire was provided by a sandbagged machine gun emplacement at the junction of the A10 and Lower Road.

A machine gun post with sandbag revetments on the south-east corner of the junction of Hoe Lane and Walnut Tree Walk gave supporting fire to the pillbox in

The spigot mortar 'thimble'.

Thieves Lane. A Blacker Bombard spigot mortar emplacement was sited opposite the Girl's Grammar School on the north side of the New River under the shade of a large chestnut tree, its distinctive "thimble" is still a local land mark, and covered the approaches to Amwell End from the east and west. The spigot mortar threw a twenty pound bomb some 600 yards, if on target it was an effective anti-tank weapon but it had a nasty habit of veering off course! Sniper positions were to be located within the School, in the Victoria Malting and the Railway Yard.

The northern defence line covered the town's approaches from Wareside, Wadesmill and Westmill Hill. The road from Wareside and Holycross was to be guarded by No.5 platoon under the command of Lt. Matthews with his headquarters at Northmet House where the plate glass windows were to be removed and replaced with sandbagged walls. Outposts had already been established at Widbury Hill and at Trinity Road where patrols consisting of an N.C.O. and seven men were based. The platoon would also man a Blacker Bombard spigot mortar located in a concrete emplacement in a wood yard at the foot of Widbury Hill probably near the entrance to present day AXA's warehouse complex since it had a direct line of fire up the hill. A second Blacker Bombard was sited some 350 yards to the east of the first near the brow of the hill, both emplacements were lost when the road at Widbury Hill was realigned several years ago. Sniper positions were to be sited in Northmet House covering the High Street, Star Street and Viaduct Road, in the Co-op Society Building covering Amwell End and Star Street and the Saracens Head covering New Road and the river.

No.6 platoon under Lt. Harris was responsible for the defence of the northern approaches to Ware with outposts at Cannons and the Cemetery, from here patrols were sent to Moles, Poles, the Sanatorium at Ware Park and Westmill Hill areas. Two Blacker Bombard spigot mortars were located on the higher ground to the east of Cannons to give protection to the pillbox at the Ridgeway as well as covering the A10 from Wadesmill and its junction with Watton Road

The Emergency Plan

In the event of a break down to the telephone service the Emergency Committee proposed to use the ATC and the Boy Scouts as messengers within the town backed up by motor cyclists supplied by the ARP County Control for inter-town communication. Information was also to be given to householders by the Police under Inspector Hollands, the Air Raid Wardens Service and the Home Guard. Lists of able bodied men and women who could be called upon to dig slit trenches for the Home Guard were prepared and the survey undertaken by the WVS to determine the number of beds available for evacuees was updated to see how many more people could be accommodated in private homes.

To ensure a fair distribution of food supplies and to feed the anticipated influx of refugees in the event of "Action Stations" Ware's plan was to shut all food shops and catering establishments until a return of stock had been sent to Leslie Southall and Norman Daker to assess and to set emergency ration levels. An emergency milk and bread scheme was also prepared with distribution points appointed together with personnel to man them. Since there were no "Buffer Depots" in the immediate district the larger of the town's food retailers were asked by the Ministry of Food to keep one month's stock of sugar and fourteen days supply of margarine, cooking fats and cheese in hand, others were obliged to stock items of food for the Home Guard personnel. The Town Clerk and his Deputy were in charge of emergency food supplies or iron rations which included tins of soup, baked beans, meat roll, tea, sugar, milk (probably that nice thick sweet sticky stuff that all us who were kids at the time loved to lick from the spoon!) and biscuits (probably the "iron rations" type used by the army which were so hard you had to "dunk" them or loose your front teeth!). The iron rations were stored at Western House for both the public and the Civil Defence.

To overcome the problem of bomb damage to the town's water mains emergency drinking water tanks were installed at the Central and Technical schools in August, the Council also purchased a small rotary pump, pipes and couplings to use as surface mains together with a 500 gallon water tank to enable supplies to be restored quickly. It was also thought that any problems with the sewerage system could be overcome by the use of mobile latrines.

To cope with the anticipated influx of refugees temporary rest centres were set up for 750 persons in the following buildings:

First line centre: Congregational Hall and school room in the High Street with places for 300.

Second line or reserve centres: Gladstone Hall in Gladstone Road (70 places), the Catholic Hall in King Edward's Road (50 places), the Salvation Army Hall in Baldock Street (50 places), the Scout's Hut in Church Street (50 places), St Mary's C.E. School (120 places) and the Central School (110 places).

In the event of these proving insufficient it was proposed to use places of worship. Mr C Parker of Little Widbury was appointed as the Public Assistance Officer to run the main centre at the Congregational Hall assisted by the ubiquitous WVS who kept stocks of blankets and gifts from abroad there. The Senior School under its headmaster, Albert Evans, was designated and equipped for any local incident.

Chapter 19
THE CALL TO ARMS

Ware has had a long associatoin with the volunteer units of the armed forces, dating from the Volunteer Infantry units formed in 1798. The tradition continued with the Territorial Army and a company of the 1st Battalion, Hertfordshire Regiment was always based in Ware as was the regiment's Corps of Drums. Shooting at the rifle ranges played a significant part of their training routine: apart from the obligatory annual shoots at either Panshanger or Youngsbury, a team from Ware always competed in the County Shoot and the Sir H. P. Croft Challenge Cup. Three "Terriers" from Ware, Ted Chivers, Ted Titmarsh and "Bomber Wells" also shot for the Hertfordshire Regiment at Bisley in 1934 and 1935. Social life has always played its part with the Territorials and so it was with the Ware "Terriers". The Ware T.A Football Club was a very successful pre-war team – not only did they compete in the local league and cups but they travelled to Belgium on an Easter tour combining sight- seeing with matches against local sides.

The "Terriers" mobilised on the 2nd September 1939 but remained at their drill halls. There was some reorganisation with men from Ware in the H.Q Company's mortar section being posted to Hertford while others from Bishops Stortford came to Ware – two from Bishops Stortford were billeted at 55 Musley Hill with Dorothy Gilbert's family. Training continued until October when the Battalion was split into two, the Ware platoons and the Corps of Drums together with other units in the eastern part of the county remained in the 1st Battalion while those in the western half became the 2nd Battalion. The 1st Battalion was deployed with the 162nd Infantry Brigade within the 54th (East Anglian) Division and spent the next three years on home defence work serving at Dovercourt where they provided the gun crews on civilian ships. Postings to Cheltenham, Northumberland, Burnham in Buckinghamshire and Kessingland followed before moving to Briggs in Lincolnshire where they mobilised for overseas service.

While at Dovercourt a call came for volunteers to join the 1st Battalion of the Beds and Herts stationed in Palestine, and one of the twenty-two men to step forward was John Stockwell whose four brothers also served in the forces during the war. John had joined the Herts Territorials at the age of fourteen as a drummer boy in 1931 and later played for the T.A football team. The volunteers travelled to Palestine by boat to Cherbourg, train to Marseilles, the troopship *Devonshire* to Haifa where they met up with their new regiment at the Allenby Barracks outside Jerusalem. John, it seems, disagreed with the old army adage that you never volunteer for anything and when men were required to man the anti-aircraft guns on the *Empress of Britain*

Ware Territorial Football Club in 1938 – back row: J Crane, E Head, R Head, F Taylor and B Crane; middle row: J Crane, Joe Crane, H Williams, E Chivers, G Walker, J Perry, Vic Penn and trainer C Trundell; front row: C Coombes, J Long, G Wallace*, G Crane*, and Jack Neal. (* Killed in action).

from Haifa to Durban to collect troops for the Western Desert offensive he took two paces forward. He returned to Blighty on the *Andes* and joined the 71st Young Soldiers Battalion at Bedford as an instructor.

To return to the Hertfordshire Regiment, the Battalion, minus the "Drums" who followed later, embarked at Glasgow on 13th April 1943 and much to their disappointment found themselves destined for Gibraltar where they arrived nine days later. "The Rock" was their station for the next fourteen months although they did go to Oran on the North African coast periodically for training exercises. With the Allies on the offensive several of the married men from Ware were lucky enough to receive messages from their wives broadcast on the B.B.C overseas service programme "Gibraltar Calling" just before Christmas 1943. Vera Crane of 2 West Street spoke to her husband George, Nancy Penn of 93 High Street spoke to her husband Joe while Mrs Haines of 24 Star Street sent birthday greetings to her husband Aubrey. Mrs V Hancock of 7 Crane Mead broadcast a message to her husband in February 1944. Sadly both George Crane and Aubrey Haines were killed later in the year while fighting in Italy. Hilda Perry and her daughter Ellen of 9 Clements Street spoke to

Bill Perry in June a couple of weeks before the Battalion moved to pastures new.

In July 1944 the Battalion transferred to the 66th Infantry Brigade in Italy and by the 18th August were stationed a few miles south of Florence where they prepared to attack the heavily fortified Gothic Line set high in the mountains. Their advanced started on the 23rd August when patrols moved through the foothills to Fiesole. By the 12th September they reached the forward slopes of the Gothic Line towering some 2,000 feet above them and together with American troops were the first to break through the defensive stronghold. The terrain was difficult and supplies to the forward troops had to be taken were taken by jeep, then by mule train and finally by carrying parties. The administrative support encouraged by RQSM J Crane from Ware never failed to supply the front line troops. While fighting in the Monte Ceco area three Ware men were killed, Aubrey Haines and George Wallace on 18th October and George Crane on 13th November. When the Battalion marched out of the line on 7th January 1945 little did they know that they were bound for Palestine and Syria to play a less rewarding role combating terrorism. They arrived at Haifa on 31st January and remained in this theatre until the Battalion was stood down in 1946.

The comradeship developed within the Regiment continued after the war with the formation of the Hertfordshire Old Comrades Association, a branch was established in Ware early in the New Year of 1947 at the French Horn in the High Street. Lord Croft was elected as the branch president, the vice-presidents were Major Kenyon, Colonel E C M Phillips, Colonel Glynn and Major Christie. The chairman was Major Stanley Burr, J Perry was the secretary with E Adams and E Chivers serving as joint secretaries, Messrs Arthur Rand, E Selby, J Crane, A Hulls, E Head, Bill Perry and John Stockwell formed the committee.

Hore-Belisha's Conscripts

The National Service (Armed Forces) Act of 1939 enabled the Secretary of State for War, Lord Hore-Belisha, to direct young men of certain age groups to register for a period of six months military training followed by three and a half years as reservists who would be called up in the event of war. Jack Gilbert registered in April 1939 and was called up for service on 15th July together with Les Beard and Sid Wallace. They were posted to the Beds and Herts Regiment and did their basic training at Kempston Barracks, Bedford. All three were transferred to the 8th Battalion of the Royal Warwickshire Regiment in October 1939 and went to France during the bitterly cold January of 1940. Jack recalls that at one stage when they were accommodated in a barn it was so cold that they were given permission to sleep in pairs (fully clothed) so that the two men could share six blankets instead of the regulation three. The 8th Battalion were eventually moved to Halle, near Waterloo, on the Belgium – German border in May 1940 where they were ordered to dig trenches – the 1914/18 mentality still prevailed in the British Army. Jack's experiences during the withdrawal from France appear in the next chapter. Kempston Barracks at Bedford was the Beds and Herts Regiments training depot and is well remembered by other Ware who were drafted into the Regiment under the National Service Act. After their basic training they joined one of the Regiment's Battalions such as the 2nd and 30th both of which were to serve in North Africa and Italy.

National Service

Once war was declared, the 1939 act enabled the Government to call up men between the ages of twenty and twenty-two. By December 1941 all men between the ages of eighteen and a half to fifty-one were liable for service; unmarried women between twenty to thirty could be called up for service in the women's forces or directed into either full-time civil defence duties or factories engaged on war production. The age at which young men had to register was lowered to seventeen and a half in 1944 although they did not receive their call up papers until after their eighteen birthday. The first registration for National Service took place on Saturday the 21st August at the nearest Employment Office which, in the case of Ware, was at Hertford. Here they stated the service their preferred choice of service and some weeks later they were required to attend a medical board held at Lattimore Road in St Albans, those who were fit would be called up within a few weeks. Some employers, mainly in the public sector and including Ware UDC, made up the conscripted employees' pay to 80% of their pre-service pay packet and in some cases war service counted towards their pensionable service. Men and women called to the services were guaranteed their jobs back when they were demobilised. This had its problems too since many were called up in their late teens they returned as men to their old jobs at boy's or apprentice's rates of pay.

Soon after the war the Ministry of Information released the population distribution based on the "average town" during the war years, these show that 10% of men and women would have been called up for military service and of these 4.5% would have been killed or missing in action and that 3.4% would have been taken prisoner. So how did Ware compare with the average town? The broad answer is that the town contributed slightly more than the average. The key to this comparison is the town's population in 1939 assessed at 8,000 by the Town Council in their salvage returns and confirmed by the number of gas masks received.

	"Average town"	Ware
Called up	800	865*
Killed in action	36	53
Prisoners of war	27	23

* Taken from the Ware Boys at the Front Fund

Comforts for the Forces

Ware had a tradition of looking after its service people who served their country in time of war and many ex-service men from W.W.I remembered the parcels and comforts sent to them by the town so they, together with their wives and daughters, were determined to see that their relatives now fighting aggression received similar gifts. The main organisation set up in the town was the "Ware Boys at the Front Fund" but there were others too. Besides the Priory knitting circle and the school children already mentioned in chapters 14 and 15 the town played its part in raising money for a Hertford based fund organised for the men serving in the Hertfordshire Regiment, for the Beds and Herts Regiment Comfort Fund, the RAF Benevolent Fund as well as several associated with the Royal Navy.

Ware Boys at the Front Fund

The origins of this fund date from the First World War when a group of prominent people in the town set up a fund to send a few luxuries to "Our Boys" in the trenches at Ypres and on the Somme. These gifts were much appreciated and were moral boosting since the troops felt that they were not forgotten by their home town. It is not surprising that these same veterans, now members of the British Legion, should resurrect the fund soon after war was declared. The Legion decided it would be better if it were made a public affair, accordingly they called a meeting on Wednesday the 25th October to which all interested organisations and members of the public were invited. At the meeting Lt-Col. T H Walker DSO, TD of Hoe Lane was elected President of "The Ware Boys at the Front Fund", Fred Weatherly as chairman (he was also the chairman of the Ware Branch of the British Legion), Ernie Whybrew as vice chairman, Bertie Clare as secretary and Mr Theobold as treasurer. Committee members were Miss Garforth, Miss Webster, Miss Seacombe, Miss Violet Castle, Messrs E J Collins, J Chapman, F Beazley, J Wells, R Harrandence, C Ward, J Spencer, G Sayers and McDonald. Apart from the British Legion the Conservative Club, the Football Club, the Labour Party and the Boy Scouts were enthusiastic supporters of the fund. Within a couple of weeks the first batch of comforts had been sent to twenty Ware men serving overseas.

The initial objective of the Fund was limited to sending parcels to Ware men serving in France or elsewhere overseas but after the evacuation from of Dunkirk it was decided to send gifts to all Ware men serving in the armed Forces in the form of postal orders. The fund was later extended to the women's services and the Nursing Services attached to the forces. A couple of years later Ware, to its everlasting credit, recognised that young men conscripted into the coal mines as Bevin Boys would have gone into the forces through choice and should therefore receive gifts from the Ware Boys at the Front Fund like their compatriots in uniform. In this respect our

WARE BOYS AT THE FRONT FUND (1939)

Formed in October, 1939 for the purpose of providing comforts for Ware Boys serving with H.M. Forces. First distribution on November 8th 1939, was sent to 20 Ware men serving overseas. Latest distribution was sent to 792 Ware men and girls serving in all theatres of war at home, on the sea and overseas, at a cost of £303 12 0. Total cost of distributions to date, approximately £3261.

This money has been contributed from many sources, chiefly from—

House Collections £2031
Dances and other social events £350
Donations and other sources £1190

We thank you for your past generous help and ask you to favour us with your continued support to enable us to keep up this good work.

Don't forget to write to your relative or friend on the inside of this programme.

Printed and presented by The Star Press, Ware

In aid of Ware Boys at Front Fund

Programme

WHIT-MONDAY (1944)

CARNIVAL and FETE

. in .

The RECREATION GROUND, Ware

Gates open 1.30 p.m.

Admission 6d.   Children 3d.

FANCY DRESS PARADE FOR CHILDREN
1.30 p.m., Car Park.
SPORTS FOR CHILDREN, entries on the field
BOXING & JU-JITSU DISPLAY by the local A.T.C.
NUMEROUS SIDE-SHOWS, PONY RIDES
Teas & Refreshments (please bring your own cups)

PROGRAMME TWOPENCE

Do not put this Programme to salvage, but write on the inside to your relative or friend, he will be interested to know what we are doing!

town was fifty years ahead of the rest of the country since it was not until 1998 that the part the "Bevin Boys" played during the war was finally recognised when they were invited to take part in the annual Armistice Day Parade at the Cenotaph. It was also agreed that any surplus moneys at the end of the war were to be given to the British Legion Benevolent Fund.

Fund raising commenced immediately with appeals to individuals for donations and for local organisations to run money raising events. Whist drives were held on a regular basis, dances were held in the Drill Hall at Amwell End often with Harry Munt as M.C and Stan Bloomfield providing the music for upto 200 people. St Mary's Choir raised money through carol singing and Western House formed a "Farthing Club". However it was realised that a steady income was needed and it was decided to initiate a house to house collection on a regular basis, the prime mover for this scheme was Ernie Whybrew of King Edward's Road. Ernie had served as a Lieutenant with the Rifle Brigade during the First World War receiving crippling wounds to a knee in 1918 which left him with a stiff leg. Like so many others who had fought and survived the first world war he was determined to do all he could to support the war effort, his stiff leg prevented him from joining the Home Guard so his energies were directed to the "Ware Boys at the Front Fund". Ernie was a whiskey connoisseur and soon after war was declared he was told that spirits were needed for the war effort, as a result his opened bottle remained untouched until Victory was achieved! The town was divided into street areas and the necessary Home Office permits for weekly house to house collections were obtained by Leslie Southall, the Town Clerk. Everyone who wanted to contribute was given a card on which the volunteer collectors recorded the amount given. It was estimated that if every house contributed one penny then £10 a week would be raised – the average weekly sum raised was between £7 and £8. Whybrew's son Ted can well remember as a young lad going round the streets with his mother and aunt collecting the weekly penny. The following report appeared in the *Mercury* dated the 23rd February 1940:

Ware Boys at the Front Fund
RESIDENTS CONTRIBUTE £100 IN 13 WEEKS

Since the formation of the committee to arrange for parcels to be sent to Ware men on active service known popularly as "Ware Boys at the Front Fund" 18 weeks ago 174 parcels have been despatched to local men in France, the Near East and on H M Ships. Besides various despatches of cigarettes two special parcels have been sent, and in addition books have been sent as received.

So far each man has had one scarf, one pair of mittens or gloves and one balaclava helmet. Cards for the acknowledgement of the parcels are included as well as cards on which suggestions can be made. So far 153 acknowledgements have been received including one from Ware men on board a ship which has often been mentioned by the notorious Hamburg commentator (sic William Joyce nicknamed "Lord Haw Haw"). The committee state that in the 13 weeks the card collection has been in operation over £100 has been paid into the bank, the weekly contributions ranged from 1d to 6d.

The knitted items included within the parcels were donated by the Priory Comforts Fund and the Hertford Comforts Fund which supplied socks for the men in the Hertfordshire Regiment. Four Ware men were taken prisoner during the retreat and evacuation from Dunkirk so in November the Committee agreed that they would "adopt" the four under the British Red Cross scheme, this entailed a weekly payment of £1.10s.0d (£1.50) per week for six months to ensure that 2Lt. William Dixon, SQMS Alec Childs, Gunner Richard Goodship and Private Cecil Lee received a regular supply of food parcels.

The audited accounts for the year ending September 1940 presented to the fund's first annual general meeting show that £498 had been raised and that 340 Ware men had received gifts. Over 400 postal orders valued at 7s.6d each were sent out for Christmas 1940, among the recipients were men serving in the Middle East, two in Iceland, two RAF pilots and a sailor serving in a submarine. By August 1941 the numbers had risen to 443 including six of "Our Girls", at Christmas the fund sent out

501 postal orders to the value of 7s.6d (38p). Further contributions were made to the Red Cross so that more parcels could be sent to the prisoners of war, now numbering five.   Towards the end of 1942 eighteen year olds were receiving their call-up papers and 650 service people received a postal order for Christmas 1942. The main sources of income came from the street collections and the dances held in the Drill Hall. Other fundraising events included charity football matches, Christmas pantomimes organised by Miss M. Gleadowes of Amwell End, boxing matches and fetes – the last of these was held on the Buryfield Recreation Ground on Whit Monday 1945.

The committee met for the last time on 11th September 1945 when the fund was disbanded, a final distribution of 16s.0d (£0.80) was made to 865 members. During its six years the town collected £6009.18s.8d and spent £5969.0s.1d, the balance of £40.18s.7d was handed to the Ware British Legion Benevolent Fund. The monumental administration and organisation behind the fund was a credit to everyone involved. A copy of the final balance sheet was framed and given to the Council to hang in the Council Chamber and is now in the Ware Museum collection.

The committee received many letters of thanks of sincere appreciation from the recipients of the parcels and gifts. One from the ordinary "squaddie", Private Fish serving in Egypt, sums up their feelings when he wrote "I knew Ware would not forget us, we will not forget Ware". Driver J Newman of the Royal Army Service Corps serving in the Middle East wrote "during my travels I have met four boys from Ware and I must say that the Ware boys have received more gifts than others in my Company". In May 1945 a number of ex-servicemen organised a dance at the Drill Hall in appreciation for the work carried out by Bertie Clare's committee and team of collectors. Colonel Peter McMullen presented Clare with a certificate of thanks and a wallet, the other seventy-eight team members were to be given a certificate together with a wallet for the men and a purse for the ladies.

Regimental Comfort Funds

A considerable number of men from the town served in various Battalions of the Hertfordshire Regiment and the Beds & Herts Regiment. Occasional dances were held throughout the war with the proceeds being forwarded to Hertford for the County Regiment Comfort Fund. The only recorded fund raising event recorded in the town for the Beds and Herts Fund took place in February 1944 when the Stars in Battledress put on a performance of "Men in Shadow" at the Drill Hall.

Royal and Merchant Navy Funds

Towards the end of 1944 the Lord Mayor of London, the figure head for "Navy Comfort Funds", suggested to the Town Council that they ran a "Navy Week" to raise money for his funds and suggested a target of £500. The initial reaction within the council chamber was not to support the Lord Mayor's proposal on the grounds that the Royal Navy Comforts Fund had unspent moneys, however they did agree to join forces with the District Council to raise £500 for the Merchant Navy Comfort Fund. The 26th April to 6th May was declared "Merchant Navy Week" with Tom Burgess as its organising chairman. The proceedings started with the crowning of Barbara Burgess, Tom's daughter, as the Navy Week Queen at the Drill Hall. Barbara and her Maids of Honour, Joanna Chapman, Margaret Tillcock, Anita Titmarsh, Audrey Rowden, Betty Crook and Doreen Penny were presented with gold and silver pins by Mr Kirkland Bridge, the fund's national secretary. A series of events followed throughout the ensuing week to raise money and with Victory in sight Ware was in a buoyant mood. Apart from the usual whist drives, rummage sales etc. one could almost say it was a rehearsal for V E Day with children's fancy dress parades, a variety show at the Drill Hall and numerous concerts by Ware Brass Band. The weeks events raised the grand sum of £1480 and a grateful Kirkland Bridge returned to town to express his gratitude, Tom Burgess was given a certificate and the main organisers, Mr A H Andrews, Mrs L J Dale and Mrs Cooper received gold badges.

RAF Benevolent Fund

Money was collected in a novel way in the town for this fund through the "Raiders Past" box, everyone who left an air raid shelter when the all clear sounded was invited to place a coin in a collecting box. Every now and then these boxes were taken to H Ward and Sons shop at No.63 the High Street from where the moneys collected were forwarded to the fund headquarters, in the first couple of years of the war the amounted donated averaged £10 every three months. It may seem strange that as the raids became less frequent the quarterly amount collected remained static, the simple answer is that many families took to their shelter nightly throughout the war.

Girls from the Grammar School and the lads from the Air Training Corps acted as collectors for the fund when moral boosting films such as "Target for Tonight" were shown at the Ware Cinema. A concerted effort was made in August 1945 to collect more funds, the proprietor of a circus visiting the town allowed collections to be made both performances. Peter Coleman, whose father died as serving officer with the RAF, ran a fun fair in the Priory grounds assisted by the ladies of the Ware Comforts Fund while Henry Campkin organised a dance at the Drill Hall where the music was played by Billy Hills' band. (Billy had been a drummer with the "Herts Guards" in W.W.I becoming a regular soldier after the war, several others in his band such as Eddie Parker were his band colleagues in 1914-1918.)

Chapter 20
'OUR BOYS AND GIRLS'
Service men and women from Ware

The story of Ware at War would incomplete without relating the experiences of some of the 865 men and women from the town who were either regular service men, volunteers or called up under the National Service Act to serve their country; tribute to those who paid the ultimate sacrifice will be found in the final chapter. They served in every branch of the services and played their part in every theatre of the war. Others were in the auxiliary services such as the Merchant Navy, the Nursing Services, Bevin Boys or transferred elsewhere in the country on vital war work. Who should be included and their stories told? Since everyone did "their bit" in one form or another there is no easy answer, the final selection is an attempt to give a broad view across the entire spectrum of the part Ware people played and it is inevitable and with regret that many other interesting stories have been omitted. By far the largest number of Ware men and women who joined services served with the Army and by the Spring of 1940 they were in France with the British Expeditionary Force (the BEF), in the Middle and Far East. Others were abroad with the Navy and Air Force.

Royal Navy

Stoker Joseph Wilson DSM, a time-served regular on the Royal Navy Reserve List, was recalled to the colours when war was declared. Joe, married to Eleanor (Nell) Gilbert of 55 Musley Hill, served on the minesweeper *HMS Skipjack* during the BEF's evacuation from the Dunkirk beaches. On 1st June 1940 the *Skipjack* was in a small flotilla of naval boats off Bray-Dunes some six miles to the east of Dunkirk harbour loaded with some 250 to 300 troops taken aboard from the beaches. Shortly after 8.00 am Stuka dive bombers made the first of five attacks against the *Skipjack's* flotilla. Their command ship, *HMS Keith,* was sunk in the first onslaught and at 8.20 the *Skipjack* was hit, turned turtle and sank some twenty minutes later taking most of the troops with her. By now the sea was covered in oil from the sunken ships with the survivors coated in oil, half blinded and vomiting as they tried to stay afloat. Joe helped the many non-swimmers and is probably the reason why he was awarded his DSM. The survivors were picked up by the tug *St Abbs* which briefly steamed away in peace when at 9.20 a single bomber passed overhead and dropped a stick of four delayed action bombs which exploded as she passed over them and blew out her hull. Those who survived, including Joe, found themselves struggling against a strong tide sweeping them eastwards towards German held coast. Suddenly they spotted a wrecked cargo liner, the *Clan McAlister*, bombed, abandoned and aground off La Panne. The more agile swimmers managed to get to her and were eventually picked up by a Thames lighter and transferred to a humble cement carrier with no name – just the Sheerness Yard Craft No.63. Joe arrived home relieved to hear that his brother-in-law Jack Gilbert had escaped from the Dunkirk beaches, he spent the rest of the war on Atlantic and Arctic Sea convoy duties and never fully recovered from his ordeal at Dunkirk.

Joe and Nell Gilbert at their wedding in July 1930

Wrens

55410 Wren Charlotte (Lottie) Chamberlain (nee Fagg). Charlotte was one of a dozen or so young girls who came to Ware when Allen & Hanburys' Bethnal Green factory was bombed in November 1940. Six of the girls including Charlotte were billeted in a bungalow in Watton Road where they shared one room, although conditions were cramped it was their first break from their parental homes and had a great time! Within a matter of days the packaged drug department in which they worked in London had been set up in the milk factory and their work resumed. Lottie could have continued work at in the Ware factory for the rest of the war but she fancied service life and particular in the Navy so she volunteered to join the Wrens. She received her call up papers in February 1943 reporting to the shore based *HMS President III* in London where she trained as a steward eventually serving in the officer's mess. Her work experiences in the services were typical of most girls in uniform – they released men from administration to active service duties. Still as a steward she was transferred to *HMS Badger* at Dovercourt twelve months later where, with a twinkle in her eye, she says she had a very good social life being entertained aboard ships returning to port. Lottie returned to London for training as a Fleet Mail Clerk and once the course was completed she was posted to *HMS President I* at Chatham and the static ship *HMS St.Tudno* at Sheerness dealing with the Fleet's mail. Lottie was demobbed from Sheerness in September 1945 and returned to her old job at Allen & Hanburys.

Army

When France fell in June 1940 the majority of Ware men serving with the BEF escaped from the beaches at Dunkirk although some returned from the harbours at Calais and Boulogne before these fell into German hands. The last to return left France from St. Nazaire. Two paid the ultimate sacrifice, four were taken prisoner of war while others were wounded. Doctor Fellows who held his surgery in the High Street was one of dozens of small boat owners who crossed the Channel to help with the evacuation from the Dunkirk beaches.

One of the luckiest and hair raising escapes from the Dunkirk beaches was by 2613781 Sergeant Ken (John) Bridges, a pre-war regular with the 1st Battalion Grenadier Guards. John's Battalion arrived at the small Belgian town of Furnes on the edge of the Dunkirk perimeter after a rear guard action starting three weeks earlier at Leuvenon the outskirts of Brussels. Nervous and edgy they sheltered in cellars at Furnes before a night withdrawal to the beach at La Panne some three miles away where they expected to be picked up for England the next day. The Germans knew that this was their only route of escape and the road was constantly under shell fire.

Once on the sandy beaches John and his section soon realised that they were in for a long wait when one spotted an apparently empty life boat about 100 yards off shore. John, a strong swimmer, stripped of his clothing but still wearing his steel helmet set out to the boat which he intended to bring back for his men. Others beat him to it, they were prepared to take John but not his comrades so he declined the

offer and returned to the shore only to find that his section apart from one man, Corporal Martin, had dispersed during another aerial attack. Martin was a non swimmer but in spite of this they decided to swim out to a destroyer some half a mile off shore, John swam on his back towing his comrade. They were picked up in a small rowing boat commanded by a white haired, fatherly-looking Brigadier and headed to the destroyer *HMS Ivanhoe* which was grounded on the bottom and trying to free herself. Tragedy struck, as John was hauled aboard the rowing boat ran foul of the destroyer's propellers and the rest were drowned.

If this was not enough at 7.41 am the destroyer was attacked by Stukas and a bomb crashed through the base of the forward funnel

Sgt John Bridges, Grenadier Guards

into the boiler room. John, seeing the crew taking off their shoes, decided that the *Ivanhoe* was sinking so he dived overboard before it sank (the *Ivanhoe* didn't in fact sink and by a miracle limped home). He swam towards the minesweeper *HMS Speedwell* which plucked him out of the water. The rescued men thought they had landed safely in England when the engines slowed down and they berthed against a harbour wall, they had a very rude awakening since they had docked against the eastern mole of Dunkirk harbour to pick up more people! Within an hour 300 French troops had boarded and the *Speedwell* was ordered to leave. She was one of the last ships to leave Dunkirk and eventually made her way back to Dover, dodging bombs and skirting minefields on the way. John had survived to fight another day with the 201st Guards Brigade in North Africa and the with the Resistance Groups in Greece.

We have already seen in the previous chapter that Jack Gilbert, Les Beard and Sid Wallace were in France serving with the 8th Battalion of the Royal Warwickshire Regiment and pick up their story again at Halle near the German border sitting in their trenches awaiting the mechanised German Army. As the Germans broke through the Battalion began a forced march back to Tournai (near Lille) where part of the Battalion held a defensive line on the banks of the River Scheldt and it is here that Les Beard was killed on the 20th May. Jack Gilbert's company sheltered in a cement factory from which they eventually emerged as "grey ghosts" since every shell which landed nearby showered them with clouds of dislodged cement dust! The retreat continued towards Dunkirk and as they neared the French port they were told "its every man for himself – make for that cloud of smoke." Jack and two colleagues "acquired" three bikes and set of for Dunkirk passing two soldiers astride a commandeered shire horse on the way. At a checkpoint near the beaches they were relieved of their transport by Military Police and the bikes were thrown on a pile of burning cars since no equipment was to fall into enemy hands – one wonders what happened to the horse! Near the checkpoint a group of soldiers gave the trio what Jack describes as "the best pork chop I've ever eaten complete with bristles from a freshly slaughter pig!" Reluctantly he admits that for previous ten days or so they not had a proper meal. From here they were directed to the beaches where, in theory, they were to gather in groups of thirty forming lines down to the water, in practice the groups scattered as the Stuka dive bombers came screeching down. Eventually Jack was picked up and transported by *HMS Worcester* to Dover where the ragged passengers were herded onto waiting trains, their ordeal endured showed in their faces, unshaven, hollow eyed and infinitely weary from their march. They were taken to Aldershot where they slept in the open and Jack's lasting memory is of the utter peace and tranquillity after the continuous noise of small arms fire, shells and bombs. A visit to the local barbers followed for a shave to remove the last of the Tournai cement dust lodged in two weeks growth! Jack spent the rest of his war on the east coast of England and as a Pay Sergeant in Kenya.

7361399 L/Cpl. Fred Munt joined the Royal Army Medical Corps on 1st November 1939 and, once qualified, was posted to the 7th Ambulance Train bound for France. They left Harwich with men from the Hertfordshire Regiment manning the ship's guns. The train moved into Belgium in the middle of May and soon return to England via Calais, Dover and Southampton loaded with wounded troops. Fred returned home to Ware on a 48 hour pass and immediately married his sweetheart, Mary Plumb. He was also interviewed by the *Hertfordshire Mercury* on his experiences in France and the following report appeared on 7th June 1940:

He went to France in the early part of the year and was stationed with a hospital train. Until the invasion of the Netherlands things were very quiet. The troops were, he said, enjoying themselves. About five days after Germany attacked Belgium our hospital train moved into Belgium. Not long after we spotted a number of enemy planes hedge hopping a short distance away. They discovered a group of refugees and promptly began to machine gun them. It was a pitiful sight. Women and children were among the 20 or 30 wounded and they were treated by our unit. There were literally thousands of refugees travelling in every available means of transport. Some were on foot and even the youngest were doing their best to help.

On another occasion when we were in Metz German planes overhead began to drop bombs. We took shelter under the train and were fortunate not to be hit as 26 craters were made nearby. I passed through Tournai and finally embarked at Calais and it was at this town that we came under an intensive bombardment from land and air. Overhead I saw a violent dog fight involving some 30 or 40 German, British and French planes. Four German fighters crashed and one British plane was lost.

The morale of our men was high and complete order prevailed. We left Calais in a cargo steamer with about 674 of us on board. All our equipment had to be left behind. As we left harbour the shore batteries at Boulogne shelled us. When about three miles out a shell hit the ship above the water line, it finished up landing on a lorry containing a supply of petrol. By a miracle this did not catch on fire though the shell was so hot that it could not be removed until three hours later.

One of the last to leave France was Sergeant Instructor Archibald Baker of the Royal Engineers, of Cross Street. Archie, a W.W.I veteran, served as a Sergeant Instructor with the Royal Engineers and received a leg wound during the withdrawal from St. Nazaire. He was invalided out of the army and when the Ware Army Cadets were formed in 1942 he became their Regimental Sergeant Major. Archie was also sworn in as a Special Constable in October 1942. Many were not so lucky and never made it to the beaches, among those taken prisoner were:

— Second Lt. William Bloomfield Dixon, East Riding Yeomanry, the second son of Mr W T Dixon of High Oak Lodge. His tank unit was covering the retreat to Dunkirk near Cassell where he was captured and held as POW No. 767 in Stalag 07B at Eichstatt.

— S.Q.S.M Alec Childs, a solicitor's clerk and husband of Mrs A Childs of 35 Musley Lane, joined the army in 1939 serving with the Royal Army Service Corps. He went to France in 1940 were he was attached to a NAAFI supply depot. For five years he was held in POW camps in Poland, first at Dirschau near Danzig and then at Stalag XXB at Torum. Alec was liberated by the Russians and repatriated via Odessa and Cairo, arriving back in Ware at Easter after five years in captivity.

— Gunner Richard John Goodship, Royal Artillery, a newly married man from 16 Watton Road, was reported missing at Dunkirk. In September 1940 his wife was informed that he was safe and well as a prisoner of war No.11643 in camp 344. He saw his four and a half year old son for the first time when he was repatriated soon after V E Day.

— Private Cecil Lee, Pioneer Corps, of 62 High Street had only been in the army for one month when he was taken prisoner in May 1940 at Boulogne Docks. He spent three and a half years in prison camps in Germany and Poland where he was put to work on the land. Unfortunately Cecil was involved in a serious accident to his legs and spent two years in hospital before he was repatriated reaching England on the 26th of October 1943. On the way home his ship called at Gothenburg where the Crown Princess of Sweden gave Cecil a Swedish Red Cross parcel.

Norway

The Allied operations in Norway had some success at sea but deepening troubles ashore led to the evacuation of Narvick. British, Norwegian and French troops launched a seaborne attack on the Lofoten Islands in April 1940 and recaptured Narvick on the 28th May. Among the soldiers taking part was Alex Wells of Ware, however events in France dictated that Narvick was evacuated and the troops withdrew.

Greece and the Near East

Men from the town were among the troops sent to help the Greeks fight the Italians and German invaders. One of those taken prisoner during the withdrawal of British Forces was 156987 Driver C J Wilkins of Royal Army Service Corps whose wife lived at 3 Croft Road. As prisoner No.4534 in Stalag 18A at Wolfsberg (Karten) he was forced to work on the railways by his German captors and returned home to

Ware just after V E Day. Among the troops rushed to Greece in a belated and unsuccessful attempt to stem the Axis advance were the 1st Battalion of the Beds and Herts Regiment in which Ware men served throughout the war. The 1st Battalion were in Egypt when war was declared and were moved to Palestine near Tel Aviv before going to the Allenby Barracks on the outskirts of Jerusalem in May 1940. Here they were joined by newly trained recruits including Ted Wallace, Don Harris, "Froggy" French, "Tug" Wilson and 5953402 Pte. Chris Nicholls all of whom sailed from Liverpool on the *Empress of Britain*. Chris met up with John Stockwell with whom he had worked at Allen & Hanburys in the NAAFI at Allenby Barracks as John was about to join the same ship now bound for South Africa. In March 1941 the Battalion proceeded to Alexandria to board the *Breconshire* bound for the Greek Island of Lemnos in the Dardanelles Straits. Here they guarded a RAF base but as the German advance reached Athens they withdrew to Alexandria on the *Glenroy*. With a threat of a German attack through Syria the Beds and Herts moved to Damascus to build a defensive block and were one of the Regiments given the task of disarming the Vichy French troops in the Bekaa Valley.

The Fall of Malaysia and Singapore

A number of men from Ware served in the Far East and the fall of Malaysia and Singapore was a particularly anxious and trying time for many families in Ware since it was some eighteen months before they were notified of their loved ones fate. At least sixteen men were reported as missing of whom five subsequently died in the hands of their Japanese captors or were killed when the ships taking them to Japan were sunk by the Americans. The treatment of the prisoners by the Japanese was extremely harsh with one in four dying of the privations and inhuman conditions they were enforced to endure. Those taken prisoner in Malaya were:

Driver Arthur William Sharp, Royal Artillery H.A.A, of 69 Cundalls Road. It was two years before his wife received a post card saying that he was a prisoner in Thailand. L/Corporal Joseph Mead, Royal Engineers whose wife Irene lived at 63 Canons Road was informed in February 1943 that her husband was a prisoner in Thailand.

More were captured with the fall of Singapore including Lt. General Arthur E Percival the Commander in Chief of the British Forces in Malaysia who had no option but to surrender Singapore to the Japanese on 15th February 1942. The General was born at Thundridge but had lived in Ware at Scotts Hill House since 1929. In common with all Japanese prisoners his fate was unknown until he broadcast a radio message from Tokyo to his wife some twelve months after his capture in which he said he was well and had received his wife's letters. Soon after Japan surrendered on 14th August 1945 the General together with a group of other high ranking allied officers were found in a small camp 100 miles from Mukenden in Manchuria on 19th August. He was unaware that the war in Europe had been over for three months.

It must have very satisfying to the General to be one of the twelve Allies officers selected to sign the formal surrender of the Japanese on 4th September aboard the U.S battleship *Missouri*. Upon repatriation he and his wife stayed with the McMullen family at "Presdales" for a while, Mrs Percival played an active part in setting up the War Memorial Fund while the General opened the first Christmas Fair held at the Drill Hall in 1946. The couple moved from Ware to Little Hadham in 1947 and subsequently to Widford where the general died in 1966.

Lt. General Arthur Percival

Others captured at Singapore were Captain O J G McMullen, Royal Artillery, the son of Colonel and Mrs McMullen of Presdales. Gunner Claude James Scott Menzies, Royal Artillery, the son of Mrs L Cain of 31 New Road, who joined up at the outbreak of war serving in the Far East with the Agra Auxiliary. L/Corporal Horace Warner, 5th Battalion Beds and Herts Regiment, the husband of Mrs W Warner of 3 Lea Close Hertford and son of Mr and Mrs H Warner of 32 Bowling Road. Corporal E J R Campkin, 1st Battalion of The Cambridgeshire Regiment, spent a considerable time in hospital before being repatriated. He was the son of Mr and Mrs James Campkin of 50 Fanhams Road. Before he joined the forces in March 1940 he worked for Allen & Hanburys and as a keen sportsman played for his works football and cricket teams. Private A F Williams, RAMC, of 44 Cundalls Road and was repatriated via Columbo in Sri Lanka. Driver L R Davidson, RASC lived at 72 Canons Road and was reported as missing in February 1942, eighteen months later his wife received a card from him saying that he was a POW in a Malaysian camp. Subsequent post cards sent from his POW camp took five to six months to reach Ware. He was liberated by British troops and was given his the first piece of bread for three years by a Hertford man – small world isn't it! Private George Hornsey, a married man whose wife lived in King George's Road, was liberated by Australian troops. Mr and Mrs A Tillcock of 4 Tower Road waited anxiously for two and a half years for news of their son Private C W Tillcock, in August 1944 they received a card from him saying that he was well and a Japanese prisoner of war.

Civilian Internee in Japanese hands

Mr F F Payne, the son of Mr and Mrs Edward Payne of 53 Trinity Road, was a teacher in the Far East and spent the whole of the war as an internee in a Japanese camp. He returned home in October 1945 and his emaciated body was a familiar sight in the town, once he recovered he returned to Malaya where he became the Director of Education.

The Western Desert and North Africa

Meanwhile in the Western Desert Rommel had pushed the 8th Army back to El Alamein and Tobruk was under siege. The 1st Battalion of the Beds and Herts Regiment was withdrawn from Syria and moved to the Canal Zone as part of the build up to reinforce the 8th Army. Towards the end of September Chris Nicholls and his comrades boarded a destroyer and sailed under the cover of darkness to their secret destination – Tobruk – to relieve an Australian Battalion and remained there until Christmas. Two weeks leave in Cairo and Chris and his mates from Ware were on the move again boarding the *Ille de France* for an unknown destination. Speculation was rife, were they going to Malaya, Burma or to join their comrades in the 5th Battalion in Singapore? As events turned out the Japanese overran S E Asia and their ship was diverted to Bombay. We shall return to the 1st Battalion a little later in this chapter.

At least one Ware man was captured by Rommel's forces at Tobruk, he was 1749521 Gunner Frederick Capel of 52 Fanhams Road. Fred was a married man with two children. As a POW in Italy he worked on a farm, later he was transferred to Germany where he worked in a coal mine for two years before being transferred to Poland as POW No. 33605 in camp 344 together with Richard Goodship from Ware. When the Russians advanced he and his fellow prisoners were force marched by the SS back to Germany. Fred was united with his family shortly after V E Day. Another to be captured in the Western Desert was 1046878 Gunner E Overfield of 62 Canons Road who was held by the Italians as POW No. 249388 in camp No. 4G at Oschatz.

Gradually the tide turned, Rommel was defeated at El Alamein in October 1942 and the Desert Rats advanced. The following month American troops and the British 1st Army landed in Tunisia, among the follow up troops were men from Ware serving with the 2nd and 30th Battalions of the Beds and Herts Regiment. The story of Private William Gilbey is typical of many from the town who joined the Regiment. Bill, associated with the Scout movement in Ware, was called up on 15th January 1940. After his basic training at Kempston Barracks he joined the 2nd Battalion at Pagham (near Bognor) at the height of the Battle of Britain before moving to Arlesford, Totton and Inverary where the Battalion practised seaborne landings from assault boats. A short embarkation leave followed during which Bill married Doris Page at St Mary's Church. The Battalion boarded the *MV Orion* at Glasgow on 11th March 1943 bound for Algiers where they landed on the 23rd March. A seventeen mile march followed to the staging camp at camp Matafou – nothing like a good "foot slog" in the heat to acclimatise rookies to North Africa after a winter at home! The

Ted Chivers was a pre-war Territorial at Ware in the Hertfordshire Regiment in the Corps of Drums, he was a crack shot, and captain of the Terriers soccer team. The photograph shows him as a Corporal in the Yorkshire Regiment, he subsequently transferred to the 30th Battalion of the Beds and Herts serving as a CQMS in North Africa and Italy.

Battalion was soon in action chasing the Germans who launched a strong counter attack at Sidi Nsir on 13th April 1943 during which Bill was wounded and hospitalised, some fifty years later during a hospital visit it was discovered that he still had shrapnel in his legs. When he recovered he was posted to the Loyal Regiment and ended his service with this Regiment at Klagenfurt in Austria being demobbed on 12th March 1946. There were other Ware casualties in this theatre. Lt. R E Selby of Round House Lodge, High Oak Road was taken prisoner but escaped in Italy and successfully made his way to Switzerland. 5955827 L/Corporal A G Phypers 4 Century Road, a pre-war employee at Allen & Hanburys, was another to be captured and held as POW No.227971 in the Italian prison camp No.4DZ at Annaburg where he did not think too highly of the treatment or food he received from his captors. He returned to Ware soon after V E Day.

The 2nd Battalion left Algiers on 13th December 1943 sailing on *HMT Llangibby Castle* for Port Said, a couple of months later *HMT Letitia* took them to Naples where they took part in the assault on the Gustav Line near Monte Cassino, entered Rome and fought their way to Florence and on to Bologna.

Others from Ware went to North Africa when the 30th Battalion of the Beds and Herts Regiment sailed from Greenock on 12th August 1943 with Ted Chivers, Bernie Crook and Reg Waller aboard. The Battalion's main roll was that of a supply unit for operations in Italy, internal security and guarding POWs. They moved Naples in January 1945 undertaking a similar but vital roll.

Italy

With the fall of North Africa the Allies landed in Sicily in June 1943 and on the Italian mainland in the following September. One of those to take part in the assault landings was David Stockwell, one of the five brothers to serve their country. David, in the Royal Army Ordinance Corps, went to North Africa in October 1942 and took part in the combined Anglo-American assaults and landings at Salerno and Anzio. At Salerno he served on landing craft LCI 585, the flagship of a flotilla of six boats carrying ammunition. They came under air attack by Stuka dive bombers on 9th September 1943 loosing one boat before returning to North Africa. When Italy surrendered in September the Italian Navy was taken over and used by the Allies and on 13th December David sailed from Tripoli (Libya) to Taranto in southern Italy on the very fast Italian cruiser *Cadorna*. He had returned to Italy to take part in the Anzio landings on the 22nd January 1944 where he suffered shell shock, repatriated back to England David spent long spells in hospitals at Glasgow and Exeter before being discharged from the army on 9th January 1945.

Several men from the town were captured by during the North African and Italian campaigns with two being held in Stalag 11A at Attenbrow in Germany, they were 5954604 Private Ernest Osbourne of the Royal East Kent Regiment ("The Buffs") from Musley Hill and 1142578 Gunner John George Waller, 81st Anti-Tank Regiment Royal Artillery, from Collett Road. Ernest had previously served in Malta for three years when the island was under siege, both arrived home soon after V E Day.

As the war progressed more and more young men were posted overseas many decided to marry their sweethearts during their embarkation leave. One such couple were Fred Morris and Barbara Haworth. Fred, a driver in the RASC, married Barbara by licence at St. Mary's Church in 1942 a few days before he boarded the 22,284 ton P & O liner *SS Strathaird* together with some 5,000 troops including high ranking

Left: Les Gilbert from 55 Musley Hill was posted to North Africa with the Royal Artillery. His sister Dorothy remembers reading the card telling the family that he had been wounded while she was eating her dinner – it killed her appetite and in spite of rationing her nice rice pudding was left untouched! Les recovered and took part in the fighting at Anzio and the Italian campaign, ending up in Palestine. His brother Jack was at Dunkirk with the Royal Warwickshire Regiment together with his brother-in-law Joe Wilson serving in the Royal Navy. Another brother-in-law, Eddy Ward, was a part-time fireman at Ware before he joined the 5th Battalion of the Beds and Herts Regiment – he was recalled as a fire fighter during the London Blitz and so escaped the fate of his colleagues who went to Singapore. Eddy rejoined the army after the Blitz and spent the rest of the war in Northern Ireland. A third brother-in-law, George Skeggs worked as an excavator driver in the local gravel pits and was directed to open cast coal mining in Yorkshire.

American officers and British nurses one of whom was to become General Eisenhower's chauffeur later in the war. As with so many other troopships they had no idea of their destination until they passed through the Straits of Gibraltar. Soon after this on the 22nd December the *Strathaird* was hit by two torpedoes, Fred and his mate who were sitting up on deck made their way below decks to join the rest of their platoon when the order was given to abandon ship which by now had started to list. The nurses were given first priority to the life boats and by the time Fred's turn came these were full so he took to a life raft, one of the problems here was that many of the troops could not swim and even though they had life jackets were afraid to enter the water to board the rafts. Fred, who had learnt to swim in the River Lea at a young age, helped and encouraged the non-swimmers and remembered the words of an uncle who had served with the Navy "get away from the ship otherwise you will get sucked under when she goes down." Having pulled clear of the apparently stricken vessel they were practically swamped by a destroyer travelling at speed which told them via a loud hailer that they'd sunk the submarine. The *Strathaird* remained afloat and the troops were ordered back on board, Fred survived to fight another day. Others such as Richard Long of 73 New Road serving with the RASC found his romance in East Africa where he married an A.T.S girl in Nairobi during 1944.

D Day and Europe

Men from Ware took part in every facet of the liberation of Europe. Sergeant Don Gardner was in the Royal Marine Commandos landing in France on D Day the 6th June 1944, Sapper James Taylor of Musley Hill landed with the 15th Scottish Division being in sole charge of all the maps used his Division. Many of the gliders taking the troops to Arnhem came over Ware, one broke loose from its mother plane and landed to the south east of Amwell Crossroads. One wonders if 14591939 Private Roy Ives of King George's Road who took part in the airborne attack flew over his home town. Roy was captured, held as prisoner No.90118 at Stalag 12A at Limburg and arrived back home just after V E Day. Others who had fought through North Africa and Italy such as George Stockwell in the RAMC were diverted to the NW Europe theatre. Several ended their war as German prisoners including Major Philip John Roper of the Dorsetshire Regiment whose wife Sally lived at "Little Acres" in Warner Road. Philip was reported missing in October 1944, later it was confirmed that he was wounded and held as prisoner No. 91857 by the Germans in Oflag 07B at Eiehstatt, the same camp as Lt. Dixon captured at Dunkirk. Philip returned home to Warner Road in May 1945 soon after V E Day. Another was Private F Stringer, a twin son of Mr and Mrs Reuben Stringer of 57 New Road, who spent much of his seven months as a prisoner of war in hospital suffering from diphtheria and tonsillitis. At least one RAF crew was held prisoner having been shot down over Germany, he was Flt. Sergeant S D P Goodey of 103 Star Street.

Several pages ago we saw that L/Cpl. Fred Munt returned from Dunkirk and married Mary Plumb, Fred continued to serve with the "Medics" and joined the 14th Light Field Ambulance attached to the 4th Armoured Division. On D Day his unit landed at Sword Beach (Queen sector) with the 13/18th Hussars and their amphibious tanks in rough seas. Fred was transferred to the 42nd Independent Guards Division in German and on 12th April 1945 the Chief of Staff of the 1st German Parachute Regiment approached the British and said that a terrible condition had arisen at Barden-Belsen where typhus was raging and requested that the British take over. A truce was drawn up, a neutral area defined around Belsen and the British agreed to go in. Fred's unit was one of the first medical units to enter the camp a few days later being attacked by the Lufwaffe on the way there. The scene they met on 15th April beggars description, there

Czech Military Medal for Merit awarded to Fred Munt for the part he played at Belsen by the Czech President Eduard Benes.

were approximately 50,000 people in the camp of which about 10,000 lay dead in the huts or about the camp. Those still alive had had no food or water for about seven days and mistakes were made by feeding them too much food too quickly. Kramer, the butcher of Belsen, and the notorious Irma Griese were still there were Fred arrived. Bert Chapman, a former Mayor of Ware, also went to Belsen. In spite receiving booster jabs before entering the camp twenty-eight of the one hundred and one British troops caught typhus. When the camp was burnt down Fred and his colleagues were flown to Stavanger in Norway in his words "to breath some pure air for a couple of weeks before coming home."

The Far East and the Chindits

The might of the American resources gradually turned the tide against the Japanese and the British were formulating plans to retake Burma and the Malaysia Peninsular. The 1st Battalion of the Beds and Herts Regiment were to play their part in this so we pick up Chris Nicholls's story from the time he landed in Bombay in March 1942. The Battalion was stationed near Poona until September 1943 when it moved to Bangalore where the men heard that they had been selected to form part of the proposed Long Range Penetration Columns to operate in Burma – they were to become part of Orde Wingate's famous Chindits. Jungle training and learning to survive as independent units started immediately and was to last for the best part of six months. Everything they needed was carried either in 70lb backpacks or by mule. On 18th March 1944 they entrained for an advanced airfield in Assam and flew into Burma in Dakotas, the famous workhorse of W.W.II. They landed at a previously prepared jungle airstrip code named *Whitechapel*, strapped to the internal sides of the planes were their de-voiced mules (to stop them braying), South African bullocks to be used as meat at the base as well as their equipment. The Beds and Herts formed column numbers 16 and 61 with Chris in the former. The Chindits job was to infiltrate and harass the Japanese lines of communication to cause as much disruption as possible. Chris, a very modest man, glosses over many of the hardships they endured. Every night they slept in a circle on the ground with a rope tied to each man's ankle as a signalling aid should any of them hear an odd noise, for five months they lived on K rations which they received from airdrops – what he didn't say that these often went astray and seven days rations had to be stretched to cover a much longer period. Water was always a problem and every drop in their water bottles was sterilised by tablets, washing was unheard of unless they came across a suitable and safe river, they were always wet and plagued by leeches. When they finally came out of the jungle unshaven and their clothing in tatters they had covered some 600 miles, from Burma they were flown to Poona where Chris says "they cleaned up and stripped the clothing from their skins!" They soon left India and made their way to Blighty for demob – Chris had been away for five years

Two curates from St. Mary's Church served their country: the Revd George Church joined the forces in September 1939. His replacement, Percy Kingston of 94 Park Road, resigned his position in July 1942 to join the Army Chaplaincy as a captain and went to India and joined the Chindits. Percy was attached to a column which spent forty days marching through the Naga Hills, river beds and jungle to the rear of the Japanese lines. He conducted services during the march when the opportunity offered with the altar and seating being made out of bamboo. Supplies of Bibles, Communion wine and wafers were dropped by parachute. As a padre he attended the wounded and in spite of wearing the Red Cross emblem was shot at several times – it is not surprising that he had a very low opinion of the Japanese soldier.

The ATS

Several girls from the town served in the ATS, including Subaltern Millicent Bishop, the daughter of Mr and Mrs R F Bishop who ran a grocery and provisions shop at 3 Amwell End, who served in East Africa. Others were L/Cpl Rose Scales of 30 Tower Road, Millicent (Billie) Ginn of 70 Canons Road and Private Kay Long of 33 Mount Street.

The Royal Air Force

Flt Lt. Alan Wallis,RAFVR, DFC

The ambition of many a young lad within the town was to join the Royal Air Force and fly, some did so following a successful apprenticeship with 936 Squadron of the Air Training Corps while many others provided the backup required to keep the air crews flying.

Although 159703 Flight Lieutenant Alan Wallis RAFVR, DFC, was never in the Cadets his experiences are typical of many from the Squadron who qualified as air crew. Alan was the son of Alfred Wallis MM of 46 Vicarage Road and a former pupil of Ware Central School. Before he volunteered for service with the RAF he had joined the LDV and was a fire watcher at Ware Post Office where he worked. Alan was called to the colours in July 1941 reporting for duty at Regents Park, his billet was in an empty block of luxury flats where he spent an uncomfortable first night on a wire framed bed devoid of any form of bedding. Following further training at Paignton he and his colleagues travelled to Wilmslow before boarding the *Highland Princess* at Liverpool bound for Halifax, Nova Scotia. The voyage across the Atlantic was far from a luxury cruise since the *Highland Princess* was on the Argentine meat run and in Alan's words "we took the place of sides of beef"! Their final destination was to be the Pan American School of Navigation at Coral Gables, Miami.

Having qualified as a navigator, Alan returned to England in December 1942 joining No.10 OTU (Operations Training Unit) at Abingdon for familiarisation flying on Whitley Mk.5 bombers. Alan married his wife Nona, a Western House nurse, at Christ Church where he had been a chorister, in March 1943 only to be recalled from his honeymoon when a detachment from No.10 OTU transferred to St. Eval (Cornwall) to undertake anti-submarine work in the western Atlantic. After eight such trips in a month Alan and his four colleagues bade farewell to their Whitley and transferred to No.1663 CU (Conversion Unit) at Rufforth, Yorkshire, to learn the ins and outs of the four engine Halifax bomber. On 24th June 1943, he transferred to No.76 Squadron at Holme-on-Spalding-Moor (East Yorkshire).

Alan made the first of his twenty-four operational flights over Germany four nights later when 76 Squadron took part in a raid on Cologne, the ensuing months saw raids on places such as Peenemunde (the rocket development centre on the Baltic), Gelsenkirchen, Aachen, Berlin, Nuremberg and Hamburg where he witnessed the fireball rising to some 18,000 feet. Berlin was an unpopular mission for two reasons.

First it was a long flight subject to radar directed "flak" and fighter attacks the whole time with bombers incurring high losses; secondly these were often "retaliatory raids" ordered by Churchill with no specific target in mind and many of the crews resented the lose of their comrades on a pointless mission. Most of Alan's flights were made in Halifax J for "Jack", he modestly fails to point out that when the crew flew in other aircraft it was only because "Jack" was unserviceable for various reasons often as a result of damage from a previous raid.

Bad weather had its advantages and disadvantages to flying. On one occasion when his wife visited Holme the weather was so bad that all flying operations were suspended and is probably the only time in Alan and Nona's lives that they relished a holiday with inclement weather! On the negative side "Jack" returning from a raid iced up at 20,000 feet, with the crew preparing to bail out it plummeted to 6,000 feet where fortunately it de-iced. Alan, now a Pilot Officer, ended his tour with a raid to Berlin in 1944. Following leave at Cross Street where Nona's parents lived Alan was posted to No.10 0TU passing on his knowledge to others. He was awarded his DFC in July 1944 for "completing many operations against the enemy in which he displayed high skill, fortitude and devotion to duty". He made his last flight on the 6th June 1945. After demob in 1946 he returned to work at Ware Post Office.

1874576 LAC Arthur J North, the son of Mr and Mrs George North of 71 Cundalls Road, served his country in many ways throughout the war. Arthur was a former Central School boy, a keen sportsman and chorister at St Mary's Church who worked for the Northmet Power Company as an electrician. Numerous references have already been made to Arthur in earlier chapters relating to his work, his experiences as an ARP messenger, with the ATC and his fire watching duties.

Arthur volunteered for the RAF and was called up for duty in March 1943 reporting to Cardington where he was kitted out and it was decreed that he should be an FME – Flight Mechanic Engineer. For the first time for a couple of years he slept in the same bed for more than two nights running! He underwent basic RAF training and "square bashing" at Skegness followed by a spell at RAF Swinderby in Lincolnshire. From Lincolnshire he went to Blackpool for technical and practical training on engine maintenance, here his billet was a seaside holiday home run by a middle-aged widow who treated the "erks" as holiday guests – post war National Service was never like that! Sport and the company of young ladies from the Lancashire cotton towns at the Blackpool Tower Ballroom or at the South Shore Pleasure Beach and the Tunnel of Love filled his spare time!

All good things have to come to and end, Arthur's did when he passed his trade exams, a weeks leave in Ware and he joined the ground crews at RAF Coningsby, on to RAF Fiskerton, servicing the Lancasters of 49 Squadron, and then to RAF Dunholme Lodge where he discovered that Flight Engineer Eric Wren of 44 Squadron, a class mate from the Central School, was in the next nissen hut. The ground and air crews had a close affinity, every time the Squadron was on a mission the ground crews would lay awake on their beds counting the returning planes and hoping that those missing had landed at other airfields, in Arthur's words "their thoughts were the loss of all the lives of men they considered were so much braver than us."

When D-Day arrived Arthur and a few mates thought life would be more interesting on the continent so they volunteered to serve across the Channel. The outcome was that they were posted to Hazelmere to join 423 AFAP under canvas, they had to ask what sort of unit it was and were told that it an Aviation Fuel & Ammunition Park and they were to be mechanics in the Motor Maintenance Section. Eventually they left for France at the end of September 1944 travelling from Tilbury to the newly liberated

Hilda Long

port of Antwerp. A few years ago Arthur wrote down his memories of service life in Europe entitled "The Memoirs of an Erk", having read these he should have taken his cue from Lesley Thomas and called it "The Virgin Erks"! Leaving aside the amorous escapades Arthur and 423 AFAP spent the winter of 1944 in the outbuildings and stables at Chateau Geni near Lille, from here they serviced and travelled with vehicles carrying bombs, petrol and ammunition to RAF bases throughout northern France.

2021513 Corporal Hilda F Long WAAF – a former captain of her school netball team and the first Ware schoolgirl to win a county badge for representing Hertfordshire at athletics – volunteered for the WAAF rather than facing the prospect of factory work. She joined up in 1941 being sent to Bridgenorth for three weeks "square bashing" and job assessment tests. A posting to Bridlington followed where Hilda learnt the intricacies of RAF stores and equipment, at the end of the course was promoted to ACWI and bound for RAF Innsworth (near Gloucester). In Hilda's words the camp was grim, the food awful but she enjoyed her job of being in charge of an engine parts store. A spell of ten months at RAF Locking followed where the roles were reversed, a lovely camp with good food but a rotten job refuelling aircraft and transport. It was not all work on the RAF bases, Hilda continued with her athletics and joined in all the various camp activities. With a twinkle in her eye Hilda relates that when they went out for a social evening the girls booked out at the guardroom and at the same time booked themselves back in again to beat the curfew. The way back to camp was via the perimeter fence but the camp authorities got wise to this and soon RAF guard dogs were on patrol at night! With the approach of D-Day Hilda went to a newly established maintenance unit at RAF Bicester. After the landings in France they worked throughout the hours of daylight packing every conceivable piece of equipment the RAF needed to equip airfields as the Allies advanced into

Europe. Hilda left the WAAFs in 1946 returning to civvy street in Ware, looking back she says she had lots of fun, lots of laughter which outweighed the grim times. Her brother Arthur served with the Irish Guards and was badly wounded shortly after D-Day when his tank was blown up, her sister Win was a Land Army Girl. Other girls from the town in the WAAFs were LACW Gwendoline Pope of "Frome" in Warner Road and Corporal Violet Page of 32 Musley Hill.

The Bevin Boys

Postal worker Reg Rand of Tower Road wanted to go in the Fleet Air Arm as a wireless operator/air gunner when his time to join up came so, as a result of a Government appeal for youth to do pre-service training, he became a member of the local ATC Squadron rising to the rank of Corporal. He also joined the Home Guard as a boy messenger and one of his tasks was to degrease the P14 and P17 rifles when they arrived from the U.S.A. When his call-up papers arrived much to his disappointment he found that he had been directed into the mines – his two years training with the ATC was of no avail. Reg appealed against the directive which was refused and like his pal Percy Storey he was also prepared to go to prison rather than become a miner but was dissuaded from doing so by his fellow postal workers who had fought in World War I.

Reg left Ware for Cramlington Lamb Colliery on 1st April 1944 where he spent a month training and body hardening before going to the Maria Colliery, Thockley some six miles from Newcastle-on-Tyne. It wasn't long before he came to terms with his fate and sensibly decided to show willingness to listen and learn to improve his position. This attitude was appreciated by the Geordie miners who became understanding and sympathetic to a southern boy "wet behind the ears" and he got on extremely well with them. The major seams at the Maria were 2ft 7ins thick with a white sandstone roof in which there were plenty of interesting fossil imprints which the miners often gave to Reg. Among the jobs he did were loading and unloading the coal tubs, marshalling the tubs, serving the working coal face, working with the pit ponies and lying in water for eight hours operating a hand pump which the local lads refused to do. Among the more pleasant tasks were working with the pit surveyor to establish new working faces.

During his stay at the *Maria* he lived with a mining family unlike many who were in barracks, as a manual worker he received extra rations. He was released Friday the 16th October 1947 and started back at Ware Post Office the next Monday! What were Reg's final thoughts on being a Bevin Boy? In his own words he says "In retrospect I had an easy war. I was relatively safe underground and did not have to suffer the privations, terror, anxieties and mutilations so many of my generation endured. I confess I am grateful to Ernest Bevin for having shielded me from the horrors of war and at the same time given me such a wide experience of life". Words of a modest man bearing in mind that mining was a dangerous and hazardous work in the nineteen forties.

Reg's father, CSM Arthur Rand, was in the Herts Terriers and was mobilised with the Battalion at the outbreak of war but in his son's words "was a bit old in the tooth for war," and so after a while was transferred to the Royal Fusiliers via the Sherwood Foresters and served at Southborough (Kent) on the staff of a Home Guard training unit. While he was away his wife was a collector for the "Our Boys at the Front" Fund. After the war Arthur was a committee member of the local branch of the Hertfordshire Regiment's Old Comrades Association

Charlie Stockwell was another Ware lad who became a Bevin Boy. Charlie joined the Ware Home Guard as a sixteen year old serving

Reg Rand at the Maria Colliery, near Newcastle-on-Tyne

with the machine gun platoon at the Drill Hall before he received his call up papers. His initial training was at Cresswell Colliery in Nottingham before moving south to the Derbyshire pits being based at a Coal Board hostel at Shipley Coppice near Eastwood. However having spent sometime underground he was released on medical grounds and transferred to the Royal Army Service Corps at Bury St. Edmonds prior to military training on Salisbury Plain. Postings to Nottingham, East Kirby and York followed and he ended his army service at Blenheim Barracks, Aldershot, as a pay sergeant.

The Nursing services

Dorothy Cockman, QAIMNS served as a Nursing Sister in a hospital in Gibraltar. Her parents, Mr and Mrs Charles Cockman of 25 Crib Street, spoke to her on the radio programme "Gibraltar Calling."

MEDALS AND AWARDS

Distinguished Service Order and bar

Lt. Colonel Robert McMullen DSO, MBE was the son of Colonel O R McMullen of Presdales. He joined the 1st Battalion the Hertfordshire Regiment (T.A) in 1932 and at the outbreak of war was the CO of the headquarters company based at Hertford. After a short course at the Staff College at Camberley he was posted to the War Office and then to the Special Operations Section of the Middle East Headquarters which was concerned with operations behind enemy lines. Colonel McMullen had a adventurous war career parachuting three times behind enemy lines as a Liaison Officer with resistance groups; he landed in Greece twice and later in northern Italy. For these operations he was awarded his DSO and bar together with the US Bronze Star.

Distinguished Service Order

Lt. Colonel P H M May MC, Durham Light Infantry, of New Road.

Distinguished Service Medal

Chief Engine Room Artificer James Clark, Royal Navy was a regular sailor with nearly twenty years service when he was awarded his DSM in June 1943. He was the son of Mr and Mrs W Clark of 72 King George's Road who watched his investiture by the King at Buckingham Palace. His medal citation reads:- *" Continued devotion to duty in the face of enemy action"*. James had spent two years facing the Italian fleet while escorting convoys to Malta.

Stoker Joseph Wilson, Royal Navy was another regular sailor married to Eleanor Gilbert from Musley Hill who won his medal at Dunkirk.

Military Medal

Sapper Edward Dives, 564 Field Company Royal Engineers, the only son of Mr and Mrs Cecil Dives of "Endcote", Warner Road was awarded his Military Medal for gallantry in Italy on the 23rd December 1944. Edward was seriously wounded at the time and was repatriated to a hospital "somewhere in England". Before the war he was employed by Mr W S Shepherd, electrical engineer, at Hertford.

Sergeant D H Gardner the twenty two year old son of Mr and Mrs Herbert Gardner of 8 Hampden Hill served with the Royal Marine Commandos. He won his Military Medal for gallant and distinguished service while operating with the Army in Normandy.

Corporal A F Wright of No.4 Church Street. The Wright family probably came to Ware London during the early part of the war. Corporal Wright was awarded his Military Medal during the Burma Campaign early in 1944 while serving with the Queen's Regiment. During a fighting patrol he was in charge of the stretcher bearers and his citation reads:-*"Throughout the whole of the action he organised his men and attended the wounded coolly and without regard to his personal safety. As a result of his personal courage and devotion to duty most of the wounded were attended to on the field and brought to safety"*.

Distinguished Flying Cross
The Distinguished Flying Cross (DFC) and the Distinguished Flying Medal (DFM) were usually awarded to air crew who had completed a tour of thirty successful operational flights over enemy territory.

Pilot Officer James H Catlin of 67 High Oak Road, a former pupil at Ware Central School, a member of the Ware Air Training Corps, worked at Wickhams before joining the RAF. He underwent flying training at Moody Fields in the U.S.A where he appeared in a Ministry of Information photograph taken in February 1943. As a twenty-one year old he was flying Lancaster bombers over Germany, on one raid to Leipzig his plane Q for "Queenie" was lucky to survive since it was attacked by a German fighter and hit by heavy "flak" with several members of his crew receiving wounds, he was awarded his DFC shortly afterwards. Later he was awarded a bar to his medal having completed an operational tour. His brother Peter served in the Royal Navy.

Pilot Officer Wallace attended Ware Central School and was a member of the Air Training Corps in Ware.

159703 Flight Lieutenant Alan Wallis RAFVR, details of Alan's Air Force career have already been mentioned earlier in this chapter.

Flying Officer John Edgar, the adopted son of Mrs J Robinson of 66 Vicarage Road, was an Observer in the RAF. He was educated at York College and came to Ware in 1938 as a teacher at St Mary's School and became a member of St. Mary's Church choir. John joined the Air Force in 1940 and went to North Africa in 1941 as a Flight Sergeant, was promoted to Warrant Officer and awarded the DFC in May 1943. His medal citation reads:-*"W.O Edgar has an exceptional operational record. He took part in many sorties when based in the United Kingdom before proceeding to the Middle East and has fought in Libya, Malta and Tripolitania. He is an Observer of great skill and has taken part in the destruction of six enemy aircraft"*. He was killed while on flying operations in April 1944, he left a sister who lived at Leadgate in County Durham.

Distinguished Flying Medal
Sgt Ernest Morris RAF of 41 Star Street, an Air Bombardier (a bomb aimer) with 49 Squadron of the RAF was awarded his DFM in May 1943. He had taken part in the daylight bombing raids on the German capital ships the Scharnhorst and Gneisenau, raids on Creusot, Milan and also the 1,000 bomber raids on Cologne. His

medal citation reads:- *"his courage, skill and determination have been of the highest quality throughout these operations and the efficiency with which he completes his allotted tasks has been an inspiration and example to his crew"*. Ernest was born in 1908 and enlisted in 1940.

Flight Sergeant Richard E Bush RAF, the son of Mabel and Charlie Bush of 27 Cundalls Road was another Ware Central School old boy who joined the ATC in 1940 achieving the rank of sergeant. Before he joined up in 1941 he worked at County Hall in Hertford. He was awarded his DFM in March 1945.

Sergeant Eric C Wren RAFVR was a Flight Engineer serving in Lancaster bombers flying out of RAF Dunholme Lodge. He won his medal for high skill, fortitude and devotion to duty in operations against the enemy on completion of twenty-eight operations over occupied Europe and Germany. Eric was a former pupil of Ware Central School and a member of the ATC in Ware.

Warrant Officer Edward Hughes RAF, the son of Mrs Hughes of 30 High Oak Road.

Sergeant P Pexton, a member of the ATC in Ware who came from Great Amwell.

Flight Sergeant (Engineer) Alan Hollands RAFVR., another member of the Ware ATC, was killed on active service. His father was the Police Inspector in Ware during the war.

Order of the British Empire

Brigadier G W F Stewart, Royal Artillery, son of Dr Walter Stewart of Baldock Street, was awarded his OBE in November 1943 for gallantry and distinguished services in North Africa.

Member of the British Empire (Military)

Major Cyril Wieland, son of the late A P Wieland of Gladstone Road, was awarded his MBE in March 1943 for distinguished services in the Middle East. He went to the Middle East as a Lieutenant in 1941, promoted to Captain and captured by the Germans. He was released during General Wavell's offensive in 1942. His wife was a Section Officer in the WAAF.

Corporal F J Wood, RAF of 11 Canons Road was awarded his medal in August 1946, he had served in South East Asia for three years.

The American Bronze Medal

Lieutenant M G Farley, Royal Engineers, of 17 Collett was decorated in Cairo with his medal for his part in the Anzio (Italy) operations, he was also mentioned in despatches.

Lt. Colonel Robert Peter McMullen DSO, MBE, see notes above for his DSO.

Czech Military Medal for Merit

7361399 Private F Munt, Royal Army Medical Corps, was one of four British soldiers awarded this medal for services rendered at Belsen concentration camp.

Mentioned in Despatches

Temporary Sub-Lt. B G Richards BEM, RNVR of Ware mentioned in despatches "for outstanding bravery, skill and devotion to duty in successful patrols in submarines.

Signalman G J Walker, **Royal Corps of Signals,** was mentioned in despatches in October 1944, he was the twenty-eight year old son of Mr and Mrs J L Walker of 72 High Street and had served in the Middle East for three years.

Signaller Frank Chapman, Royal Corps of Signals, an ex pupil of Ware Central School and the son of James Chapman of Bluecoat Nurseries was mentioned in despatches in November 1944, before joining up in 1940 he worked for the London Transport Board at Hertford and subsequently served with the 8th Army.

Sergeant T J Speed, Royal Army Service Corps, of 50 Vicarage Road was mentioned in despatches for devotion to duty. He was a "Duck" (amphibious vehicle) driver in the D-Day landings and the assault across the river Rhine. He was another London Transport Board driver before he was called up operating from their Hertford garage.

Signalman E H King, Royal Corps of Signals, of 44 Musley Lane was mentioned in despatches for services in Italy. He worked for Crook Brothers, the builders, before the war.

Police Citation

P.C Alick Wright, serving with "X" Division of the Metropolitan Police was commended by the King on the recommendation of the Home Secretary for his courage and bravery when he rescued a man from the debris of a demolished house in London in 1944. Alick was the fifth son of Mr and Mrs George Wright of 10 Park Road.

Chapter 21
VICTORY

In April 1942 the country's morale was at its lowest ebb but the tide began to turn that autumn with General Montgomery's victory at El Alamein on the 23rd October. To mark this success, in common with the rest of the nation, Ware's church bells rang out in celebration. They had been silent since 1940 under the Control of Noise Order and were only to be rung as a warning to the local army garrison that parachutists had been seen in the neighbourhood of the church in question and not, as commonly thought, for a general warning of an invasion. In May 1943 the Order was repealed and hence forth the bells could be rung on all occasions.

Limited street lighting was reintroduced from the 27th September 1944 using low powered bulbs, the relaxation only applied to classified roads such as the High Street and then only from 10 pm until midnight. Gradually more lights were allowed until approximately one third of the pre-war total were in service. Another 40 lamps were commissioned at the onset of winter in 1945 which had to be extinguished at 10.30 pm except for thirteen between Amwell End and Baldock Street to conserve fuel. The number of lamps now lit nightly was two thirds of the pre-war total. It was not until Victory in Europe was achieved that all lighting restrictions were lifted.

Thoughts both nationally and locally started to focus on post-war Britain. The County and Ware Town Councils began to consider the effects of the Butler Education Act, the Beveridge plan for social reform, and Sir Patrick Abercrombie's report on New Towns. Abercrombie proposed to create new towns at Hatfield, Stevenage and Harlow at the same time limiting Ware's expansion to some five hundred people although, following pressure from the Ware Councillors, this figure was eventually revised to four thousand. Included within his plan was the route of the Ware Bypass the alignment of which was hardly changed when it was built some thirty years later. The Council had sufficient land for a further 132 houses on the Vineyard estate and by December 1944 plans had been drawn up so that work could be put in hand as soon as permission was received from the Ministry of Health. G Davis and Sons of Broxbourne started to construct the first twenty houses in April 1945.

The Town Council were reluctant to apply to the Ministry of Health for prefab houses so in February 1945 the Ware British Legion came up with a novel idea to pressurise the Councillors into action. The Legion suggested that at least 200 out of the town's servicemen would require council housing when they were demobbed and contacted servicemen suggesting that they wrote to the Town Council immediately requesting housing when they left the forces, the ploy worked since within a week or so sixty-four applications had been received at the Priory. Shortly after this the Council

A V.E Day Street Party at Cundalls Road, among the families in the photograph are:
Watson, Storey, Franklyn, Sell, Chalkley, Hills, Gumble, Homewood, Warren, Taylor,
Buttery, Newton, Heffer, Sharp, Presland, Hart, Wright, Clark, Bush, Barnes, Smith,
Heathfield, Cockman, Andrews, Barrett and Middleton.

submitted an application to the Ministry of Health for fifty prefabs!

V E Day

By the late spring of 1945 the allies were advancing into and Austria, the Russians were making huge advances in the East and the Anglo-American forces advanced rapidly from the west. The war in Europe was practically over. Fighting on the Italian front ceased on the 29th April and by the 5th May the war in Western Europe was over. A Home Office circular arrived at The Priory on 4th May detailing the arrangements for "V E" Day; the Prime Minister, Winston Churchill, was to broadcast to the nation at 3.00 pm on 8th May followed by HM King George VI the same evening, the 9th May was to be a public holiday and church bells would be rung on Sunday which would be a special day of thanksgiving for victory.

Ware was already in a festive mood since the "Merchant Navy" fund raising entertainments were still in progress on 5th May, the High Street and many of the local roads were quickly bedecked with flags and fairy lights ready for V E Day on 8th when the Ware Town Band paraded through the town ending up in the Priory grounds for community singing. A loud speaker relayed the broadcast by the King for the benefit of the crowd listening to the band. The festivities continued until the early hours with many bonfires blazing in and around the town. The Reverend Lloyd Phillips held a thanksgiving service in St. Mary's Church the same evening and an open air service was conducted by the Salvation Army. A grand Victory Dance was quickly organised at the Drill Hall for the Saturday evening and street parties were held throughout the town over the ensuing days. Baldock Street, Fanhams Road, Fanshawe Crescent, Croft Road, Musley Hill, Canons Road, Trinity Road, Cundalls Road, King George's Road, High Oak Road, Bowling Road and Watton Road are all recorded as having parties.

General election

On 18th May the Prime Minister invited the leaders in the wartime coalition government to continue in partnership until the defeat of Japan. The Labour Party declined and so a general election had to be held. Nominations closed on the 25th June with Ware Town Councillor Arthur Swain standing as an Independent candidate. Polling took place on Thursday the 7th July and the votes cast were:-

Lt. Colonel Derek Walker Smith, Conservative	19,877
Councillor Lynton Smith, Labour	17,349
Captain Peter Hughes, Liberal	7,587
Councillor Arthur Bernard Swain, Independent	1,005

V J Day

The war in the Far East came to a rapid close after the atomic bombs were dropped on the cities of Hiroshima and Nagasaki. On 10th August 1945 the Japanese government indicated that they would accept unconditional surrender demanded at the Potsdam agreement and fighting ceased on 14th August. Clement Attle, now the Prime Minister, announced the news at midnight and declared that Wednesday and Thursday, the 15th and 16th August, would be public holidays. Although there was general relief in Ware that the war was finally over the scenes of euphoria and celebrations seen on V E Day were not repeated, the town was in a much more sombre mood with all churches holding thanksgiving services on the Sunday.

With the town's young men returning Ware Football Club reformed and held trial matches and the town gradually returned to normal although plagued by shortages of every commodity – food rationing did not finally end until the early fifties. The finale of the War in Ware was to provide a fitting Memorial to the Fallen, this proved to be an ongoing saga which finally ended on 8th July 1978 when the Queen Mother opened the restored Place House as a Memorial Hall.

Chapter 22
THE WAR MEMORIAL AND HALL SAGA

When hostilities in Europe finally ceased, thoughts turned towards a suitable memorial to the fallen and in June 1945 the British Legion proposed that this should be Memorial Hall. A public meeting was held in the Priory on Thursday the 11th October when a motion proposed by Miss Woodhead (Headmistress of Ware Grammar School) and seconded by Mrs Margaret Percival (General Percival's wife) resolved "that a fund be opened for a War Memorial at Ware to engrave the names of the fallen of the last war on the present memorial and to provide:

(1)   A hall, and if funds are sufficient
(2)   A community centre,
(3)   A recreation ground, and
(4)   Alterations to the existing memorial – "the various schemes to be executed in that order."

A sub-committee was set up to arrange for the names of the fallen to be inscribed on the War Memorial, a list of names was requested from relatives via advertisements and lists posted in the town's churches, the Priory, the British Legion, the Gas and the Electricity show rooms. It was agreed that the names would be added to the flank walls of the Memorial which was rededicated on Armistice Sunday, the 8th November 1947. In spite of the appeals for names several appear to be missing although one, that of Flight Sergeant Ron Bentley, was added when the Memorial was refurbished and rededicated on the 6th June 1999.

A fund raising committee was formed, Tom Burgess was appointed chairman with Leslie Southall as its secretary, the committee members were Fred Weatherly (British Legion), Jimmy Crane (ex servicemen), Ernie Whybrew (Ware Football Club), Gwen Dixon (Red Cross & St. John Ambulance Brigade), The Reverend A Lloyd Phillips (the town's churches), William S Ward (the general public), G J Risby (the town's youth), Alderman Charles Ward, Mrs Weatherly (British Legion Ladies Section) and Albert Evans (the town's schools). Fund raising functions started immediately with the whole town taking part.

Some £750 had been raised by July 1946 when a grand fete was held in the Priory Grounds the highlight of which was a display by the Dagenham Girl Pipers. The fete, in reality a revival of the Ware Carnival Queen event last held in June 1939, raised some £170 for the Fund. The summer fete became an annual event raising money for the Fund although its format gradually changed with the formation of the

Ware Festival Committee in 1950 when, for the first time, the Town Band led a parade of children in fancy dress through the town to the Priory ground where the traditional side shows were held. The fetes continued to be run in conjunction with a swimming gala at the Priory Street pool and until 1953 all the proceeds went to the Memorial Fund. The embryo of Ware Week had been formed.

Ernie Whybrew who had been heavily involved with the quarterly house to house collections for Ware Boys at the Front Fund was keen to set up a similar scheme for the Memorial Fund, this took time to organised but through a lack of volunteers not all the town was covered. Many of the town's business companies and banks gave donations, Barclays and the Westminster Banks each gave £350 with Allen & Hanburys contributing £250 to name but a few.

Another fund raising event, which was to become part of the Ware scene for several years to come, took place in 1946 when a Christmas Fair, opened by General Percival, was held at the Drill Hall. Again many of the organisations in the town ran stalls with the town's youth taking part too, the Army Cadets put up the decorations and various schools ran side shows such as the bran tub. The fair always raised over £200 and was usually more successful than the summer fete. Charles Ballands put the Astoria Cinema at the Committee's disposal for a special children's matinee on Tuesday the 7th January. By 1948 the fund had amassed some £3,000.

In 1948 the thoughts of the Town Clerk, Leslie Southall, were turning towards the design of the hall. It is clear from correspondence that Southall had set his targets on a new building capable of holding some 500 people complete with a stage capable of accommodating 130 people, a foyer and a bar. He suggested that an architect be engaged to design the building. Twelve members of the Committee met on the 21st March 1949 to review progress, several members realised that building costs had soared and that the proposed hall would cost three to four times the sum originally envisaged, but they remained determined to reach their goal.

1954 saw the relaxation of building controls and licences so building works were now possible. The Memorial Fund stood at some £7500 – far below the cost of the building Southall envisaged. Over the ensuing years, various sites were looked at and proposals to incorporate the hall within other projects were studied, but these were all beyond the fund's means. There was a new twist in 1960 when the Town Council sold its water undertakings and had a considerable surplus of funds. The Memorial Committee seized on this and Southall wrote to the Council asking if the Fund was reopened and further subscriptions were raised would they, the Council, double the amount of the contributions. The Council's resolution was that the Memorial Committee would never raise sufficient money for a hall and that a public meeting should be convened in order that a project within their financial means could be set. The real death blow to the town ever building a Memorial Hall came in 1962 when the Fund had to be registered as a charity under the Charity Act of 1960, the Charity Commission laid down the ground rules on how the money could be spent and it is evident that Leslie Southall did not make ther rules public which would have saved further acrimony. To quote but two of the conditions which put paid to many proposals which had been suggested in the past or were to be proposed in the future:

(1)   The Hall had to be for the benefit of the whole of the town and not a few selected organisations.

(2)   The Hall had to be run as a Trust and be on a long lease, this effectively   ruled   out incorporating it within building owned by either Ware UDC or a commercial organisation.

Leslie Southall, Clerk to Ware Urban District Council

Various proposals were made and rejected, but in 1962 the Town Council reversed its decision taken in 1960 and agreed that £52,000 of the money raised from the sale of their water undertakings could be spent on a new hall. Their proposal was to relocate their town depot behind the Library to a new site in Priory Street and use the vacated area for the hall. However, by the time the new depot was completed the national economic situation was such that Central Government placed spending restrictions on councils which precluded the construction of public halls. With a "squeeze" in place the Council purchased the Drill Hall in Amwell End and the Memorial Committee agreed to hand over their funds to help with its conversion provided their mandate was fulfilled, there was yet another body blow because the Ministry of Housing would not sanction the loan for the necessary conversion work and it could only be used for sporting activities so the Memorial Committee were forced to withdraw their support.

Hopes were raised yet again in July 1971 when a public meeting was held to discuss the County Council's proposals for the redevelopment of Church Street and construction of the Ware Inner Relief Road. The scheme, approved by the County Council backed by the Ware Town Council, included the provision of a 200 seat public hall built within a multi-storey car park to the north of the High Street. Moving ahead of the chronological sequence of events, with the reorganisation of local government in 1974 Ware UDC became part of East Hertfordshire District Council and the surplus money set aside by the Town Council for the Memorial Hall disappeared into the District Council's coffers never to be seen in Ware again.

August 1973 saw a flourish of letters in the *Mercury* backing a proposal for at least some of the Memorial Fund to be spent on the Old People's Centre in Priory Street. The British Legion together with some of the town councillors were on the attack but had not checked the original mandate prior going into print – the same can be said about the press as well. Again Southall could have diffused the situation if he had given a frank and open statement explaining the objects of the Fund and the conditions laid down by the Charity Commission – public relations was not his forte.

There was a glimmer of light at long last in 1975, when the "Ware 4" Group were proposing to establish an arts centre in an old malting in Kibes Lane. Leslie Southall, now retired, approached David Perman of the Ware Society to see if some or part of the Memorial Fund could be used for this project. David, keen to preserve the town's unique heritage, did his research and pointed out that the Kibes Lane arts centre would present problems since the District Council were prepared to grant only a five year lease. By talking to EHDC Director of Planning, who was equally keen to regenerate the town's historic buildings, he came up with two other possibilities. The first was the United Reform Church (Leaside behind Sketchlys) who at that time were keen to sell their building and move into St Mary's Church. The second possibility was Place House in Blue Coat Yard which had been acquired by the Hertfordshire Building Preservation Trust who wanted to restore it to its former medieval state including the original aisled hall which was probably the oldest building in Ware. Southall responded by saying that the United Reform was too small and thought that there were certain conditions attached by the Donors and considered Place House did not meet the purpose the Fund was raised for. In other words the former Town Clerk was not keen on either of the schemes.

For many years the Town Council had been represented on the Ware War Memorial Committee by seven Councillors. In December 1975 all seven signed a letter to Southall which basically stated that it had come to their attention that the Hertfordshire Building Preservation Trust had acquired Place House and that they considered the restoration work to be a worthy scheme to spend the Memorial Fund on – they requested an early meeting to discuss the subject. Before convening a meeting Southall visited the Charity Commission, armed with a synopsis of the history of Place House and an argument as to why the medieval hall would be unsuitable, i.e. it was too small since it would only hold fifty people and that fire regulations would undoubtedly prevent the restoration to its former state. However, the Commissioners were keen to see the Fund spent on a suitable project and were amenable to the Place House scheme; their only requirements were that the Fund was spent on an area available to the general public and that they approved of the form of Trust. The Committee met on 8th April 1976 (the seven councillors with the British Legion and the Hertfordshire Regiment Old Comrades Association representatives were the only members to attend) and unanimously agreed that their Fund should be spent on Place Hall subject to a site inspection and meeting with the Preservation Trust. Over the ensuing months they agreed to donate £11,000 to the Preservation Trust with the balance of the

Memorial Fund set up as an endowment fund run by the Town Council for maintenance purposes and these endowments were inscribed on plaques erected in the hall. The Place House Trust was formed with John Bishop as its first chairman and a start made on the restoration work.

Place House was formerly opened by the late Queen Mother on 8th July 1978 although it was another two years before the final meeting of the Ware War Memorial Committee was held at the Priory on 16th September 1980, nearly thirty-five years after its formation. Leslie Southall received a well earned vote of thanks for his thirty-five years of service as its secretary and in the latter years as treasurer as well. The total amount raised amounted to £19,341.67

Her Majesty Queen Elizabeth the Queen Mother at the opening of Place House on 8th July 1978. Place House, tucked away in Bluecoat Yard, is thought to have been the medieval manor house of Ware. In the early 1970s it was badly in need of repair when it was acquired by the Hertfordshire Buildings Preservation Trust and comprehensively restored. It is now a Grade I listed building. The freehold is still owned by the Preservation Trust but it is maintained and managed as a sort of village hall for the town by the Place House Charity, described above. Photograph by courtesy of Russ Craig of BEAMS.

Chapter 23
ROLL OF HONOUR OF WARE'S MEN AND WOMEN

They shall not grow old, as
We that are left grow old:
Age shall not weary them,
Nor the years condemn.
At the going down of the
Sun and in the morning
We will remember them.

Laurence Binyon's *For the Fallen*

Royal Navy

D/JX Able Seaman Edward E. Anson, the husband of Mrs A L Anson of 4 Redan Road died on 18th February 1942 when *S.S.Somme* was sunk by a U-boat some 200 miles S.W of Iceland enroute from London to Bermuda with the loss of all crew members. Edward was based *HMS President III* at Bristol for all personnel allocated for service in defensively equipped merchant ships. The *Somme*, a Royal Mail and Nelson Line ship, was a 5265t vessel launched in 1919. Edward has no known grave and his name is commemorated on the Plymouth Naval Memorial.

Seaman Dennis Story, the nineteen year old son of Percy Story, a baker at 7 Amwell End (now Down to Earth) was reported missing and presumed killed when *HMS Ellesmere* was sunk in the Channel on the 24th February 1945. The *Ellesmere* was a 580 ton Whaler built in Smith's Yard at Middlesborough (the same yard as *HMS Tulip*) in 1939 and was used as an anti-submarine vessel. Dennis went to St Mary's and Ware Central School and had been in the Navy for two years. Dennis's elder brother, Percy Junior, was a pre-war "Terrier" with the Hertfordshire Regiment with whom he served throughout the war.

Royal Marines

PLY/X1374 Marine John D. Greenhill, Royal Marines, the third son of Mrs R Greenhill of 8 Fanhams Road served on the cruiser *HMS Exeter* which was sunk in the Java Sea during an encounter with the Japanese on the night of 27/28th February 1942 off the Dutch East Indies (Indonesia). John, always known as Jack, was taken prisoner by the Japanese and died on a Dutch hospital ship the 24th April at Macassar at the age of twenty-six. Jack was a former pupil of Christ Church school and before he joined the Marines in 1935 he worked for A B Swain. He is buried in the Ambou British Cemetery in Indonesia. John's three brothers also served in the forces, Bill and George served in the army and met up at Monte Casino in Italy while James (Jim) served with the Royal Artillery.

Marine John Greenhill

Army

801106 Private Charles Barker, 2/6th Bn., The Queen's Royal Regt. (West Surrey) was the thirty year old husband of Muriel and the father of a young child who were living at 26 Fanhams Road when he was killed in Italy on the 26th February 1944. Charles has no known grave and his name is commemorated on the Commonwealth War Graves Commission Cassino Memorial. Before joining the regular army in 1936 he had been a member of the Ware Territorials.

Sapper Herbert G. Bassill, 262 Army Field Coy., Royal Engineers, died on the 29th November 1942 aged 27 years. Herbert was born in Ware but had moved to Luton. His final resting place is marked by a Commonwealth War Graves Commission headstone in Ware Cemetery.

5781515 Corporal Edward (Teddy) John Bartlett, 3rd Bn., Army Air Corps, the twenty-one year old son of Edward and Mary Bartlett of 8 Raynsford Road was killed during the invasion of Sicily on 14th July 1943. His name is commemorated on the Commonwealth War Graves Commission Memorial at Casino which is dedicated to all those soldiers who died in Italy and have no known grave. Teddy had served in the army for two years spending his last year in North Africa. Prior to the war he was employed by Walter Thurgood.

Bateman J. It is believed that John came from Fanshawe Crescent but insufficient information has been found to make a positive identification.

5952031 Private Leslie Albert Beard, 8th Bn., Royal Warwickshire Regiment, was the twenty-two year old son of Charles and Bessie Beard of 65 Star Street. Les went to France in January 1940 and was killed defending the River Scheldt near Tournai on the 20th May 1940 as the B.E.F withdrew towards Dunkirk. He is buried in the Commonwealth War Graves Commission Cemetery at Esquelmes in Belgium.

7259757 Sergeant Harry O. Carter, 225 Parachute Field Amb., Royal Army Medical Corps, was the husband of Anna Carter of 21a Trinity Road and the eldest son of Henry and Maud Carter of 35 Trinity Road. Harry died on 7th August 1944 at the age of thirty-four and is buried in the Ranville War Cemetery. Ranville was the first village to be liberated by the 6th airborne Division in the early hours of D-Day.

Before joining up he was a male nurse in a Billericay hospital. His youngest sister Nora served in the WAAF.

14271774 Gunner Ernest W. Chappell, East African Artillery, Royal Artillery, was the twenty two year old son of Mr and Mrs Ernest Chappell of 18 Watton Road. Ernest had been a signaller with the Gunners for two years and was onboard the 7513 ton *SS Khedive Ismail* chartered as a troopship enroute from Mombassa to Colombo when she was attacked and sunk by a submarine near the equator some 700 miles S W of Ceylon on 12th February 1944. Only 136 men from a total of 2407 on board survived the attack. Ernest has no known grave other than the sea and is commemorated on the East Africa Memorial in Nairobi, Kenya. Before the war he managed Dimock's butchers shop in Hoddesdon.

9650611 Gunner Wallace (Wally) Clark, 75 Field Regt., Royal Artillery, is believed to be the son of Mr and Mrs William Clark of Cundalls Road and the husband of Mrs V E Clark who lived at 204 Rye Road Hoddesdon with her parents, he died on the 27th September 1942 at Salisbury. Wally was twenty-five years old and is buried in Hoddesdon Cemetery.

5955782 L/Cpl. George Crane, 1st Battalion The Hertfordshire Regiment, a pre-war "Terrier" was a twenty-nine year old married man living at 24 George Street, Hertford with his wife Vera and young daughter Betty. George, the sixth son of Alfred and Ruth Crane of 2 West Street, Ware was serving with No. 3 Company of the Hertfordshires in Italy where he was killed on 13th November during an attack on the Gothic Line. His eldest brother was the Regiment's Quartermaster Sergeant and attended George's funeral at the Fanza War Cemetery. Before the war George worked as a linesman with the G.P.O and played football for both the "Ware Terriers" and Ware Town Football Clubs.

5951112 Cpl. Edward F (Eddie) Gayler, 5th Battalion The Bedfordshire and Hertfordshire Regiment (TA). Eddie was a thirty-one year old married man who was reported as missing after the fall of Singapore in February 1942. Before the war he was employed by the Tottenham and District Gas Board and a member of Ware Football Club. In October his Battalion moved to Liverpool where they embarked on the *SS Reina Del Pacifico* on the 27th with an anticipated destination of the Middle East. However with the entry of Japan in the war their ship was diverted to the Far East. The voyage took Eddie to Halifax, Newfoundland, where they were transhipped to the *USS West Point* travelling via Cape Town to Bombay, and then on to Singapore, which they reached on the 29th January. Here they went to Birdwood Camp and assumed the defence of the north coast line.

Following the Japanese capture of the colony and the cease fire on 15th February, Eddie and his comrades were held as prisoners of war at Changi until October 1942 when they trekked northwards for five days in overcrowded cattle trucks with little food and no sanitation to Banpong in Thailand. They now faced a march of some sixty miles through virgin jungle to the site of the railway the Japanese proposed to build into Burma. For twelve months they toiled under horrendous conditions, under nourished, little or no clothing or footwear, stricken with malaria and dysentery and without little or no medicines, awful camp conditions without proper sanitation yet with morale high they completed the line on the 23rd October 1943. During this time some seventy of their original number had died. After the line was opened the Japanese relaxed a little concentrating on getting the survivors away from the jungle into camps in the vicinity of Banpong, here the food improved slightly but there were few amenities. This period of "relaxation" ended abruptly in May 1944 when an order went about that as many fit men as possible were to be shipped to Japan.

Major Robert Grantham, RE

Eddie was among sixty-three from his Battalion who went by train to Singapore on 9th June where they were to embark on the *Hofoku Maru* along with others including another Ware lad, Charlie Taylor, serving with the 1st Bn. of the Cambridgeshire Regiment. The *Hofoku Maru* left Singapore in July and proceeded in convoy to Manila (in the Philippines) where she was detained with engine trouble. She set sail again on the 20th September and the following morning the convoy she had joined was attacked by American planes, the *Hofoku Maru* was hit and went down very quickly taking Eddie and fifty of his comrades in the Beds and Herts with her. Charlie Taylor lost his life as well. Eddie's name is recorded on the Commonwealth War Graves Commission Memorial in Singapore to those who have no known grave.

5574729 Private John J. Gordine, 5th Bn., Wiltshire Regiment, the twenty-nine year old son of James and Ellen Gordine of Ware was killed in the vicinity of Tilly-sur-Seulles, near Bayeux, Normandy, on 7th August 1944. John is buried in the Commonwealth War Graves Commission Cemetery at Tilly-Sur-Seulles.

116347 Major Robert W. Grantham, Royal Engineers, came to Ware as the town's Engineer and Surveyor in 1931. Apart from his slum clearance work his most notable landmark still remains in use today – the Priory Street swimming pool. Robert designed and constructed most of the town's civil defence works before he received his call-up papers in 1940. He died of malaria in Cairo on 31st August 1941 at the age of thirty-five and is buried in the Cairo War Cemetery. His wife Majorie left Ware soon after Robert's death. For many years after his sad death his photograph was hung in the Council Chamber and is now in the Town Clerk's Office. On 4th April 1946 Alderman C Ward said in the Council Chamber that Robert had done so much to improve the town that his name should be perpetuated and proposed that

East Mead Estate, a close of fifteen houses for elderly people, designed and developed by him should be renamed in his memory. The proposal was carried unanimously and Robert's name lives on in the town in Grantham Gardens.

320521 Trooper William (Billy) S Greenhill, 1st King's Dragoon Guards (Royal Armoured Corps, the son of Mrs Emily Greenhill of 57 Musley Hill, died of wounds in Lybia on 12th June 1942. He is buried in the Knightsbridge War Cemetery.

5988962 Private Aubrey T Haines, 1st Battalion The Hertfordshire Regiment, a thirty-three year old married man lived at 24 Star Street left a widow with a five year old daughter. His parents lived 12 Parker Avenue, Bengeo. Aubrey, well known as a bandsman in peacetime in both the Hertfordshire Regiment and in the Ware Town Bands, had served with the Territorials for nine years before the war and was mobilised with his T.A colleagues at the outbreak of hostilities. He served with the Regiment's H.Q Company acting as a stretcher bearer. On 19th October part of "3" Company were attacking a position known as Point 677 near Monte Ceco in northern Italy when they came under heavy and accurate fire. A relief party was organised by a Major Bone who was wounded as they advanced to the front. Aubrey was in the stretcher bearing party carrying the major back for treatment when they were hit by a stray shell from a British 25lb howitzer. Another Ware lad, George Wallace, was killed the same night. In peacetime Aubrey worked as a lorry driver with the builders Henry Norris and Son of Hertford, three of his brothers also served in the Army.

1911276 L/Cpl Silvester B. Hart, 663 Artisan Works Coy., Royal Engineers, was another who lost his life at Dunkirk. Affectionately known as "Nutty Hart" by his colleagues Silvester was a thirty-five year old married man with a five year old son who lived at 60 Star Street when he volunteered for army service in January 1940. Mrs Hart learnt that her husband was one of the six thousand plus troops (the crew gave up counting the numbers after this number had boarded her) who had embarked on the 20,000ton P & O liner *"Lancastria"* at St Nazaire during the evacuation from France. The ship left port on 17th June 1940 and was waiting some ten miles offshore for an escort home when she was attacked by dive bombers and hit by four bombs at 3.50 pm. Some five thousand troops perished as she rolled over and sank, it was the worst individual sea disaster in British marine history and the least publicised. Silvester was among those reported missing, his body was washed up on the French coast in July 1940 but it wasn't until May 1941 that the Red Cross was able to confirm his death to his wife. "Nutty" is buried in the in the Commonwealth War Graves Commision's Cemetery in the seaside village of La Bernerie-en-Retz to the south west of Nantes.

The Hatherill family of 17 Redan Road

Ernest and Dorothy Hatherill lost their two sons during the war. **932189 Sergeant (Pilot) Reginald E. Hatherill**, RAFVR, their eldest son Reg left Ware Central Senior

Sgt Reg Hatherill RAFVR (left) and Corporal Charles Hatherill.

School in 1936 and joined Ware UDC at The Priory working a junior clerk in the Clerk's Department. At the outbreak of war, Reg went to the RAF at Uxbridge to volunteer as a pilot. He died at the age of twenty-one when the Whitley bomber he was in crashed during a training flight on the 6th November 1941. A Commonwealth War Graves Commission headstone in Ware Cemetery marks his final resting place.
14205750 Corporal Charles E. Hatherill, 5th Bn., East Lancashire Regiment, Charlie, their younger son, was killed while on a night patrol near Bayeux in France on the 20th July 1944. He was also twenty-one and is buried in the Bayeux War Cemetery.

974532 Gunner Benjamin Holtby, 124 Field Regt., Royal Artillery, the twenty-two year old son of Albert and Lily Holtby of 29 the Bourne died of wounds received at El Alamein, Egypt, on the 29th September 1942 and is buried in the Alamein Cemetery.

998988 Gunner John F. Hyatt, 127 Field Regt., Royal Artillery, served as a Battery Surveyor with the Gunners. John was the only son of the late F R Hyatt and Mrs Lydia Hyatt of Ware. He was killed in Tunisia on the 6th April 1943 at the age of thirty-one and is buried in the Medjez-El-Bab War Cemetery.

5833826 Private Jonathan J. Linfoot, 1st Bn., The Cambridgeshire Regiment, the twenty-seven year old son of Daniel Linfoot of Tumbling Bay, Star Street was killed in action on 13th February 1942 just a couple of days before the fall of Singapore. Jonathan has no known grave and his name is commemorated on the Singapore Memorial located in the idyllic Kranji Cemetery overlooking the Straits of Johore. Two of his colleagues from Ware serving with the Cambridgeshires died as prisoners of war. His name is also on the Allen & Hanburys memorial.

The Luck family of 16 Watton Road

Alfred and Sarah Luck had four sons serving with the forces two of whom were killed in action. **14646633 Private Albert Luck**, 4th Bn., Wiltshire Regiment, their youngest son was killed in the battle of the Rhineland on the 23rd November 1944. Albert, aged nineteen, is buried in the Rhineland War Cemetery. Before joining the Army Albert was employed as a baker's roundsman with the Co-op in Hertford. **11407392 Gunner Ernest C. Luck**, 266 Bty,. 101 HAA Regt., Royal Artillery, was a twenty-two year old married man, he and his wife Gladys lived at 10 Crane Mead. Ernest, like his brother Albert, worked as a bakers roundsman with the Co-op in Hertford joined up in 1940. He had been abroad for two years before he died of wounds in Burma on 18th April 1945 and is buried in the Taukkyn War Cemetery, Myanmar.

Sayers J. Probably related to the Sayers family living at Musley Hill but insufficient information has been found to make a positive identification.

5831306 Private Charles W. Taylor, 1st Bn., The Cambridgeshire Regiment, was the son of Mr and Mrs John Taylor of 37 Croft Road and was taken prisoner at the fall of Singapore. He worked on the Burma-Thailand railway, possibly on the same section as Eddie Gaylor (see above). Once the railway was complete Charlie was being transferred to Japan on the *SS Hofoku Maru* which was sunk off Manilla by American aircraft on the 21st September 1944, he went down with the ship together with Eddie Gayler and his name is also recorded on the Commonwealth War Graves Commission Memorial in Singapore to those who have no known grave.

Todd A E. Insufficient information has been found to make a positive identification.

5989105 Private George R. Wallace, 1st Battalion The Hertfordshire Regiment, another pre-war "Terrier" and a member of Ware Football club was the son of Mr and Mrs George Wallace of 131 Musley Hill. On 18th October 1944, in pitch darkness and driving rain, a platoon under Lt. Jackson advanced, attacked and captured an enemy strong position known as Point 677 near Monte Ceco in northern Italy. It was in this action that George was killed. He is buried in the Commonwealth War Graves Commission Cemetery at Faenza.

Leslie Ernest Walters, the son of Mr and Mrs Ernest Walters of 39 Croft Road was killed in action during January 1945.

Ward W T. Insufficient information has been found to make a positive identification.

7537363 Private Gordon A. Whybrew, Army Dental Corps, the twenty-one year old son of Susan Empson and step-son of Thomas Epsom of 6 Fanshawe Crescent, was attached to the Royal Army Medical Corps. Late in the evening of the 17th September 1940 he was off duty and walking in Sefton Park, Liverpool, with a young lady during an air raid. Bombs fell in the park and Gordon was killed outright, the girl however escaped uninjured and suffered only slight shock. Gordon is buried in the churchyard at Wareside where the Whybrew family lived before coming to Ware during the period between the two world wars.

The Wright family

William and Mary Wright were the third family in the town to loose two sons during the war. The Wrights came to Ware from Poplar during the war and were living in West Street at the time of their son John's death. **14270126 Gunner John W T Wright**, 1 H.A.A. Regt., Royal Artillery, was twenty-one when he was killed in a traffic accident in Italy on 8th July 1945 and is buried in the Padua War Cemetery. **14428075 L/Corporal Sydney C. Wright**, 2nd Bn., King's Royal Rifle Corps, was killed on the 22nd June 1944 during the invasion of Normandy at the age of eighteen. He is buried in the Ryes War Cemetery to the east of Bayeaux.

Royal Air Force

1376923 Sergeant Pilot Peter L. Chapman RAFVR, 101 Sqdn., was the eldest son of the Ware Postmaster. On the 20th January 1942 Peter's Wellington Ic bomber No.21110 took off from RAF Oakington (north of Cambridge) with his five crew members bound for Emden. Nothing was heard of the plane after takeoff which failed to return to base. Peter has no known grave so his name is commemorated on the Runnymede Memorial. His sister Margery served with the WAAF and a brother with the Fleet Air Arm. Ralph, his youngest brother, died in a tragic shooting accident with the Ware Home Guard.

657578 Flight Sergeant (Airgunner) Lawrence C. Hartman RAFVR, 7 Sqdn., the thirty-one year old son of Cecil and Ann Hartman of 21 Bluecoat Yard. Lawrence's Squadron was also based at RAF Oakington and at 16.59 pm on 14th January 1944 his Lancaster III No.JA935, Squadron letter "E", took off for a raid on Brunswick and was shot down over Hanover. Lawrence is buried in the Hanover War Cemetery.

1180254 Sergeant Pilot Aubrey G. Hutchinson RAFVR, 150 Sqdn., was the twenty-six year old husband of Grace Hutchinson living at 119 Watton Road. His parents lived in Bournemouth. Aubrey lost his life during a raid on Cologne during the night of the 27th/28th April 1942. His Squadron were based at Snaith, near Goole in East Yorkshire, and flew Wellington IIICs. Fourteen aircraft from Snaith took part in this raid, it was a clear night and over their target they encountered intense and accurate ack-ack fire. Two planes failed to return including X3288 piloted by Aubrey who is buried in the Rheinberg War Cemetery near Wessel.

50657 Flight Lieutenant Pilot Ronald D. Rayment RAF, 619 Sqdn., was the twenty three old son of William and Lilian Rayment of 9 Collett Road and husband of Alice Rayment of 12 Wellington Street Hertford. Ronald, a former pupil of Hertford

Grammar School, flew in Lancaster III bombers out of RAF Woodhall Spa in Lincolnshire. At 17.22 pm on the evening of the 26 November 1943 Ronald as the skipper of Lancaster DV 381 with the Squadron letter "E" took off for a raid on Berlin, one of 463 bombers to attack the German capital that night. Nothing more of "E" was heard that night although several other crews from the Squadron believed it had ditched in the North Sea on the return flight. Ronald and one of his crew are buried in the Becklingen Cemetery on the road from Hanover to Hamburg, the remainder are commemorated on the Runnymede Memorial.

Pilot Officer Don Skipp

627136 Sergeant John Henry Reed RAF, 206 Sqdn., the son of John and Annie Reed of Cricklewood and nephew of Mr and Mrs James Greenhill of 16 New Road, was well known in Ware football and cricket circles. John joined the RAF in 1938 after seeing service with the Hertfordshire Territorials and was among the first detachments to serve in France; subsequently he was evacuated from Dunkirk. After the fall of France he went on flying operations taking parts in many operations as a wireless operator-air gunner in Hudson aircraft from RAF Bircham Newton in Norfolk. On 11th February 1941 John flew on two missions with his pilot Sergeant Bracker over the North Sea in Hudson T9289. The first was on convoy patrol lasting from 16.55 – 18.05 pm, they took off again on a a Euro patrol at 21.20 pm from which they did not return.

162984 Pilot Officer Donald H Skipp RAFVR, 107 Sqdn., was the twenty-two year old son of Mr and Mrs Horace Skipp who ran Ware Garage in the Market Square and lived at 21 King Edward's Road. After leaving Hertford Grammar School he was a draughtsman with the Northmet Power Company at Bridgefoot (now The Bridge pub) and joined the LDV on its inception. Don trained as a Sergeant navigator/ bomb aimer in South Africa and in 1943 was flying in twin engine Boston IIIAs from RAF Hartford Bridge (near Hartley Wintney). His usual pilot was Californian Lt Art Truxler of the American Air Force who, together with another crew member Pilot Officer MacConnell of the Australian Air Force, used to spend their leaves with the Skipp family (the fourth crew member, the wireless operator/gunner was an Englishman Flight Sergeant Naisbit). On the 6th January 1944 eleven Bostons from Hartford Bridge including Don's Boston BZ 387 with the Squadron letter "L" rendezvoused over Beachy Head with others from 88 and 342 Squadrons to attack targets in the St Valery area. The overall operation was a success but Don's plane

Flight Sergeant Ronald Bentley and his headstone at the Commonwealth Ware Graves Commission Cemetery at Sage

was hit by flack putting one engine out of action and they were forced to return with the engine "feathered". On the approach circuit to their home station "L" crashed at Little Sandhurst and exploded killing all four crew members. Don's funeral service was held at Holy Trinity, Bengeo and his final resting place is in the Hertford North Road Cemetery where he is buried with his parents. The Ware ATC provided a Guard of Honour under Cadet Sergeant Norman Murphy. Truxler and McDonnell are buried at Brookwood American Cemetery in Surrey. Written in their Squadron log book are the words "we shall miss this experienced crew. They were all very pleasant colleagues". Don's name also appears on the Northmet Power Company's memorial.

1873484 Flight Sergeant Ronald W Bentley RAFVR, 35 Sqdn., another Hertford Grammar School boy, was the twenty year old son of Mr and Mrs William Bentley of 34 Croft Road and served as an rear gunner with Bomber Command. Ron flew in Lancaster bombers primarily engaged on path finding duties from RAF Graveley in Huntingdonshire. On 5th January 1945 Ron's Lancaster PB 364, Squadron letter "M", took off at 16.27 pm bound for Hanover under the command of Flying Office K Potts. They flew at 18000 feet and as their target was obscured by low cloud they dropped their flares and bombs by instrument. Nothing more was heard of "M" but it is known from entries in the Squadron records that it was shot down over Oldenburg. Ron is buried in the Commonwealth War Graves Commission Cemetery at Sage along with his colleagues Flt Sgt M B Sharp (Flight Engineer), Flt Sgt G A Pope

(Wireless Operator/Air Gunner) and Sgt V M B Halls (Air Gunner). His name was not added to Ware's war memorial until the 6th June 1999.

127874 Flt Lt Peter James Timmons RAFVR, 107 Sqdn., the husband of Irene, father of Patricia and the third son of Edward and Eunice Timmons of 22 Baldock Street, died in a flying accident on 15th October 1944 at the age of twenty-six. Peter, a pupil at Hertford Grammar School, was in the Metropolitan Police before he joined up and had been a keen member of Ware Swimming Club. At the time of his death Peter was flying Mosquito HR 239, Squadron letter "E", from RAF Lasham near Alton in Hampshire. He and his navigator, Pilot Officer Hughes, had taken part in many operations over occupied territory. In clear weather on the afternoon of the 15th October Peter had taken off on a routine flight when his aircraft crashed near Alton and went up in flames, no reason for the crash was found. Peter is buried in a private grave in Ware New Cemetery.

WAAF

442133 A.C.W 2 Annie Henrietta Taylor, WAAF, was killed in a road accident at Roydon on Monday, 15 September 1941. Annie was the twenty year old daughter of William and Charlotte Emma Taylor of 13 Cundalls Road had joined the WAAF the previous February. She was buried in Ware Cemetery where her final resting place is marked by a Commonwealth War Graves Commission headstone.

Merchant Navy

Able Seaman Frank L. Harris, was a twenty year old seaman serving on 1473 ton Leith registered *S.S Brandenburg* which was sunk by a U-boat with the loss of all hands some 450 miles west of Portugal on 10th February 1941. The *Brandenburg*, owned by the Currue Line, was en route from Villa Real to Oban carrying 1800 tons of sulphur and pyrites when she was lost. Frank has no known grave and his name is commemorated on the Merchant Navy Memorial at Tower Hill, London.

Fred Cyril Peacock, a twenty-eight year old ship's carpenter serving on the 6578 ton London registered *S.S Orfor* sunk by a U-boat with the loss of all hands some 600 miles east of the Barbados at 3.00 am on 14th December 1942. At the time she was lost she was enroute from Calcutta to Kingston Jamaica carrying 7000 tons of gunnies or jute. His parents, Edwin and Priscilla, lived at 40 Watton Road. Fred has no known grave other than the sea and his name is commemorated on the Merchant Navy Memorial at Tower Hill, London. Fred had served with the Ware Territorials.

Cadet Peter John Wilbourn, the son of Henry and Grace Wilbourn of 63 Vicarage Road joined the Merchant Navy from Hertford Grammar School. He was serving on 13,000 ton tanker the *S.S San Gaspar* of the Eagle Oil and Shipping Company when she was torpedoed at set on fire by the German U-575 submarine on 18th July 1942 some 100 miles east of Trinidad. Her master, Captain D K Blyth, was forced to abandon ship and thirteen lives were lost including sixteen year old Peter. He is buried along with his fellow seamen in the Port of Spain (St. James) Military Cemetery Trinidad and Tobago in the West Indies. The U-boat surfaced shortly afterwards, interrogated Chief Engineer J M Sayer's lifeboat and presented the crew with a bottle of cognac. Despite the extent and severity of the damage the *San Gaspar* remained afloat, was towed into Trinidad, repaired and survived the rest of the war.

Servicemen associated with Ware whose names do not appear on the Town's War Memorial

948893 Gunner Stanley Baker, 135 Field Regt., Royal Artillery, formerly of Stapleford was killed in Malaya on the 26th January 1942 yet it was not until March 1946 that his wife who lived at 96 King George's Road was officially notified of his death. Stanley who was twenty-five when he died has no known grave as is commemorated on the Kranji Memorial overlooking the Straits of Johore.

864641 Fusilier George E. Barrett, 1st Bn., Royal Fusiliers (City of London Regt.), was the twenty-two year son of Charles and Daisy Barrett and the husband of Jean, who, at the time of his death was living with her parents, Mr and Mrs Frederick Ward, at 14 Cross Street. George died on the 23rd November 1943 while fighting with the 5th Army Corps on the Italian Adriatic sector and is buried in the Sangro River War Cemetery. Jean remarried at Ware Congregational Church after the war.

954912 Lance-Sergeant Edward F. Barnes, 155 (The Lanarkshire Yeomanry) Field Regt., Royal Artillery, a thirty-five year old married man from Croft Road was yet another Ware man to be taken prisoner at the fall of Singapore. He died in a Japanese Prisoner of War Camp in Thailand on the 23rd December 1943 and is buried in the Chungkai War Cemetery near Kanchanaburi. Chungkai was one of the base camps on the infamous Burma Siam railway and this particular burial ground was started by the prisoners themselves and most who rest there are men who died in the camp hospital on the banks of the river Kwai Noi. It wasn't until August 1945 that his wife, Phyliss, was notified of his death. Before joining the forces Edward was employed by Crook Brothers in Ware.

114181 Pilot Officer Geoffery E. Coleman RAFVR, a member of the London Stock Exchange and a married man with two children who lived at "Hillside" in Scotts Road. During the early part of the war he had been a Lieutenant in the Ware Home Guard. In December 1941 he volunteered for service with the RAF Regiment. The following March he was taken ill and died in Westminster Hospital, London on the May 1942. His funeral service was held at Ware followed by cremation at Enfield where his name is commemorated on a panel by the Commonwealth War Graves Commission within the Crematorium grounds. His wife Lilian continued to live in Ware for several years being an active member and treasurer of the Ware Music

Club, his son Peter organised a fun fair at the Priory in August 1945 in aid of the RAF Benevolent Fund.

158305 Sergeant Pilot Victor D. Farmer, 57 Sqdn., RAF, was the twenty-five year old husband of Winifred Ellen (nee Tilston) living at "Downside" in Scotts Road. Victor died on 5th May 1943 and is buried in the Reichswald Forest War Cemetery in Germany. His parents lived at Worthing in Sussex where his name is commemorated on that town's War Memorial.

2939686 Private David Finlayson, 5th Bn., Queen's Own Cameron Highlanders, a twenty-two year old possibly married to the daughter of Fred Shambrook, the shoe repairer of 1 East Street. He served in Holland and towards the end of November 1944 he was slightly injured by a grenade. As he made his way back to his Regimental First Aid Post he saw a group of soldiers standing near a building, "some of our Company" he thought and made his way towards them. They were in fact Germans. There were ten of them, young and fully armed but when they saw him they rushed towards him with cries of joy! They were parachute troops and had only been in the army for six weeks and were only too glad to surrender. David found another six hiding in a cellar in the building who also surrendered giving him a "bag" of sixteen. Sadly David was killed in action a few months later on 9th February 1945 when the Allies started their advance into Germany. His final resting place is in the Mook Commonwealth War Graves Commission Cemetery near Nijmegen in Holland.

14523347 Private Arthur FitzJohn, General Service Corps, came to Ware from Walkern and lived at 25 Gladstone Road with his wife Beatrice. Arthur died on 30th October 1943 aged 31 years and his final resting place is marked by a Commonwealth War Graves Commission headstone in War Cemetery. His mother, Ellen FitzJohn, may have lived in Star Street.

1801850 Flight Sergeant (Engineer) Alan S. Hollands DFM, RAFVR 101 Sqdn., was the twenty year old son Police Inspector Charles Stanley Hollands of Ware. Alan, a former ATC cadet, worked for the Northmet Power Company before he joined the RAF. His Squadron was based at RAF Ludford Magna and his Lancaster 1 (LL860 SR-1) took off at 2120 hours on the 26th April 1944 to take part in Operation Schweinfurt. His plane was one of twenty-two lost during the operation. Alan and the other seven crew members are buried in the Viroflat New Communal Cemetery some four miles to the east of Versailles in France. Most unusually all the crew were decorated, though it seems none of the DFMs were immediate decorations, details not being announced until the 21st December 1945. His parents moved to Hitchen during the war. Alan is commemorated on his works memorial.

1413694 Corporal Cyril Ernest Storey, RAFVR, was the twenty-five year old son Ernest and Minnie Storey of 12 Canons Road. Cyril was an ex-pupil of Ware Central School and before he joined the RAF worked as an overhead linesman for the Northmet Power Company based at Hertford. He was a member of the Veralanium Cycle Club at St. Albans. Cyril had been in the RAF for six years four of which he had served overseas, he died on 3rd January 1947 and his funeral at St Mary's Church was attended by airmen from the RAF station at Gosport. His final resting place is marked by a Commonwealth War Graves Commission headstone in Ware Cemetery.

Private Kenneth Williams, Black Watch, the son of Mr and Mrs Abraham Williams of 25 Vicarage Road was killed when a group of the Black Watch who had secured the Empel Bridge were separated from their main Company and came under heavy fire from German self-propelled guns. Kenneth, who was twenty-one, joined the army in 1942 and had previously served in the Ware Home Guard.

Three memorial tablets

After the war there were three other memorial tablets in the town. One can be found in Ware New Cemetery near the entrance from Watton Road and its inscription reads:

> *In Undying Memory of our comrades of the Hertfordshire Regiment*
> *who laid down their lives in the wars of 1914-18 and 1939-1945 and*
> *of the following members of the Ware Territorial Club who gave*
> *their lives in the 1939-1945 war:*
>> *G C Crane*
>> *F C Peacock*
>> *J H Reed*
>> *C R W Wallace.*

The second memorial commemorating the Allen and Hanburys men who died in the Second World War is now located in the main reception area at GlaxoSmithKline's premises in Priory Street:

The third memorial tablet used to hang in the Northmet Power Company's offices at Bridgefoot (now The Bridge public house) and is now in the safe custody of the Northmet's former employees association.

Appendix No1
The Civil Defence Establishment and the numbers of volunteers in February 1938

	Men	Women	Totals	War establishment including reserves
	—————Volunteers—————			
Wardens	72	3	75	107
First Aid Parties	20	-	20	30
First Aid Post	17	50	67	25
Ambulance Drivers and attendants	-	2	2	30
Drivers for sitting casualties	1	1	2	8
Rescue Parties	4	–	4	21
Decontamination Squad	6	–	6	11
Report & Communications				26
Indoor duties	1	5	6	
Messengers	2	–	2	
Miscellaneous duties	6	–	6	
Totals	**129**	**61**	**189***	**258**

* Excludes 25 volunteers in the Auxiliary Fire Service.

Members of the National Service Advisory Committee 1938.

Mr Charles Ward of "Muree", Collett Road
Mrs Carew Jones of Scotts Hill Cottage

Mrs R M May of 95 New Road
Mr Nigel Hanbury of Green End House

ARP certificate holders in May 1938

J F Johnson	R W Jackson	A Brazier	E Devonshire
B Chappell	R W Grantham	A G Raison	W Masters*
A Trundle	J Trundle	T McKenzie	A Arnold
G Gilbert	A E Wright	– Hammond	C J Lucas
S F Smith	E Haggar	D Patmore	R Charville

* Walter Masters of King George's Road was a long serving member of the St John Ambulance Brigade and had helped with the wounded soldiers at the Priory in WW1; ill health forced him to leave the Brigade so he became a Special Constable.

Appendix No 2

Civil Defence Establishment and actual strength in 1939

| | Establishment | | | | | |
	Men	Women	Total	Reserves	Total est'ment	Actual strength
Air Raid Wardens (including Heads)	68	17	85	25% = 22	107	92
Four First Aid parties (including car drivers)	20	–	20	50% = 10	10	21
First Aid Post *	4	16	20	25% = 5	25	108
Six ambulance drivers and attendants	–	24	24	25% = 6	30	7
Drivers for four cars– sitting casualties.	–	6	6	25% = 2	8	8
Two light rescue parties including drivers	14	–	14	50% = 7	21	5
Gas Decontamination squad including drivers	7	–	7	50% = 4	11	6
Control Centre	4	6	10	25% = 3	13	14
Messengers	10	–	10	25% = 3	13	4
Miscellaneous	–	–	–	–	–	28
Totals	**127**	**69**	**196**	**62**	**258**	**193**

* Excluding doctors and nurses.

The wartime establishment set including reserves was 258 being the sum of columns 4 & 6.

Appendix No 3
Revised Civil Defence Establishment and strengths 2nd September 1941

	Unit Establishment	*Personnel Establishment*	*Effective strength*
Public Baths F.A.P & cleansing centre	6 men & 13 women	7 men & 51 women	25 men & 33 women incl 3 women full time
Bridgefoot Cleansing Station	4 men & 4 women	–	–
Ambulance Drivers	15 men or women	17 men & 10 women	27 men incl 2 full time
First Aid Parties	20 men	43 men	43 incl 4 full time
Rescue Parties	20 men	31 men	15 men
Decontamination Squad	7 men	7men	7 men
Wardens	43 men	116 men	116 men incl 3 full time
Control Centre	8 men	18 men	18 men incl 1 full time
Outdoor messengers	6	15 men	15 men
Totals	**146**	**315**	**299**

Unit establishment was the maximum number considered necessary.
Personnel strength was the number required in order to maintain the unit establishment.
Effective strength was the number based on the number on "effective strength register".
13 people employed full time.

Revised Civil Defence Establishment and strength 1st November 1944.

	Unit Establishment	*Personnel (part-time Establishment*	*Effective strength*
Public Baths F.A.P & cleansing Centre	6 men & 13 women	33	33 and Miss Cannon on full time basis.
Bridgefoot Cleansing Station	4 men & 4 women	–	–
Ambulance Drivers	15 men or women	8 part time	8 and 4 men full time
First Aid Parties	20 men	43 men	43 and 4 men full time
Rescue Parties	20 men	37 men*	37 men
Decontamination Squad	7 men	7men	7 men
Wardens	43 men	84 part time	84 men and 2 full time
Control Centre	8 men	14 part time	14 men incl 1 full time
Outdoor messengers	6	6 part time	6
Totals	**146**	**232**	**243**

* Rescue party includes men drafted in from the Home Guard.

Appendix No 4
Ambulances and Drivers

(a) Vehicles earmarked as ambulances:-
St. John Ambulance Association, Austin ambulance index number JH 8881.
Snowdrop Laundries Ltd., Baldock Street, Ford van index number HV 8787.
Snowdrop Laundries Ltd., Baldock Street, Ford van index number BRO 519.
Snowdrop Laundries Ltd., Baldock Street, Ford van index number ABD 78.
Ware Hardware Stores, High Street, Morris 14 index number UR 5062.
Crooks Stores, High Street, Morris index number DUN 153.

(b) The following light vehicles were earmarked for the conveyance of stores etc.:-
Mr W Harwood, 37 Fanshawe Crescent, Morris 8 van index number JH 5771.
Mr E Nicholls, 94 High Street, Ford 14 van index number JH 3092.
Mr Skinner, Watton Road, van index number ENK 782.

(c) People who qualified as ambulance drivers were:-
Messrs H Skipp, G Parker, C Adams and C B Carter all from Ware Garage.
Mr Mathews, The Garage Baldock Street. Mr Gideon Talbot, High Street Garage.
Mr S Caudle, 39 Baldock Street. Mr H Laver, 9 Cundalls Road.
Mr J R Goodey, 26 Watton Road. Mr A H Skinner, 26 Watton Road.

(d) Private cars judged suitable as "ambulances" to carry sitting casualties :-
Mr D W Lee, 21 High Street, Hillman Ten index number REO 318.
Mr T Crook, 8 High Oak Road, Austin Fourteen index number DAR 41.
Mr A E Wright, 8 Jefferies Road, Morris Fourteen index number VE 6570.
Mr C Ward, Collett Road, Morris Fourteen index number DAH 465.
Mr G Bishop, Musley Lane, Morris Ten index number GL 3792.
Lady Garforth, Widbury House, Austin Eighteen index number BML 590 and Wolsley Fourteen
    index number EJH 597.
Mr A C Ledger, Alban House, Little Widbury, Saloon car index no. ENK 791.
Mr C Forbes, High Street, Saloon car index number JH 2872.
Mr H Skipp, Market Place, car index number BAR 688.
Others known to have volunteered their services were Mr R Kay of 11 Chadwell, Mr Sayers,
    Mr Reed of 46 Trinity Road, Mr Porter of New Hall Farm Wareside, Mr G Brooks of 40
    King Edward's Road and Mr Jenkinson of the French Horn.

Appendix No.5.

Staffing lists at the First Aid & Ambulance posts in September 1939.

First Aid Post at the swimming baths

Officer in charge Dr Stewart, Deputy Dr Lempriere.

Senior V.A.D Personnel:- Commandant Miss C M Garforth, Deputy Miss G Dixon.

Personnel. First four hour shift:-

Miss Garforth, Miss Sibthorpe, Mesdames Lempriere, Clark, Lond, Blake, Prior and Payne.

Second four hour shift:-

Mesdames Gardner, Goldstone, Bailey, Slater and Hiam, Miss Fairbain and Miss Chetwood.

Third four hour shift:-

The Misses Mason, Cooper and Dixon, Mesdames King, Smith, Nurse, Long and Hems.

The Misses Pearce, Cleadow and Simmers were reserves covering the three shifts.

Transport allocated at the baths to convey stores and sitting casualties were the vans belonging to Mr Nicholls and Mr Harwood together with the cars owned by Lady Garforth and Mr Bishop. The drivers were Messrs Nicholls, Harwood, Bishop and Private E Dyer Lady Garforth's chauffeur).

First Aid Party No 1 based at the Priory

Corporals A Blake and J Ives, Privates A C Trundle, E Long A G Page (the Brigade's Divisional Secretary of 22 Princess Street), J Brinklow and Messrs R Jackson, S F Smith, E Beazley, H Hammond, C Smith and C West were based here, Mr A E Wright and Mr A C Ledger completed the Party with their cars. Private Alf Trundle worked for the Council and was seconded as a full-time First Aid worker in October 1940, Alfred Wright also worked for the Council as the Rating Officer.

First Aid Party No 2 based at the Waterworks

Mr H Lond, a full time First Aid worker, together with Privates H Campkin, E Cadmore R Davies formed the nucleus for this post with Messrs B Smith F Milton, D Adams and D Parker turning out when the siren sounded. The third Snowdrop Laundry van converted to an ambulance was used here on a part time basis with volunteer ambulance drivers G Parker and J R Goodey. The cars used for sitting casualties belonged to and were driven by Mr T Crook and Mr C Ward. Mr Smith worked for the Council and was seconded as a full-time First Aid worker in October 1940.

First Aid Party No. 3 at Ware Grammar School

Here the Party were based in the domestic science room under two full time First Aiders, Privates A Flood and F Woodhouse who were backed up by Private P Lawrence and Messrs S Clarke, S French, A Long and R Rouse. Mr Kay's third van (BRO 519) converted to an ambulance was stationed here together with Mr Skinner's van and the cars belonging to Mr D W Lee and Mr H Skipp. The designated drivers were Mr C B Carter, Mr F Francis of Chadwell Lodge, Mr Skinner, Mr D W Lee and Mr H Skipp.

Chief Ambulance Officer Tom Burgess and Tom Forbes (with his car) were in charge of the depot assisted by Bob Jackson. The St. John's ambulance together with one of Mr Kay's Ford vans (ABD 78) were based here on a whole time basis, a second of Mr Kay's vans together with the one from Crooks Stores on a part time basis, the ambulance drivers allocated were Messrs Adams, Mathews, Talbot and Forbes. An attendant or first aider was allocated to each ambulance. At the outbreak of the war the ambulances were housed in lean-to garages near the Priory shrubbery (near the site of the present day Priory timber annexe).

Appendix No.6.

First Aid Headquarters duty rota for Sundays 1939.

Sunday	10.00 am to 1.00 pm		2.30 pm to 5.00 pm	
	Drivers	Attendants	Drivers	Attendants
Oct. 29th	Pte P Lawrence	Pte E Cadmore	Pte E Dyer	Pte P Blogg
Nov. 5th	Pte A Trundle	Pte S Clarke	A/Cpl A Blake	Pte H Hammond
Nov. 12th	Mr Parker	Pte E Long	Pte A Flood	Pte J Webb
Nov. 19th	Mr Talbot	Pte S French	Mr Skipp	Pte J Trundle
Nov. 26th	Mr Carter	Pte R Davis	Supt T H Burgess	Pte J Freestone
Dec. 3rd	Pte E Dyer	Pte A Page	Pte P Lawrence	Sgt H A Brown*
Dec. 10th	A/Cpl A Blake	A/Cpl F Beazley	Mr Parker	Pte L Goldstone
Dec. 17th	Supt T H Burgess	Pte F Woodhouse	Mr Talbot	Pte G Smith
Dec. 24th	Pte E Flood	Pte J Brinklow	Pte A Trundle	Sgt W Masters
Dec. 31st	Mr Skipp	Pte C Garrett	Mr Carter	A/Cpl J Ives

* Sgt H A Brown was the St John Ambulance Brigade's Divisional Secretary after Mr A G Page.

Members First Aid Parties in 1940 or 1941
(based on undated list prepared by Tom Burgess)

No.1 Party at the Priory		No.2 Party at Musley Hill	
Shift 1	Shift 2	Shift 1	Shift 2
F Woodhouse	A Blake	E Andrews	T Coptcoat
L Wallace	H Mole	S Burdwell	F Beazley
A Trundle	P Blake	W Wilbourne	C Lond
W Roberson	W Gladding	J Cooper	A List
	A Wright	D Devile	
P Lawrence (driver)	A Stalley	H Freeman (driver)	
C Haggar	W Hall	J Baker	
(sitting driver)		(sitting driver)	
C Adams (ambulance)			

Appendix No 7
Members of the First Aid Ambulance section 28th January 1942

First Aiders

E Andrews	C Bailey*	F Beazley*+	A Blake*+
T H Burgess	E Cadmore	S Clarke	W C Clibbon
E Dyer	H Flood	T Forbes	W Groom
C Garrett	H Hodgkinson	J Ives*+	R Jackson
P Lawrence*	A G Lise	C H Lond	E N Long
F Milton	S J Salmon	A C Trundle*	F W Woodhouse*+
W Wilbourne			

Ambulance drivers

C Adams*	C Carter	H Lee	G Parker
W J Reed	R Shambrook	G Talbot	

Car drivers

E Crook	T Crook	H Skipp	W Ward

*   Full time personnel.   +   Party Leaders.

Appendix No 8
AFS members in 1940

A Armstrong	E Barrett	B Camp
H Hall	J Page*	E H Riddle
F J Wilbourne	W G Clark	T Want
W R Orger	H J Sapsford	A W Chaplin
A W Wilburn	P G Greengrass	T C Wallace
R Wilson	A T Grey	L Harwood
G A Wilkinson	J E Warren	W Want
E W Godfrey	W W Clift	H Staward
C Walsh	L Moody	A J Homewood
W T Thorby	E Timmons	F Wheeler
H H Taylor	G E Gould	C G Chappel
G H Skeggs	E C Turner	R Howarth
P G Knight	C E Ward	H G Webb
A H W Salmons	H C Barker	W C Clemo
J Dyke	G W G Mardell	H S Finn
A Halfhide	H F Gillet	F E Hills
H Giblean	C W Page	R H Cruse
F G Cutmore	G E Albany	G Presland
A E Chapman	E J Stewart	H W Decks
F C Wallace	J W Cook	A G Adams
W J Devonshire	– Parker	– Merville
– Bonney	– Barker	– Osbourne
– Parnell	– Beckett	– Tancock
– Cain	– Warner	– Francis
C E Dorrington		

*   John Page left the A.F.S to join the Home Guard.

Appendix No 9
The Food Control Committee August 1939

Trade Representatives.
Chairman Mr A H Rogers
Mr E Neave, grocers.
Mr W R Attwood, dairymen.
Mr R F Burgess - J W French & Co Ltd.
Mr J Royce - A B Swain Co Ltd.
Mr E K Samways - Allan & Hanbury.

Vice chairman Mr A Chapman.
W G Clark, butchers.
Mr G Edwards , bakers.
Mr H W Chancellor- D Wickham.
Mr E Way – the Co-op.

The Food Control Committee August 1942

Consumer representatives
Miss I G C Abbot
Mr G Bland
Mr R F Burgess
Trade representatives.
Mr W R Attwood, Dairyman
Mr A Neave, Grocers
Trade Union representatives
Mr S Goody

Lady H G Chapman
Mr A Chapman
Mr E K Samways

Mr W G Clark, Butchers
Mr E Way of the Co-op

Mr F Watson

Mr A H Rogers
Mr A V Golstone

Mr G Edwards, Bakers

Priory Comforts Fund Committee November 1939

Mrs E P Sewell, treasurer
Mrs A H Andrew
Mrs H D Apperly
Mrs J R Colville
Mrs W T Dixon

Mrs J Cooper
Mrs C Lempriere
Mrs F Williams
Mrs May
Mrs Nurse

Mrs Reed
Mrs Richard Croft
Miss Munt
Miss Woodhead

Appendix No 10
Dates St. Mary's Junior Girls School went into their air raid shelters

3rd September **1940**	10.20 am to 11.45 am	2.45 pm to 3.45 pm
4th September	9.20 am to 9.55 am	
11th September	9.45 am to 10.40 am	
29th September	9.00 am to 9.30 am	1.35 pm to 2.00 pm
1st October		2.10 pm to 2.20 pm
2nd October	9.40 am to 10.45 am	
7th October	9.40 am to 10.30 am	1.40 pm to 2.10 pm
		2.20 pm to 3.05 pm
8th October	9.00 am to 10.05 am	
15th October	10.10 am to 10.25 am	11.35 am to 11.50 am
21st October	10.55 am to 1.20 pm	
25th October	9.10 am to 9.50 am	1.30 pm to 3.45 pm
28th October		2.55 pm to 3.35 pm
29th October	11.00 am to 11.30 am	
30thOctober	11.55 am to 12.30 pm	
5th November		2.30 pm to 3.35 pm
13th November		1.30 pm to 2.40 pm
7th January **1941**		2.20 pm to 4.20 pm
21st January	10.30 am to 11.00 am	11.15 am to 12.20 pm
29th January		2.40 pm to 3.40 pm
30th January	9.40 am to 10.00 am	2.10 pm to 4.20 pm*
31st January	9.25 am to 9.45 am	11.25 am to 12 noon.
21st February	9.45 am to 10.00 am	
27th February	10.25 am to 11.30 am+	
30th September **1942**	10.56 am to 11.15 am	
19th October	10.15 am to 10.30 am	10.50 am to 11.00 am
11th January**1943**	9.50 am to 10.20 am	
20th April	11.50 am to 12.05 pm	
3rd July **1944**		3.10 pm to 4.30 pm
10th July		2.40 pm to 3.20 pm
19th July	10.15 am to 11.15 am	
27th July		3.20 pm to 3.45 pm
28th August		2.20 pm to 4.00 pm
29th August	1.10 pm to 1.25 pm	1.55 pm to 2.20 pm
31st August	8.55 am to 9.40 am	9.55 am to 10.20 am
	11.00 am to 11.10 am	11.55 am to 12.10 pm
31st October	8.58 am to 9.10 am	
16th March **1945**		4.10 pm to 4.20 pm
19th March	8.45 am to 8.55 am	9.10 am to 9.20 am

*   All clear sounded at 6.00 pm - all children sent home in small parties.
+   Children sent home as they were so cold.

Appendix No 11
Home Guard
Nominal Roll for No. 1 Rifle Platoon, Mobile Reserve Company
(Formerly No.7 Platoon of Ware Home Guard)

Platoon Commander
2 Lt. F Cavandish of 80 Cannons Road

Platoon Sergeant
Sgt. A R Cole M.B.E of Little Widbury

Intelligence Sergeant
H G Mayes of 81 Musley Lane

Signals Section
Pte R J Mott of 29 Cannons Road
Pte R H Sharp of 20 Coronation Road

Pte D A Bardell of 2 Jefferies Road

Riflemen
L/Cpl E Osbourne
Pte J A Adams*
Pte W C Cadmore*
Pte E A Chappell
Pte W J B Dell
Pte G E W Fish
Pte P E Gold
Pte J Hiam
Pte E E Johnson
Pte W C Lathrope
Pte G F Mitchell
Pte F H Stockwell (King George's Road)
Pte W J Storey
Pte F F Tidy
Pte R Wood

L/Cpl W R Spencer
Pte R H Barnes
Pte P J Catlin
Pte A J Crane
Pte A A Davy
Pte S G Francis
Pte M Harris
Pte H Hollingsworth
Pte B J Kingsbury
Pte J R Mayoss
Pte J E Moss
Pte T C Pearce
Pte J C Taylor
Pte A Tyler

*   Served in 1914 - 1918 war.

Appendix No 12
Air Training Corps

The names of the founder members of 936 Squadron are inscribed on a WW1 aircraft propeller which now hangs in the Squadron's headquarters at Broadmeads and shows the branch of the services in which they served.

Cpl. A Goldstone	RNVR	Cpl P French	RAFVR
Sgt R Bush	RAFVR	Cpl K Hollands	RAFVR
Cadet P Davey	RAFVR	F/Sgt E Smith	RAFVR
Cadet R Davis	RNVR	F/Sgt N Murphy	RAFVR
Cadet J Catlin	RAFVR	Sgt A North	RAFVR
Cadet R Blake	RAFVR	Cadet L Timmons	RAFVR
Cadet K Sheppard	RAFVR	Cadet G Perry	RAFVR
Cpl D Elred	RAFVR	Cadet D Guy	RAFVR
F/Sgt R Smith	RAFVR	Cadet M Chapman	RAFVR
Sgt A Hollands+	RAFVR	Cpl P Leigh	RAFVR
Cadet E Wren*	RAFVR	Sgt S Morgan	RAFVR
Cadet J Lake	RAFVR	Cpl A Warby	RAFVR
Sgt P Pexton	RAFVR	Sgt D Taylor	RNVR
F/Sgt W Campkin	RAFVR	F/Sgt F Church	RAFVR
F/Sgt F Prior	RAFVR	Cadet F Freeman	MN
Sgt J Spencer	RAFVR	Cpl R Skeeles	FAA
Cadet P Burling	RAFVR	Cadet L Thompson	RAFVR
Cpl R Rand	Mines	Cadet M Seymour	RAFVR
Cadet R Daniels	RAFVR	Cadet D Bird	RAFVR
Cadet P Crane	RAFVR	Cadet J Tarry	RAFVR
Cadet H Allen	RN	Cadet A Coxall	RAFVR
Cadet E Clibbon	RN	Cadet D Woods	RN
Cadet D Pugh	RN	Sgt G West	RAFVR
Cadet W Capel	FAA	Cpl R Jackson	RN
Cadet J Carter	RAFVR		

+ Killed in action   * Awarded the DFM